A lucid book, learned and practical, written with grace and passion by a master teacher.

Setting out to tell how he teaches the Rules, Gallagher actually describes the experience of living them. He takes each Rule and shows how he presents it, weaving together clear explanations and illustrations from daily life. Meant as a handbook for teachers—and excellent as that—the book will be helpful to those engaged in adult formation or teaching spiritual direction. Anyone who reads it will say of the book what it says of the Rules: "Such clarity is obviously an enormous gift for the spiritual life."

—**Joseph Tetlow, SJ**, Ignatian scholar, author, and retreat director

Having taught the Rules for the discernment of spirits to varied groups over many decades, Father Gallagher now generously shares his insights and pedagogical methods with a broader audience. He has witnessed the Lord "setting captives free" as listeners receive this great gift of St. Ignatius and now desires to help others offer this gift as well. In his usual clear and encouraging style, Father Gallagher provides future teachers with the essential tools, a "blueprint for this teaching." May Father Gallagher's generosity serve to equip a new generation of teachers who will in turn become witnesses to the Lord's redeeming love!

—**Rev. Richard J. Gabuzda, S.T.D.**, Executive Director,
  The Institute for Priestly Formation

This highly practical and lucidly written book is yet another example of why Father Timothy M. Gallagher, OMV, is America's preeminent interpreter of and writer on Ignatian discernment and spiritual direction.

—**Harvey D. Egan, S.J.**, Emeritus Professor of Systematic and
  Mystical Theology, Boston College

Through *Teaching Discernment*, Fr. Timothy Gallagher places in the hands of all who read, study, instruct, and implement the Fourteen Rules for the discernment of spirits an indispensable key for unlocking St. Ignatius' teaching within the New Evangelization of the universal Church. This masterfully designed "Pedagogy for Ignatian Discernment" is certain to find great welcome among those called to the sacred task of presenting the instrumental key of discernment, which through grace, unlocks the chains of captivity found within the human heart and sets the captives free. With warmth, generosity, patience, and untiring reverence for the human heart, Fr. Gallagher's *Teaching Discernment: A Pedagogy for Presenting Ignatian Discernment of Spirits* is a fruitful sign of future blessings to generations of teachers of discernment. May this book unlock within the heart of the universal Church a springtime of discernment!

—**Elizabeth M. Gengle,** Heart of the Interior Life Retreat Ministry, BA Theology, Franciscan University of Steubenville

As one who has benefited from receiving Fr. Timothy Gallagher's teaching on the Ignatian Rules for the discernment of spirits, I can attest that Fr. Gallagher is a renowned master in the Rules for the discernment of spirits of Saint Ignatius of Loyola. He has honed decades of scholarship into his extensive writing and teaching on the Rules. Now Fr. Gallagher opens up the pedagogy that he has found to be successful in introducing others into the art of discernment. By explaining his pedagogical insights, refined and proven over many presentations on the rules, Fr. Gallagher's latest effort equips others to be able to effectively communicate the inestimable spiritual value of the practice of the rules as teachers themselves. In this new book, Fr. Gallagher shares not just the wisdom of the content of the rules, but he also shares how to teach the rules in a way that allows the depth of Ignatius's understanding to reach many more who desire to live discerning lives.

—**Rev. James Rafferty, S.T.D.,** Director of Mission and Communications, The Institute for Priestly Formation

Father Gallagher is a master teacher and very few in the world today know the Rules for Discernment as well as he does. This book will be an excellent guide for all who desire to share the wisdom of St. Ignatius with those they direct and teach. I cannot recommend this book more highly for those desiring to learn and hand on the wisdom and practical examples it contains.

—**Msgr. David L. Toups, STD,** Rector/President,
St. Vincent de Paul Regional Seminary, Boynton Beach, Florida

I am pleased to have read this new book by Fr. Timothy Gallagher before its publication. I can affirm that I read it with even greater interest than his earlier book, *The Discernment of Spirits: An Ignatian Guide to Everyday Living*, which I found excellent. It would be difficult to find to find a more clear and practical book on Ignatian spiritual discernment. In this new book, he explains the foundations of his competence in this topic and his pedagogy. He does so, however, as a personal sharing with the reader, and this gives the book a special attraction: that of direct conversation.

In his own life, this is an author convinced of and enthusiastic for his topic, and clear and direct in his exposition. He loves St. Ignatius of Loyola and his spirituality, a richness that he understands, with reason, to be the inspiration of his own founder, Venerable Bruno Lanteri. Fr. Gallagher's style is accessible, precise, and illuminating. Behind it lies profound study and reflection on the subject he discusses. The book reveals many years of analysis, teaching, and practical application in his own life and pastoral practice, of the Ignatian rules for the discernment of spirits.

Experience has taught Father Gallagher that a well-chosen example is worth more than many words to help a person who desires to apply the rules in the concrete practice of his life. His original way of linking each rule to examples and his pedagogical approach in doing this is, I believe, especially valuable. May God continue to help him to exercise for the good of the Church this gift he has received.

—**Manuel Ruiz Jurado, SJ,** Emeritus Professor of Spiritual
Theology, The Pontifical Gregorian University, Ignatian scholar, author, and retreat director

In our formation program for spiritual directors, we have used Fr. Gallagher's books as our foundation for teaching the discernment of spirits. In this latest book, *Teaching Discernment: A Pedagogy for Presenting Ignatian Discernment of Spirits*, Fr. Gallagher has given us another treasure. The ability to discern the spirits at work within your directee is crucial for any spiritual director. Fr. Gallagher's teachings are clear and solid. He has done a great service in making St. Ignatius of Loyola's Rules for the discernment of spirits available and easy to understand. They are a must for any spiritual director, or any person desiring to grow closer to the Lord.

—**Kay Davis, M.A.**, Program Director and Formator, Lanteri Center for Ignatian Spirituality

Having learned from some of the masters, Father Gallagher has a unique perspective on Christian discernment. Father's own reverent discernment allows him to present riveting examples of discernment that help students grasp the principles. I have referred dozens of people to Father Gallagher's works and am happy for this new volume.

—**Monsignor Daniel Trapp**, Associate Professor of Systematic Theology, Liturgy and Sacraments, Sacred Heart Major Seminary, Detroit

Fr. Gallagher has been perfecting Ignatian pedagogy for decades. Now he shares with us—and future generations—his secrets of teaching the Rules for discernment. Spiritual Guides everywhere will give thanks for this treasure!

—**Father Daniel Barron, OMV**, Director of Spiritual Formation, St. John Vianney Theological Seminary

Fr. Gallagher's book would benefit every seminary faculty. Because St. Ignatius' Rules of discernment have a universal application, they speak to all four dimensions of formation (human, spiritual, intellectual, and pastoral). In particular, this book will be an essential tool in forming the formators. Whether we see the parish as a school of prayer (St. John Paul II) or a field hospital (Pope Francis), having a solid grasp of the Rules will help our faculty form our future priests to be the spiritual fathers and physicians they are called to be.

—**Rev. James Mason**, President-Rector, Kenrick-Glennon Seminary

This book will be a fountain of blessing for many. Father Gallagher shares his Christ-like pedagogy that he has so carefully developed over thirty-five years of fruitful ministry, with open-hearted generosity and evident passion for the redemptive quality of this material. The underlying wisdom with which he has taught these liberating rules of St. Ignatius to so many, is revealed throughout these pages with authority, humility and gentleness. For those of us who have been blessed with the hope and renewal of energy that Father Gallagher's clear presentation of the rules for discernment has engendered in our own lives, it now seems possible that we can share it with others ourselves.

The spiritual life is lived daily in our depths, a hidden place where educated awareness and resolve can bring us freedom and hope, even as we live through the vicissitudes and heavily distracted climate of our culture. We need Spirit-filled guides to teach us how to discern the movements of our hearts, and Father Gallagher shows us a pedagogy that is accessible, charged with the love of God, and models patient reverence for every human person.

Freshly exhorted, those of us who have been blessed ourselves by these grace-filled Rules begin to hear a call to be a further instrument in bringing this transforming wisdom to as many people as possible. I deeply appreciate Father Gallagher's willingness to share so openly his life-giving pedagogy.

—**Sally Harrington Philippo**, wife, mother, spiritual director, leadership of Vita Nova

Gifted teachers are first and foremost gifted listeners. This pedagogy is the fruit of Fr. Gallagher's thirty-five years of listening to the Rules and the people who have received his reverent, insightful instruction. Paying attention to his experienced counsels will now permit more teachers and listeners to realize the hopeful power of the Rules for "setting captives free."

My spiritual director recommended that I read Fr. Gallagher's *Discernment of Spirits: An Ignatian Guide for Everyday Living* soon after it surfaced in 2005. I was radically reoriented to how powerful, liberating and hopeful the Rules could be. Since then, I have had the privilege of teaching the Rules to priests and seminarians. With this book, I can now offer them the next step for learning the Rules by heart—teach someone and share the gift of discernment."

—**Father Paul Hoesing, S.T.L**, Dean of Seminarians, Director of Human Formation, Kenrick-Glennon Seminary

In this generous new book, *Teaching Discernment: A Pedagogy for Presenting Ignatian Discernment*, Fr. Timothy Gallagher presents with his characteristic gentle reverence, depth and precise clarity not only Ignatius's fourteen Rules of discernment, but also Fr. Gallagher's masterful pedagogy developed through his many years of teaching those rules to thousands. Fr. Gallagher's work is that of a skilled guide who illuminates the Ignatian signposts of discernment, equipping each of us to better discern the path God has laid out in our lives. His pedagogy always hues closely to the intent and words of Ignatius. Fr. Gallagher shares with us his own intent in each step he takes as a teacher. He also generously shares his carefully curated stories and apt examples and his decisions and methods as an instructor that make these Rules come alive for a contemporary audience.

As a psychologist who has worked for many years with laity, clergy and seminarians, I have seen many clients gain clarity and freedom from a basic understanding of these Rules, as have I in my own life. Now, with this fine guidebook, I find myself equipped to systematically teach those Rules as well. I strongly recommend this book to those in a position to help teach the freeing power of these Rules to others.

—**Paul Ruff, M.A.**, Licensed Psychologist, Saint Paul Seminary, Saint Paul, Minnesota

Teaching Discernment

A Pedagogy for Presenting Ignatian Discernment of Spirits

TIMOTHY M. GALLAGHER, OMV

A Crossroad Book
The Crossroad Publishing Company

The Crossroad Publishing Company
www.CrossroadPublishing.com
© 2020 by Timothy M. Gallagher

Crossroad, Herder & Herder, and the crossed C logo/colophon are registered trademarks of The Crossroad Publishing Company.

All rights reserved. No part of this book may be copied, scanned, reproduced in any way, or stored in a retrieval system, or transmitted, in any form or by any means, electronic, mechanical, photocopying, recording, or otherwise, without the written permission of The Crossroad Publishing Company. For permission please write to rights@crossroadpublishing.com

In continuation of our 200-year tradition of independent publishing, The Crossroad Publishing Company proudly offers a variety of books with strong, original voices and diverse perspectives. The viewpoints expressed in our books are not necessarily those of The Crossroad Publishing Company, any of its imprints or of its employees, executives, owners. Although the author and publisher have made every effort to ensure that the information in this book was correct at press time, the author and publisher do not assume and hereby disclaim any liability to any party for any loss, damage, or disruption caused by errors or omissions, whether such errors or omissions result from negligence, accident, or any other cause. No claims are made or responsibility assumed for any health or other benefits.

Book design by Tim Holtz

Library of Congress Cataloging-in-Publication Data
Names: Gallagher, Timothy M., author.
Title: Teaching discernment : a pedagogy for presenting Ignatian discernment of spirits / Timothy M. Gallagher, OMV.
Description: New York : Crossroad Publishing Company, [2020] | Includes bibliographical references and index.
Identifiers: LCCN 2019018398 | ISBN 9780824599355 (pbk. : alk. paper)
Subjects: LCSH: Discernment of spirits. | Ignatius, of Loyola, Saint, 1491-1556. Exercitia spiritualia.
Classification: LCC BV5083 .G353 2019 | DDC 248.3--dc23
LC record available at https://lccn.loc.gov/2019018398

ISBN 978-0-8245-9935-5

Books published by The Crossroad Publishing Company may be purchased at special quantity discount rates for classes and institutional use. For information, please email sales@CrossroadPublishing.com.

Contents

Acknowledgments	xiii
Introduction	xv
Text of the Rules	xix

Part One
Preparing to Teach

1	How This Pedagogy Developed	3
2	The Fruit of This Pedagogy	11
3	The Heart of the Pedagogy	15
4	Getting to Know the Text	22
5	Choosing Examples	24
6	Living the Rules Personally	31

Part Two
Teaching the Rules

7	General Principles	37
8	Start with the Basics—the Title Statement	50
9	The Spirits in Persons Far from God: Clarity for Your Listeners—Rule 1	60
10	The Spirits in Persons Growing Toward God: Addressing Your Listeners' Experience—Rule 2	72

11	Helping Your Listeners Recognize Spiritual Consolation—Rule 3	84
12	Helping Your Listeners Recognize Spiritual Desolation—Rule 4	99
13	The Advice That Your Listeners Never Forget—Rule 5	118
14	Liberating Your Listeners: Never Be Passive in Desolation!—Rule 6	133
15	Understanding Desolation: A Trial, Its Reason, and Its Fruit—Rule 7	150
16	Giving Hope to Your Listeners: Consolation Will Return Soon—Rule 8	158
17	Answering the Question: Why Does God Permit Desolation?—Rule 9	169
18	To Listeners in Consolation: Prepare for the Future—Rule 10	181
19	Living the Discerning Life: Humble in Consolation, Trusting in Desolation—Rule 11	192
20	Teaching Your Listeners to Resist Temptation—Rule 12	204
21	A Key Counsel: In Time of Trouble, Do Not Keep Silent!—Rule 13	217
22	Hope Where Your Listeners Have the Least Hope—Rule 14	235
23	Concluding the Teaching	244

Part Three
The Context of the Teaching

24 The Proximate Preparation for the Teaching — 249

25 Tools for the Teaching — 254

26 What about the Second Set of Rules? — 264

27 Resources for Learning the Rules — 268

    Notes — 271

    Index — 289

Acknowledgments

I am deeply grateful to the many who have helped me in the writing of this book, and in particular: to Roy Carlisle, whose editorial expertise and accompaniment contributed greatly to this book; to Emily Wichland, whose competence in copyediting and whose creative suggestions enhanced the book; to Denise Forlow of Crossroad Publishing whose sure direction guided the process of publication; to Lynda Fitzsimmons for her invaluable help with details of publication; and to Gwendolin Herder, president, and all at Crossroad Publishing for another book in what is now a long-standing, ongoing, and fruitful relationship.

Finally, I thank the following for permission to reprint copyrighted material:

Excerpts from the *New American Bible, Revised Edition* © 2010, 1991, 1986, 1970 Confraternity of Christian Doctrine, Washington, D.C. and are used by permission of the copyright owner. All Rights Reserved. No part of the New American Bible may be reproduced in any form without permission in writing from the copyright owner.

Excerpts from the *Catholic Edition of the Revised Standard Version of the Bible*, copyright 1965, 1966 by the Division of Christian Education of the National Council of the Churches of Christ in the United States of America. Used by permission. All rights reserved.

From *Story of a Soul*, translated by John Clarke, O.C.D. Copyright (c) 1975, 1976, 1996 by Washington Province of Discalced Carmelites ICS Publications, 2131 Lincoln Road, N.E. Washington, DC 20002-1199 U.S.A. www.icspublications.org.

From *St. Therese of Lisieux: Her Last Conversations* translated by John Clarke, O.C.D. Copyright (c) 1977 Washington Province of Discalced Carmelites ICS Publications 2131 Lincoln Road, N.E. Washington, DC 20002-1199 U.S.A. www.icspublications.org.

Excerpts from *St. Francis of Assisi, Writings and Early Biographies: English Omnibus of the Sources for the Life of St. Francis*, ed. Marion Habig, Franciscan Press, 1973. Used with permission of Franciscan Media. www.franciscanmedia.org.

Excerpts from *Spirit of Light or Darkness: A Casebook for Studying Discernment of Spirits*, by Jules Toner, SJ, 1995. Used with permission. Copyright Boston College, Institute for Advanced Jesuit Studies. All rights reserved.

Excerpted from *Letters of St. Ignatius of Loyola*, by Saint Ignatius of Loyola, translated by William J. Young, SJ, (Loyola Press 1959). Reprinted with permission of Loyola Press. To order copies visit www.loyolapress.com.

Introduction

I write this book to share a pedagogy. As I will tell in the book, this pedagogy developed over thirty-five years, and much of my life has been dedicated to shaping and sharing it. I know it is effective. I know, from long experience, that it imparts clarity and engenders hope. That is why I want to share it.

This pedagogy serves to teach Ignatius of Loyola's rules for the discernment of spirits (*SpirEx* 313–327).[1] I base it on close examination of Ignatius's own words and their illustration through abundant examples—"ordinary" examples, the kind we all experience, though often without understanding or knowing how to respond to them. Ignatius supplies the key.

When I teach the rules, or when others learn them through the books and digital resources in which I share this pedagogy, energy is awakened. With Ignatius's help, people understand their daily spiritual experience. They perceive more clearly in it what is of God and what is not of God. That clarity sets them doubly free, free *from* the discouraging lies of the "enemy" (Ignatius's word) and free, above all, *to* follow the Lord they love.

When people learn Ignatius's rules, often a desire is born to share them with others. This is already occurring in parishes, seminaries, religious institutions, among friends, and in many other settings. To do this, teachers, presenters, are needed. If you are among them, or if you desire to be among them, this book is for you. It offers a blueprint for this teaching.

You need not be an Ignatian scholar. You need only a certain— I would say "ordinary"—ability to present, a willingness to learn the material, a readiness to organize the group, and, above all, a love for the material and conviction of its value. If you find this disposition in yourself, then this book will supply the rest. In it, you will find the tools you need.

This is the third book I have written on these rules.[2] The first, *The Discernment of Spirits: An Ignatian Guide to Everyday Living*, provides a systematic presentation of the fourteen rules according to the pedagogy just mentioned: text and examples. The second, *Setting Captives Free: Personal Reflections on Ignatian Discernment of Spirits*, allowed me to explore further aspects of the rules and to share my own thoughts on various issues in the rules and especially what they mean in my own life.

In this book I return to these fourteen rules for a third time. The rules are the same, but the perspective is different. In this book I am speaking to teachers and prospective teachers of the rules. The focus is on how to present these rules, how to teach them to others.

The book contains three parts. In the first, I describe the pedagogy itself. In the second, I recount in some detail how I present each of the fourteen rules according to this pedagogy. In the third, I discuss various tools and resources for the teaching.

Because this book examines the same rules discussed in the two earlier books, some overlap with them is unavoidable. I have judged, however, that the present book will aid you more if it is complete in itself, without requiring constant reference to the earlier books. These earlier books can also help you, and they develop some points in greater detail. But this book provides the essential content you need to present the rules.

Teaching Discernment provides a model for presenting the rules. In it I share the various examples and metaphors—for example, the snowball at the top of the mountain and halfway down the mountainside to illustrate rule 12—that I find helpful in presenting the rules. You may use these same examples and metaphors if you choose. I presume, however, that you will find your own examples and metaphors as well. Mine are not prescriptive!

When supplying Ignatius's rules or examples of them in life, I have often inserted commentary into the text. This written commentary reflects the spoken commentary I offer as I read through these texts. What may appear somewhat cumbersome here on the written page is alive and, I believe, helpful to listeners in the actual presentation.

When I teach these rules, I employ handouts and a PowerPoint presentation, as I explain in this book. Both are available to prospective teachers, and the links are found in chapter 25 where I discuss these aids for the teaching.

I have entitled this book *Teaching Discernment: A Pedagogy for Presenting Ignatian Discernment of Spirits*. Teaching discernment—this teaching requires learning the rules and shaping an effective way to present them. It entails more, however, than a simple transmission of information. It is teaching in the sense that one teaches faith or prayer to another: instruction in a spiritual reality, yes, but one conveyed with both mind and heart, born of the conviction, life, and love of the teacher. Our listeners readily perceive this quality in us. They sense the difference. Such conviction, personal practice of discernment, and love are graces to be sought through prayer.

I have very much desired to write this book. I am glad to share this pedagogy with you and hope that it will assist your teaching of the rules. I have long understood these fourteen rules in the light of Jesus's words in Luke 4, "The Spirit of the Lord is upon me, because he has anointed me to bring glad tidings to the poor. He has sent me to proclaim *liberty to captives* . . . to *let the oppressed go free*" (Lk 4:18).[3] Ignatius's rules *set captives free*. It is beautiful to see this happen and blessed to be the instrument of this freedom. May this book contribute to the number of those who serve as such instruments.

Text of the Rules

Rules for becoming aware and understanding to some extent the different movements which are caused in the soul, the good, to receive them, and the bad to reject them. And these rules are more proper for the first week. (313)

First Rule. The first rule: In persons who are going from mortal sin to mortal sin, the enemy is ordinarily accustomed to propose apparent pleasures to them, leading them to imagine sensual delights and pleasures in order to hold them more and make them grow in their vices and sins. In these persons the good spirit uses a contrary method, stinging and biting their consciences through their rational power of moral judgment. (314)

Second Rule. The second: In persons who are going on intensely purifying their sins and rising from good to better in the service of God our Lord, the method is contrary to that in the first rule. For then it is proper to the evil spirit to bite, sadden, and place obstacles, disquieting with false reasons, so that the person may not go forward. And it is proper to the good spirit to give courage and strength, consolations, tears, inspirations and quiet, easing and taking away all obstacles, so that the person may go forward in doing good. (315)

Author's translation in *The Discernment of Spirits: An Ignatian Guide for Everyday Life* (New York: Crossroad, 2005), 7–10. The numbers in parentheses are standard usage for citing paragraphs from the *Spiritual Exercises*. Thus, "(313)" indicates paragraph 313 in the *Spiritual Exercises*. Elsewhere in this book, these paragraphs will be given together with the abbreviation "*SpirEx*."

Third Rule. The third is of spiritual consolation. I call consolation when some interior movement is caused in the soul, through which the soul comes to be inflamed with love of its Creator and Lord, and, consequently when it can love no created thing on the face of the earth in itself, but only in the Creator of them all. Likewise when it sheds tears that move to love of its Lord, whether out of sorrow for one's sins, or for the passion of Christ our Lord, or because of other things directly ordered to his service and praise. Finally, I call consolation every increase of hope, faith and charity, and all interior joy that calls and attracts to heavenly things and to the salvation of one's soul, quieting it and giving it peace in its Creator and Lord. (316)

Fourth Rule. The fourth is of spiritual desolation. I call desolation all the contrary of the third rule, such as darkness of soul, disturbance in it, movement to low and earthly things, disquiet from various agitations and temptations, moving to lack of confidence, without hope, without love, finding oneself totally slothful, tepid, sad and, as if separated from one's Creator and Lord. For just as consolation is contrary to desolation, in the same way the thoughts that come from consolation are contrary to the thoughts that come from desolation. (317)

Fifth Rule. The fifth: In time of desolation never make a change, but be firm and constant in the proposals and determination in which one was the day preceding such desolation, or in the determination in which one was in the preceding consolation. Because, as in consolation the good spirit guides and counsels us more, so in desolation the bad spirit, with whose counsels we cannot find the way to a right decision. (318)

Sixth Rule. The sixth: Although in desolation we should not change our first proposals, it is very advantageous to change ourselves intensely against the desolation itself, as by insisting more upon prayer, meditation, upon much examination, and upon extending ourselves in some suitable way of doing penance. (319)

Seventh Rule. The seventh: Let one who is in desolation consider how the Lord has left him in trial in his natural powers, so that he may resist the various agitations and temptations of the enemy; since he can resist with the divine help, which always remains with him, though he does not clearly feel it; for the Lord has taken away from him his great fervor, abundant love and intense grace, leaving him, however, sufficient grace for eternal salvation. (320)

Eighth Rule. The eighth: Let one who is in desolation work to be in patience, which is contrary to the vexations which come to him, and let him think that he will soon be consoled, diligently using the means against such desolation, as is said in the sixth rule. (321)

Ninth Rule. The ninth: There are three principal causes for which we find ourselves desolate. The first is because we are tepid, slothful or negligent in our spiritual exercises, and so through our faults spiritual consolation withdraws from us. The second, to try us and see how much we are and how much we extend ourselves in his service and praise without so much payment of consolations and increased graces. The third, to give us true recognition and understanding so that we may interiorly feel that it is not ours to attain or maintain increased devotion, intense love, tears or any other spiritual consolation, but that all is the gift and grace of God our Lord, and so that we may not build a nest in something belonging to another, raising our mind in some pride or vainglory, attributing to ourselves the devotion or the other parts of the spiritual consolation. (322)

Tenth Rule. The tenth: Let the one who is in consolation think how he will conduct himself in the desolation which will come after, taking new strength for that time. (323)

Eleventh Rule. The eleventh: Let one who is consoled seek to humble himself and lower himself as much as he can, thinking of how little he is capable in the time of desolation without such grace or consolation. On the contrary, let one who is in desolation think that he can do much with God's sufficient grace to resist all his enemies, taking strength in his Creator and Lord. (324)

Twelfth Rule. The twelfth: The enemy acts like a woman in being weak when faced with strength and strong when faced with weakness. For, as it is proper to a woman, when she is fighting with some man, to lose heart and to flee when the man confronts her firmly, and, on the contrary, if the man begins to flee, losing heart, the anger, vengeance, and ferocity of the woman grow greatly and know no bounds, in the same way, it is proper to the enemy to weaken and lose heart, fleeing and ceasing his temptations when the person who is exercising himself in spiritual things confronts the temptations of the enemy firmly, doing what is diametrically opposed to them; and, on the contrary, if the person who is exercising himself begins to be afraid and lose heart in suffering the temptations, there is no beast so fierce on the face of the earth as the enemy of human nature in following out his damnable intention with such growing malice. (325)

Thirteenth Rule. The thirteenth: Likewise he conducts himself as a false lover in wishing to remain secret and not be revealed. For a dissolute man who, speaking with evil intention, makes dishonorable advances to a daughter of a good father or a wife of a good husband, wishes his words and persuasions to be secret, and the contrary displeases him very much, when the daughter reveals to her father or the wife to her husband his false words and depraved intention, because he easily perceives that he will not be able to succeed with the undertaking begun. In the same way, when the enemy of human nature brings his wiles and persuasions to the just soul, he wishes and desires that they be received and kept in secret; but when one reveals them to one's good confessor or to another spiritual person, who knows his deceits and malicious designs, it weighs on him very much, because he perceives that he will not be able to succeed with the malicious undertaking he has begun, since his manifest deceits have been revealed. (326)

Fourteenth Rule. The fourteenth: Likewise he conducts himself as a leader, intent upon conquering and robbing what he desires. For, just as a captain and leader of an army in the field, pitching his camp and exploring the fortifications and defenses of a stronghold, attacks it at the weakest point, in the same way the enemy of human nature, roving about, looks in turn at all our theological, cardinal, and moral virtues; and where he finds us weakest and most in need for our eternal salvation, there he attacks us and attempts to take us. (327)

PART ONE
Preparing to Teach

1

How This Pedagogy Developed

I first encountered the Spiritual Exercises in my seminary years through retreats based upon them. In particular, I remember one six-day retreat led by Father Claude Boudreaux, SJ, then serving at the Jesuit General Curia in Rome. Our seminary residence was outside Rome, and Father Boudreaux spent the week with us, giving daily conferences based on the Spiritual Exercises of St. Ignatius.

I remember him seated before us in the seminary library and his calm delivery as he spoke on the Principle and Foundation, the First Week with its invitation to freedom from sinfulness, the key meditations of the Second Week—the Call of the King, the Two Standards, the Three Classes, and the Three Degrees of Humility—the contemplation of the life of Jesus and of his passion and resurrection, with the concluding Contemplation to Attain Love. Through this retreat and others like it, I and my companions were introduced to the Spiritual Exercises.

During those same years, I grew closer to the founder of my religious community, the Venerable Bruno Lanteri.[1] As I learned more about him, I increasingly perceived his love and esteem for the Ignatian Spiritual Exercises.

Then, in the summer after my second year of theology, one of the seminarians made the thirty-day Spiritual Exercises. When we met in the fall, he spoke of this experience, and a deep desire awoke in me to do the same. I went to the library and attempted to read the book of the *Spiritual Exercises*. As is often true of first contact with the book, it simply confused me with its many points, rules, notes, meditations, contemplations, repetitions, and the like. I did not persist in the effort to read.

But my interest was strong. That year, the Jesuit who had directed my companion's Exercises, Father Engelbert Lacasse, visited our residence in Rome. I spoke with him of my desire to make the thirty-day retreat, and after our conversation he told me that he would accept me for the following summer. My superior approved, and we made the necessary plans.

That next summer, I and three of my companions made the month of retreat under Father Lacasse's direction. The retreat was hosted in a convent in Shawinigan, Quebec, Canada. Father Lacasse did not speak English well, nor did I French, though both of us understood the other language well. That was how we communicated, each speaking his own language! We never had any difficulty in conversing.

Father Lacasse's approach was a mixture of old-school preaching and the more recent emphasis on personal prayer with regular meetings between retreatant and director. Father gave five conferences a day, each followed by forty-five minutes of personal prayer. He met with us every other day.

What could have been a heavy daily schedule was not so because we found Father Lacasse so inspiring. In his daily talks he simply commented on the text of the *Spiritual Exercises*, exposing us to the book and in a way that motivated prayer. I loved the whole experience. I remember that when we finished the month, I said to myself, "Someone has finally taught me how to pray."

That thirty-day retreat was my first encounter with Ignatius's rules for the discernment of spirits (*SpirEx* 313–336). They made no particular impression on me at the time; they were a part of a larger text that I now esteem, but they did not draw my attention in any special way. Father Lacasse had explained each, and I had learned from his explanation. The matter rested there.

After the retreat I continued to learn more about the Spiritual Exercises. When studying at the Pontifical Gregorian University, I met Father Manuel Ruiz Jurado, SJ. I attended his classes at the university, and he later served as director of my licentiate and doctoral theses. At his suggestion, I focused my academic writing on Venerable Bruno Lanteri's understanding of the Spiritual Exercises and the place he gave them in the work of my congregation.[2] My perception of their centrality in our ministry grew.

Father Ruiz Jurado is a leading Ignatian scholar and was well qualified to guide my studies. The licentiate and doctoral theses were solid exercises in learning. At the same time, I attended classes and conferences on the Spiritual Exercises by other leading Ignatian figures: Charles Bernard, SJ, Herbert Alphonso, SJ, Clemente Espinosa, SJ, and others.

When I finished my studies and prepared to return to the United States, I asked Father Ruiz Jurado for suggestions on Ignatian reading. Among his recommendations was Daniel Gil, SJ's recently published commentary on the rules for discernment.[3] I will be forever grateful to Father for this recommendation. I purchased the book, brought it with me to the United States, placed it on my shelf, and, at the time, left it there without reading it.

A year earlier, Jules Toner, SJ, published his commentary on the rules for discernment.[4] I was aware of this book, but likewise did not then read it. In retrospect, I find it remarkable that, to my mind, the two best commentaries on these rules in their five-hundred-year history were written within a year of each other.

Certainly busyness was involved in my slowness to read these books. I had just returned to the United States after eleven years in Italy and was absorbed in my new work with our seminarians. But that was not all. At that time I had no awareness that the rules for discernment might merit more attention than, for example, the talks Father Lacasse had given on them in the thirty-day retreat.

At this point, a classmate who had been working in Argentina returned to visit. In Argentina he had come to know Father Miguel Ángel Fiorito, SJ, another master of Ignatian discernment.[5] As we spoke, my classmate mentioned talks that he gave on the rules for discernment. One simple comment struck me and stayed with me. He told of how he would speak for a half hour on the title statement to the rules: "Rules for becoming aware and understanding to some extent the different movements which are caused in the soul, the good, to receive them, and the bad to reject them. And these rules are more proper for the first week."[6]

I had no idea how anyone could speak for a half hour on this brief text of thirty-four words (in the original Spanish), simply a title to the rules that follow. I realized that if this text could be explained for thirty minutes, it contained much more than I knew. For the first time, I felt a need to learn more about these rules.

I was teaching at the time, and it happened that a month opened for me during the fall semester. I decided that this was my opportunity to study Ignatius's rules for discernment more in depth. I took Daniel Gil's commentary on them and went to a quiet part of the house. Day after day, with Gil's guidance, I explored the rules. I can still see myself, walking up and down the corridor outside the office, wrestling with the questions that arose as I studied. I grew familiar with the original text in Spanish. Gil's phrase-by-phrase explanation of the text opened my eyes to a richness I had never seen. I began to understand how one could give a half-hour talk on the title statement or any of the rules.

From time to time I was asked to give retreats to our seminarians. In these retreats I began giving simple talks on the rules. The turning point came when I was asked to give an eight-day retreat to a group of sisters. Each morning I spoke for thirty minutes on the rules, and over the eight days presented all fourteen (*SpirEx* 313–327).[7] Something electric occurred in the transmission and reception of these rules; both the retreatants and I knew that something significant had happened.

This was the moment when I first understood that these rules contained a treasure. The study I had done and would do in subsequent years contributed further to this understanding. But that was not the primary factor. What really opened my eyes to the power in these rules was the response of people when they were explained. With varying nuances, people would say, "For the first time, I understand what is happening in my spiritual life. I can already see the difference these practical guidelines will make in my life. I feel a whole new sense of hope. Why didn't anyone tell us about this before? I wish I had known this ten (twenty, thirty, forty) years ago. Everyone should know this teaching."

That retreat with the sisters was the first time I experienced this response to the rules. It was only the first experience of an enthusiasm that I have witnessed consistently in the twenty-five years since whenever the rules were presented with the pedagogy I will discuss in this book.

After that retreat, for the next eleven years, I gave three retreats a year to these sisters, each time explaining the rules for discernment. At the end of one retreat, a sister told me that she had watched the groundskeeper go into a shed and come out carrying the tools he needed. She said, "I feel like St. Ignatius has done the same for me. His rules give me the spiritual tools I need to live my spiritual life."

Every time I prepared and then presented the rules, I learned more about them. My grasp of the pedagogy and my understanding of why it was effective continued to develop.

Requests for this teaching arrived from other groups as well, and I found myself presenting the rules often throughout the year. By now my interest in the rules was deeply awakened, and I began to read everything I could find on them. This encompassed their five-hundred-year history and included various languages. It involved all of Ignatius's writings; Jesuit writings about Ignatius's life and spirituality; early commentaries on how to give the Spiritual Exercises; writings by more recent authors such as José Calveras, SJ, Ignacio Casanovas, SJ, Ignacio Iparraguirre, SJ, Manuel Ruiz Jurado, SJ, Daniel Gil, SJ, Jules Toner, SJ, Miguel Ángel Fiorito, SJ, and Thomas Green, SJ; the many articles on discernment in *Manresa* and *The Way*; and a wide variety of contemporary writing on discernment. The reading led me deeper into the wisdom of Ignatius's rules.

During these years I made another decision that, as I realized later, contributed significantly to this developing pedagogy. Endless volumes are written on the spiritual life, and I realized that I could not read everything. Some approach to prioritizing my reading was necessary. I decided that I would focus primarily on the classics of the spiritual life, the writings, for example, of St. Teresa of Avila, St. John of the Cross, St. Francis de Sales, St. Bonaventure, St. Francis of Assisi, St. Thérèse of Lisieux, Bl. John Henry Newman, Julian of Norwich, St. Catherine of Siena, and other classic authors.

As these two streams of reading mingled—writing on Ignatius's rules for discernment and classic writing on the spiritual life—I began to see a link between them. Ignatius's text described what occurs in spiritual experience, and the classic sources supplied lived examples of that experience. Taken together, something powerful emerged.

I realized that Ignatius's text is Ignatian only in its formulation—in the structure of the fourteen rules and the words he employed to express each; the experience he illustrates in that text is universal. Any person of faith who seeks to love and follow Christ will undergo the spiritual experience Ignatius describes in his rules.

St. Augustine's spiritual struggles before and during his conversion, for example, perfectly exemplify Ignatius's first two rules.[8] A page in the spiritual diary of Raïssa Maritain, wife of the philosopher Jacques Maritain, author, and a woman of deep love of God, supplies a clear example of rule 3.[9] Again, an experience of Julian of Norwich incarnates the spiritual presupposition underlying Ignatius's rule 8.[10] The words of St. Francis of Assisi to one who was discouraged illustrate Ignatius's rule 9.[11] Examples multiplied endlessly as I read.

In my religious community, each year we make an eight-day Ignatian retreat. The days are spent in silence, praying repeatedly with Scripture as the day unfolds. Each day, the retreatant meets with a director to share the experience of prayer and receive help in discerning where God is leading. I chose to make these retreats with masters of Ignatian spirituality: Manuel Ruiz Jurado, SJ, George Aschenbrenner, SJ, Jules Toner, SJ, Dominic Maruca, SJ, and others. From these retreats I learned in a practical way about Ignatius's rules and how they apply in lived experience. I remember in particular my conversations with Jules Toner, then in his later years. Rarely have I encountered so sharp a mind. It was a delight to discuss discernment of spirits with one who understood the questions so clearly and who could offer such clear answers.

As the years passed, the convergence of these several channels of learning—reading about Ignatian discernment and about classic spiritual experience, the repeated teaching of the rules, contact with masters of Ignatian spirituality, the experience of the rules that many shared with me, and my own growing awareness of how these rules applied in my own life—coalesced in the pedagogy that is the subject of this book. It consists essentially in this: a careful exploration of Ignatius's own words in his text and an abundant exemplification of them through concrete spiritual experience. I will return to this methodology in subsequent chapters.

Eventually I was invited to teach the rules to a group of spiritual directors in training. At that point, the teaching moved beyond the context of retreats and became a teaching in its own right. Further invitations followed, and I began presenting the rules in many settings: parishes, seminaries, programs of spiritual formation, professional groups, and similar venues. After some time, my superior asked me to formulate this presentation as a book. A series of Ignatian books resulted, as one book required another for completeness.

Now, some thirty-five years since I began to explore Ignatian discernment, this pedagogy has reached thousands. For much of this time, I have traveled nationally and internationally teaching Ignatius's rules according to this pedagogy. I have shared it with people of different nationalities, cultures, ethnicities, languages, and educational backgrounds. I have seen that when the rules are taught in this way, all understand them and perceive how to apply them in their lives. One thing only is presupposed: that this person is trying, or at the very least has tried in the past, to live as a true follower of Christ—that is, that this person is making some sincere effort to pray and to live according to Christ's Word. If so, then the person has already experienced what Ignatius describes in his fourteen rules and will readily understand how to apply them in the future. And not only will these rules be understood, but they will also awaken joy, enthusiasm, and hope.

The books I have written on these rules have amplified the radius of this pedagogy.[12] At present, *The Discernment of Spirits: An Ignatian Guide to Everyday Living* is published in a number of languages.[13] I hear continually from people who tell me how this pedagogy has helped them understand, often for the first time, Ignatian discernment.[14] I have presented this pedagogy on television and through podcasts with the same response.[15]

I know now from experience that this approach to the rules widely expands the number of those who can apply them. The rules cease to be the sole property of a retreat master, Jesuit or otherwise, in a remote retreat house, and become the common possession of all who love Christ. Without exaggeration and because so many tell me this, I can say that these rules, so explained, are life changing.

Increasingly I learn of people who have themselves become teachers of Ignatius's rules. Having benefitted from these rules personally, they wish to share them with others. May their numbers grow! This book is for them and all who will join them as teachers of Ignatian discernment. It is also for those who would like to teach the rules, wonder if they have the prerequisites to attempt this, and if so, how to proceed. To all these, this book offers a blueprint.

2

The Fruit of This Pedagogy

Is it worth teaching the rules? Does this teaching merit the time and effort involved? Can Ignatius's rules for discernment really make a difference in people's lives—enough to justify the energy required to prepare and teach them? Obviously the answers to these questions matter. How a person answers these questions will determine whether or not that person will decide to teach these rules.

I imagine that anyone reading this book has most likely answered these questions affirmatively. I know from decades of experience and beyond doubt that the answers to these questions *are* affirmative. The only question is the pedagogy. If that is effective, great fruit will follow from teaching the rules for discernment.

All people of faith who seek to love Jesus experience the spiritual ups and downs Ignatius describes in his rules. At times they find themselves full of spiritual energy. God feels close, and they sense his love. Prayer is alive; they look forward to it and come from it with new hope and joy. They are grateful for their callings to marriage, priesthood, the consecrated life, or some other form of service in the world, and their daily activity feels blessed with meaning. These may also be times of creativity and new initiatives in prayer or service.

At other times, and for reasons they do not always understand, their spiritual energy seems to disappear. Now God feels distant, and it is hard to sense his love. Prayer is difficult; they struggle even to be faithful to the time of prayer, and little seems to change when they do pray. They feel little joy in their callings and daily service, and find themselves beset with doubts and disquiet.

All of us, with different individual nuances, experience this ebb and flow in our daily spiritual lives. Most of us never talk about this. We do not even have a vocabulary to describe it. When we undergo the more troubling times, we bear them in silence and with some sense of shame: our lack of energy for prayer, our sense of distance from God; the doubts, anxieties, burdens, and urgings to abandon our spiritual efforts we experience indicate to us that we are less than we ought to be—less than God wants us to be—in our spiritual lives. We feel different from others who, it appears to us, never seem to go through this. A gray sense of diminished hope or even hopelessness results. We may live our spiritual lives this way for days, weeks, months, years, or decades.

Who will set the captives free? In the synagogue of Nazareth, Jesus proclaims, "The Spirit of the Lord is upon me. . . . He has sent me to proclaim liberty to captives and . . . to let the oppressed go free" (Lk 4:18).[1] Jesus did not come that we might be held captive to spiritual anxiety, shame, and hopelessness. He came to *set captives free*. Ignatius, in his rules for discernment, is simply an instrument of that freedom.

Simply! Ignatius is not the only one to describe these spiritual ups and downs, but no one has written about them with the same clarity, practicality, and usability. When the rules are taught to people who love Jesus and yet carry such spiritual burdens, the chains of captivity begin to break. A path toward freedom opens and with it a release of hope and energy. To pursue the metaphor, the sun shines through the grayness, and the grayness dissipates.

When I was in the seminary, I read *The Hidden Treasure* by St. Leonard of Port Maurice.[2] In this little book, St. Leonard speaks of the Mass as a treasure at the disposal of all but whose depths and richness many do not know; the treasure is hidden. I often think of Ignatius's rules in this way, as a hidden treasure, a powerful and rich resource available to all but unknown to many. I have seen this change in recent years, but still too many do not know of this spiritual treasure.

The Fruit of This Pedagogy

Hardly a day passes that I do not hear from one or more persons—at this point, thousands of such persons throughout the English-speaking world and in other languages as well—about the difference Ignatius's rules has made in their lives. Whether in person or through digital means, I repeatedly hear comments such as these:

"I never even knew how to talk about this spiritual experience. Now I have a way to understand and talk about it. It is such a relief."

"It's so wonderful to know that I'm not the only one."

"I'm so glad to know that what I experience is normal in the spiritual life."

"I am amazed that five hundred years ago someone described so exactly what I experience."

"It is so good to know that there is no shame in experiencing these spiritual burdens, that all of us do, and that what matters is to resist and reject them."

"I never knew what to do about this, and now I have a way to deal with it."

"I thought that all I could say was that I'm having a bad day. Now I know that I can reject these discouraging lies."

"I thought that I just had to wait for this to end. Now I see that I don't have to be passive, that I can take action to resist this."

Almost invariably, when I teach the rules, people say, "I wish I had known this ten, twenty, thirty years ago." I love this comment when I hear it, because it tells me that these people have deeply assimilated the teaching and that the rules are now likely to make a positive difference in their lives.

One woman, who may stand for many, told me that before learning the rules she thought that the discouraging lies of the enemy—"You are not what you should be. You do not pray well. You do not love God very much. Your service is less than it ought to be."—were the voice of God telling her the truth about her spiritual life. We can easily understand the deep discouragement this entailed. And she had carried this burden for years. To know now, with Ignatius's help, how to distinguish these lies from the true voice of God *set her free* to love and serve the Lord.

I often hear these and similar comments after people have learned the rules. But most of all, I hear this: "Everyone should know this! Every Christian should know this. These rules should be taught to everyone. If they were, it would make such a difference in living our faith." They are right. So many pitfalls, so many harmful decisions, and so much "gray" suffering would be eliminated if all knew and practiced Ignatius's rules for discernment.

For that to happen, teachers of these rules are needed. You, reader, can be one of them. Whether you are single, married, ordained, or consecrated, you can learn and help others learn these rules. The tools are available. The pedagogy exists. The fruit is enormous. The following chapters will supply the means to teach a discernment that can set captives free.

3

The Heart of the Pedagogy

The key to this pedagogy is *text* and *examples*. When we guide our listeners through Ignatius's text—his own words—and then illustrate the text through concrete examples, the rules come alive for our listeners. They understand the rules and see how to apply them in their lives.

Teach the Text

Many approaches may be employed in teaching Ignatius's rules. Long experience has taught me that, if the goal is to help people apply these rules in their lives, the best way is to focus on the text itself, on *what Ignatius actually says*. Once expressed, this may seem evident, but it must be stated, because it is the first and essential key to effectively teaching the rules. I cannot recommend this approach too highly.

Focusing the teaching on Ignatius's text does two things. First, and above all, it ensures that the content of our teaching will be rich. We will be sharing the words of a saint and a uniquely gifted master of discernment. We will not wander in the presentation. We will not omit essential points. We will not need to cast about for a way to present discernment. This approach guarantees that we will remain firmly on track in our teaching.

This service to our listeners—explaining Ignatius's own words—is important because his text is highly condensed and requires patient unfolding. Only such unfolding reveals its full richness.[1] Our listeners will need our help to grasp the full depth of the text.

Second, because this approach adheres to Ignatius's own pedagogical choices, it preserves us from presenting complexities that Ignatius does not discuss and that will confuse rather than help our listeners. Certainly there are further complexities in discernment of spirits. Discussion of these with the right audience—spiritual directors, for example, or those who work professionally in this field—will have value.[2] But if the goal is to help all who love the Lord to apply the rules in their lives, such discussion is not only not necessary—Ignatius obviously did not think so—but also actually impedes the goal of the teaching.

We may have had the experience of needing help with a computer function. We approach a person skilled in computers and present our question. The expert answers the question, and we understand how to perform the function. But if the expert continues to explain and overwhelms us with information on variations of the function or problems we may face at some point, very likely our initial clarity will weaken, submerged in a wealth of related information. All that the expert says is true, and it answers real questions. Explained in other settings and when such questions have arisen, it will benefit the hearer. However, said to this person, at this time, with this need, confuses rather than helps.[3]

To exemplify a presentation based on Ignatius's text, I will cite his second rule:

> **Second Rule.** The second: in persons who are going on intensely purifying their sins and rising from good to better in the service of God our Lord, the method is contrary to that in the first rule. For then it is proper to the evil spirit to bite, sadden, and place obstacles, disquieting with false reasons, so that the person may not go forward. And it is proper to the good spirit to give courage and strength, consolations, tears, inspirations, and quiet, easing and taking away all obstacles, so that the person may go forward in doing good.[4]

How will we present this rule? What outline will we follow? What approach will we adopt? As mentioned, the simplest, easiest, clearest, and most effective approach is to present the text itself in its progressive unfolding.

Both we and our listeners will have the text in hand. We will read the text of rule out loud or ask our listeners to read it. Then we will ask, "For whom is rule 2?" This is the first point Ignatius addresses in the text. Rule 2, he says, is for persons who are "going on intensely purifying their sins" and simultaneously "rising from good to better in the service of God our Lord." We will highlight these two qualities and, through examples, show how these appear in real life. Because this is generally the spiritual situation of our listeners, we will now have their rapt attention. They will know that Ignatius *is speaking to them*.

Ignatius next explains how the enemy—a term already clear to our listeners from the similar approach taken with rule 1—works in such persons: "For then it is proper to the evil spirit to bite, sadden, and place obstacles, disquieting with false reasons, so that the person may not go forward." We, continuing to follow St. Ignatius, will now focus on how the enemy will attempt to discourage these persons who are growing toward God. Ignatius lists four tactics of the enemy: he will *bite, sadden, place obstacles*, and *disquiet with false reasons*. We will explain each of these and illustrate each through examples. The enemy will *bite*, attempt to gnaw at their peace; he will *sadden*, strive to bring a heaviness into their spiritual lives; he will *place obstacles*, presenting this spiritual journey as too difficult, as unsustainable; and he will seek to *disquiet with false* (biblically, he is the "liar") *reasons*, awakening trouble of heart where there is no cause. All of this, we will explain, is "so that the person may not go forward."

At this point, our listeners' attention will be deeply engaged. Very likely, they have experienced all these tactics. Because they could not identify them, they struggled to find freedom from them. Now, with uplift of heart, our listeners see the way to liberation.

Finally (the last word for Ignatius is always grace), Ignatius shows how the good spirit—this term also is clear to our listeners from rule 1—works in these persons who are growing toward God: "And it is proper to the good spirit to give courage and strength, consolations, tears, inspirations and quiet, easing and taking away all obstacles, so that the person may go forward in doing good." Ignatius lists five tactics of the good spirit: he will give *courage and strength, consolations, tears, inspirations, and quiet*, and will *ease and take away all obstacles*. As with the tactics of the enemy, we will present each tactic of the good spirit, explaining it and illustrating it through examples. The good spirit will give these persons *courage and strength*, bringing new energy for growth; he will give them *consolations*, joy in the Lord; he may inspire *tears* that express physically the heart's experience of God's love; he will supply *inspirations* that show the way forward and bring *quiet*, that is peace, to the person; and he will *ease and take away all obstacles*, so that the person may proceed on this spiritual journey with confidence. We will indicate that the good spirit adopts these tactics "so that the person may go forward in doing good."

We should follow this same text-centered approach with all the rules. If they do, the presentation will be rich, well focused, and complete. Each successive rule will reinforce the teaching of the preceding rules as Ignatius continues to apply the same vocabulary and the same basic concepts.

Teach with Examples

Ignatius did not write the rules in a library. They arose from experience, his and that of the many who came to him for spiritual help. When the rules are set once again in experience—their original context—they come alive: *they speak to our listeners' lives*. If the teaching is to be effective, and if our listeners are to apply it to their lives, it is critical that the connection between

The Heart of the Pedagogy

Ignatius's text and their lives be evident in the teaching. Examples are this link.

At times, when I am teaching the rules, I tell my listeners that someday I will write a book entitled "Let's Look at an Example of That." Because I use those words so often, they all laugh. When we find ourselves often repeating these or similar words, it is a sign that the teaching is on target.

In a later chapter I will say more about how to find and choose examples. My point now is that an abundant use of apposite examples is indispensable to teach the rules effectively.

Let us return, for example (!), to the teaching of rule 2. In his text, Ignatius tells us that the enemy will *bite* at those rising from good to better in God's service. We will explain this word: the enemy will bite (*morder*), gnaw, that is, attempt to trouble, to unsettle the joy these persons experience in their new closeness to God. Having explained the word, now it is time to give examples that link Ignatius's word to the experience of our listeners.

Each of us will find our own way to do this. To be concrete, I will share my approach. First, I speak generically: "One of us is experiencing growth toward God and delights in the new peace this growth brings. Faith is alive, God feels close, and there is new energy for spiritual things. Then a time comes when this delight has diminished, and now there is a sense of trouble, of disquiet, and of burden in the spiritual life." Then I ask, "Have any of us ever experienced this?" Many—often all—nod yes. At this point, my listeners are linking Ignatius's rule to their own experience.

Next I quote Ignatius's letter of spiritual direction to Sister Teresa Rejadell, one who was clearly "rising from good to better" in God's service: "The enemy is leading you into error . . . but *not in any way to make you fall into a sin* that would separate you from God our Lord. He tries rather to *upset* you and to *interfere with* your service of God and *your peace of mind*.[5] I note that the enemy does not immediately tempt one rising toward God with obvious sin—the last thing such a person wants at such a time.

The enemy does something different: he *bites*, strives to upset us, to interfere with our service of God, and to strip away our peace of mind. Again, my listeners grasp the link between Ignatius's text and their lives.

I also cite an example from Ignatius's own experience. After his conversion in Loyola, Ignatius spent three days at the Benedictine abbey of Santa Maria de Montserrat, preparing and making a life-changing confession. Some months later, in a time of great spiritual growth, a thought began to trouble him regarding that confession. Ignatius recounts of himself, "Even though the general confession he had made in Montserrat had been made with great diligence and completely in writing, as has been said, nonetheless it seemed to him at times that he had not confessed some things, and *this caused him much affliction*."[6] In a time when Ignatius is "going on intensely purifying his sins" and "rising from good to better" in God's service, the enemy does not attempt immediately to lead him into sin but simply *bites* and gnaws at the peace Ignatius would otherwise feel in God.[7]

If time allows, I may quote examples such as the following, in this case taken from my own experience of this biting:

> When I feel drawn to spend quiet time in prayer, just with the Lord and without much mental activity, and find this nourishing and joyful, there is the voice that says, "You're not really praying. You should be doing more, reflecting on a scriptural passage, using the time better." This voice awakens *a small sense of uneasiness* that weighs on my prayer. It is not clamorous; *it just saps the joy*. Because it is not clamorous, I don't easily see it.
>
> When I want to share "small" things with the Lord, ask help in daily matters, or share daily concerns about work, relationships, projects, small tensions, and similar things, there is a voice that says, "With all the real problems in the world, people in the midst of wars and

hunger, deep physical suffering, and lives torn apart, you should be ashamed to bring such small concerns to the Lord. With such great needs in the world, you are asking for help with these small burdens?" My director quoted Jesus's words that even the hairs on our head are counted, that not a single sparrow falls to the ground without our Father knowing it (Lk 12:6–7). Everything in my life matters to God, and this hesitation *that weighs on my freedom* to share these things in prayer because they are so small *is the enemy's biting*. I should reject it.[8]

At this point, my listeners understand well how the enemy's "biting" may appear in their own experience. The examples have linked the text to their lives. This is the heart of the pedagogy: text and examples.

4

Getting to Know the Text

In my second year of priesthood, I was assigned to my community's house in the Archdiocese of Milan, Italy. The archbishop at the time was Cardinal Carlo Maria Martini, SJ. For some years, like many others, I had read his books. These were based on retreat talks in which he blended biblical expertise with the Spiritual Exercises in a compelling way.

One day a week Cardinal Martini made himself available to the priests of the archdiocese. One day I met with him, and we spoke of various things. In particular, I asked his advice on how to learn the Spiritual Exercises more deeply. I have never forgotten his counsel: learn the text of the *Spiritual Exercises*, steep yourself in the text, grow familiar with the text. He said that this knowledge of the text would bless all I would ever do with the Spiritual Exercises. He was right, and I have been grateful to him ever since for that counsel.

To all who would teach Ignatius's rules for discernment, I say the same: Get to know the text. Read it attentively. Learn how Ignatius expresses himself in the text. Return to it often. Ask questions of the text if anything is not clear. Explore the answers to these questions. The more familiar with the text you become, the more prepared you will be for effective teaching of the rules.

The text of these fourteen rules is brief—1,239 words in the original Spanish. Not one word in this text is superfluous or wasted. Because it is so compact, its full richness will not appear in a first or single reading alone. Spend time with the text. Get to know it well. If you do, it will open for you in ways that will delight you and, as I have said, will bless your teaching.

Which translation in English should you use? There are many, and all have merit. I will recommend two because both were done with the same criterion, the criterion that best serves this text-and-examples approach. If the reader will permit, one is my own translation, which I have provided at the beginning of this book.[1] I made this translation from the original Spanish and with the purpose of rendering the original as nearly as English allows. I sacrificed elegance of style for closeness to Ignatius's words in Spanish. I believe that this approach to translation greatly assists a pedagogy based on close attention to the text. Years ago, Eldar Mullan, SJ, also made a translation that was intended to be "as faithful and close a reproduction of the Spanish text as could be."[2]

With a well-chosen English translation, you have all you need to teach the rules. If you read Spanish or have even a slight acquaintance with Spanish, then I recommend obtaining the text also in Spanish.[3] This will permit you to compare the English with the original if you should seek greater clarity regarding certain points.

Then, read a commentary on the rules, one based on the text. To my knowledge, my *The Discernment of Spirits: An Ignatian Guide to Everyday Living* is the only commentary in English that follows this approach.[4] I believe that if you assimilate this book well, you will have the essential knowledge you need to begin teaching the rules. My second book on these same rules, *Setting Captives Free: Personal Reflections on Ignatian Discernment of Spirits*, offers further considerations and examples for each of the rules.[5] After this basic reading, other reading on discernment may be done according to interest. Two fine commentaries on the text also exist in Spanish.[6]

As you get to know the text, your enthusiasm for the teaching will grow. New insights will open for you. You will find yourself applying the rules more often and with greater fruit in your own life. And you will know that you have something valuable to share with prospective listeners.

5

Choosing Examples

How do we find relevant examples? Where do we look? What kinds of examples best assist the teaching? These questions lie at the heart of the pedagogy, and I will offer some thoughts in reply.

Finding Examples

A first, rich source of examples is the spiritual experience of classic figures in the tradition. I use, for example, St. Ignatius's conversion experience as recounted in his autobiography; St. Augustine's experience immediately prior to his conversion as narrated in his *Confessions*; an experience from the last months of St. Thérèse of Lisieux as described by her sister; an incident in the life of St. Francis of Assisi included in one of the early biographies; a page from Julian of Norwich's *Revelations of Divine Love* that portrays her experiences of spiritual consolation and spiritual desolation; and many similar examples from sources of this nature.[1] Once you have absorbed the rules and understand their content, reading of this kind will increase your bank of examples: you will perceive the link between Ignatius's rules and what you find in such reading.

Accounts of spiritual experience—autobiographies and biographies of spiritual figures, conversion stories, and the like—are particularly rich sources of examples. Over the years, I have read extensively in such writing. At times, an entire book will yield one telling example, but that example will powerfully illustrate one of the rules. I always experience a certain thrill when I realize that this new example will strengthen the teaching. As time passes, a teacher who does such reading will not only benefit personally but also build an effective set of examples.

Examples taken from such classic figures also assist the teaching in another way. When our listeners perceive that Ignatius's rules provide language for universal spiritual experience—that, for example, saints such as Augustine, Benedict, Francis of Assisi, Thérèse, and many others have experienced what Ignatius describes in the rules—they realize that the rules are not "just Ignatian." In the rules Ignatius simply describes what all who love the Lord experience.

Other examples derive from our attention to our own experience and that of others around us. One Sunday afternoon I arrived at a seminary for a retreat that was to begin that evening. I was given a room for the afternoon and spent perhaps two hours there before we left for the retreat house. It was a gray, cold winter's day. The huge seminary building was almost empty, as many seminarians had not yet arrived. For some minutes I sat there alone in the room, in the silence, in the empty seminary, looking out the window at the overcast day. When I teach the rules to seminarians, I speak of a seminarian, alone in his room on a Sunday afternoon, in a large, empty seminary, feeling that it is too difficult, that he cannot go on. When I use this example, I make it a rainy day as well, and the seminarians laugh. But they get the point. I use this experience to illustrate Ignatius's rule 2 and the enemy's tactic of "placing obstacles" in the way of one who is growing toward God.

Examples of this kind abound if we are attentive to our own spiritual experience and that of others around us: the man or woman whose day at work has not gone well and who struggles even to pray; the parent who has had a difficult conversation with a college-age son or daughter and finds little energy for the Bible study that evening; the person who has just made a grace-filled retreat or whose prayer is blessed with a joyful sense of God's love, and who contemplates new initiatives in the Lord; the discouraged man who sits at his desk at 10:00 p.m., poised between the prayer he usually says at that time and the smartphone or tablet as an escape. There are many experiences like these in daily life, and if we note them, we can shape them into effective examples.

Finally, we may use personal examples in our teaching. Employed appropriately, judiciously, and not overdone, these can serve in various ways. Such examples interest our listeners; they give our listeners a sense of connection with us—"He/she is one of us, not teaching from on high, but our brother/sister in the struggle"; and they set our listeners at ease in their own struggles with the tactics of the enemy that Ignatius describes—"If he/she experiences this too, then it must be all right that I also have the same struggles at times."

When, for example, I teach rule 8 (in desolation, remember that consolation will return, and much sooner than the desolation tells us), I share a practice that helps me apply this rule. At times, when I am in desolation, I take my journal and describe the experience in writing. This writing helps me see it more objectively and already begins to free me from it. Then, with rule 8 in mind, I also write that a point will come, and not far distant, when the desolation will have passed and I will reread these lines in consolation. This always happens. Often, just an hour or a few hours later, the desolation is gone and I am again in peace. When I do reread the lines I wrote in desolation, I am confirmed anew in the truth of rule 8.

I tell my listeners that I am a writer, that writing is in my blood, that this is one way I apply rule 8. Obviously I have their interest in mind as I share this personal example. The sharing is appropriate—it embarrasses neither me nor my listeners—and it renders the rule concrete. I tell my listeners that they, too, will find personal ways to practice rule 8.

If we use personal examples, the focus must be on what will help our listeners. The sharing must not arise simply from our desire to speak about ourselves and our own experiences.

Examples That Serve the Teaching

The best examples are those to which our listeners can relate fully: experiences similar to their own. For this reason, I do not use examples that involve the mystical experience typical of the higher states of contemplative prayer. These are beautiful, but they will be beyond the experience of many listeners. Thus, for example, I do not quote Ignatius's mystical experiences of the Trinity to exemplify the rules, but I do quote his experiences of spiritual consolation and spiritual desolation. In the same way, I do not cite St. Teresa of Avila's mystical experiences, but I do quote her spiritual wisdom as it applies to all and illustrates Ignatius's rules. I may adopt examples from the lives and writings of such mystics, but only of their more ordinary experiences such that all can relate fully to them.

For the same reason, I do not employ examples from private revelations.[2] If approved by Church authority, these may contain many spiritual riches and nourish many people. They are, however, generally beyond the personal experience of my listeners.

Finally, I do not use examples from Jesus's experience as seen in the Gospels. I recognize that there may be other views on this, and I respect them. I do not use such examples, however, because Jesus is the only instance of the Hypostatic Union—the union of two natures, human and divine, in one Person—and there are depths here beyond our experience. Thus, for example, when on the Cross Jesus cries out, "My God, my God, why have you forsaken me?" (Mt 27:46),[3] is he experiencing spiritual desolation in Ignatius's sense? The question is real, and the answer may be yes. But, as just said, there are depths here beyond our experience, and I prefer not to enter into such questions. I believe it better to employ examples to which my listeners can relate fully from their own experience.

I believe it important that any example used be completely solid and solidly rooted in the Church's tradition. We are presenting these examples for the instruction of God's people. Consequently I avoid any example that contains some rich content mixed with other more questionable elements.

If we have built a sufficiently varied bank of examples, we can choose those that best apply to our specific group of listeners. Are these married men and women? Then do we have examples from the experience of those who live the lay and married vocation? Is this a group of men? Then do we have examples of men whose experiences illustrate the rules? A group of women? Then do we have examples of women whose experiences illustrate the rules? The same may be said of young adults, priests, religious, seminarians, or any group to whom we are presenting the rules. This norm should not be made absolute: the experience of many spiritual figures is universal—many of St. Augustine's or St. Thérèse's experiences, for example, may apply well both to those living in marriage and in the priesthood. It is good, however, to keep this principle generally in mind when choosing examples.

Some Specific Examples

We will each find our own examples and employ those we find most useful. I will mention two that I have found especially helpful, in particular for presenting the title statement (*SpirEx* 313) and the first two rules: Ignatius's conversion at age thirty on his convalescent bed, and the spiritual experience that immediately preceded and prepared Augustine's conversion.[4]

When I begin teaching the rules, after a brief introduction, I turn quickly to Ignatius's conversion at age thirty. I tell of his morally wayward life before then, his leg wound in battle, his long convalescence after three surgeries, his thoughts and feelings as he read the life of Christ and the lives of the saints, and his more worldly thoughts about pursuing a woman of high rank. Then I describe the day when "his eyes were opened a little,"[5] his subsequent identification of the first set of thoughts as from God and to be followed, and the second as not of God and to be rejected, and, finally, the powerful impact of this first experience of discernment on his life and, through him, on the lives of many others as well. The details of this striking story are found in Ignatius's own autobiography and in any biography of Ignatius.

I find that many benefits flow from beginning the teaching with this account. The story is fascinating in itself and immediately engages my listeners. A sense awakens that "this teaching is going to be good." One young man told me that he arrived for the teaching worn from long travel. When we began that evening, he fully expected to fall asleep from tiredness. He found that he wasn't able to sleep! Ignatius's story so interested him that he was immediately absorbed by the material.

Ignatius's story is so human that listeners quickly find themselves drawn to him and interested in what will follow. Those six words—"his eyes were opened a little"—provide a useful rubric for the entire teaching; learning and applying the rules does exactly that—it opens our spiritual eyes to notice, understand, and respond to spiritual experience with new precision. "His eyes were opened a little" is a perfect introduction to the first piece in the text, the title statement (*SpirEx* 313), which outlines the basic paradigm of discernment: be aware, understand, take action.

The second example is the spiritual experience that immediately preceded Augustine's dramatic conversion as he recounts in his *Confessions*.[6] I describe Augustine's conversation with his friend Ponticianus; Ponticianus's account of two young men who decisively give their lives to Christ; the torment this account awakens in Augustine as he compares his own inability to change his life with the decisiveness of these two; his anguished prayer and tears in the garden; the singsong voice of the child outside the garden chanting, "Take and read, take and read"; his opening of the Scriptures to Romans 13, Paul's injunction to put on Christ and make no provision for the desires of the flesh (Rom 13:14); Augustine's change of heart; his conversation with his mother, Monica; and the beginning of a new life in Christ.

Again, the experience is fascinating and engages my listeners. It perfectly introduces rules 1 and 2: the images of sensual pleasures that fill his imagination and propel the young Augustine toward sin (rule 1, action of the enemy), and the shame and even torment that never leave him in peace while he lives this sinful life (rule 1, action of the good spirit). When Augustine desires to change, abandon sin, and turn to Christ, a discouraging voice within insinuates that he is too weak, that he cannot do it, that he will never change in a lasting way (rule 2, action of the enemy); and an encouraging voice assures him that, with God's help, the change is indeed possible, that he can do what so many others did with God's grace (rule 2, action of the good spirit). When we read rules 1 and 2, my listeners quickly connect the text with the example.

I share these two examples not because I imagine that all teachers will use them. I simply mention them because I find them so effective.[7] You will find your own ways to exemplify the rules.

6

Living the Rules Personally

I have always considered it a blessing that I teach Ignatius's rules repeatedly during the year. Because I do, they are never far from my consciousness, and this greatly helps me apply them in my own life. In my times of spiritual consolation, I have a greater awareness of God's gift and where it may be leading. In times of spiritual desolation, the rules are an invaluable resource for naming the experience and taking appropriate steps to resist it.

Anyone who teaches these rules will experience this as well; it is one of the many personal benefits of teaching the rules to others. This fact leads me to a general principle with respect to teaching the rules: we can only teach them well to others if we are seeking to live them in our own lives.

When we apply these rules in our own lives and so experience their wonderful fruit, we will teach them to others with greater energy, conviction, and enthusiasm. Because we experience ourselves how the rules apply in daily spiritual experience, we will help our listeners make this connection as well. Our experience becomes an important resource for helping others understand how to apply the rules. We will do this with respect for the individuality of each listener—each will find a personal way to apply the rules—but we will know from lived experience how to guide each listener along this path.

How will we apply these rules in our own lives? An effective, almost indispensable means is the daily examen prayer.[1] This exercise of prayer, which might take eight to ten minutes each day, is a time to review the spiritual experience of the day. It includes the classical examination of conscience and adds to it the dimension of discernment: with the Lord, we note whether or not there have been experiences of spiritual consolation or spiritual desolation in the day and, if so, how we have responded to them. The examen prayer helps us apply Ignatius's rules to the day's experience.

We may find it helpful to keep a journal as we pray the examen prayer.[2] Even brief jottings may help us understand our experiences more clearly and perceive more clearly how the rules apply to us.

Some form of accompaniment in our efforts to live daily discernment will greatly bless the efforts themselves. What form might this accompaniment take?

- Spiritual direction, that is, regular meetings with a capable spiritual guide, is a solidly attested element of our spiritual tradition and can be of great assistance in pursuing daily discernment. If we find spiritual directors who know the rules and with whom we can share our experiences of them, we will be greatly assisted along this path. I know that spiritual direction may not always be easy to find. It is encouraging, however, that more and more directors today know these Ignatian rules.

- For some, occasional meetings with an experienced director may be the most realistic form of such accompaniment.

- Participation in groups of spiritual formation with qualified leadership may be another means to find this support.

- Conversation with spiritual friends who share the same journey may also be highly encouraging in the practice of discernment. These are simply friends in the Lord. They do not attempt to be spiritual directors, but their friendship, conversation, and support can do much to assist us.[3]

A rich means for learning the rules is to make an Ignatian retreat—the original setting of the rules. Those of us who have done so know how much this assists us personally, how a retreat helps us understand the rules and blesses our teaching of the rules.

An Ignatian retreat may be made according to the time you have available: three days, five, seven, ten, even thirty. Shorter forms of the retreat, perhaps of several days, may be made annually if you desire. The full Spiritual Exercises may also be made without leaving home, in your daily life.[4] In this case, you pray for an hour a day over several months, meeting weekly with the retreat director.

If you make retreats with directors who know the rules, you will learn much about the rules. Having experienced them in their original setting, you will see more clearly how to apply the rules in daily living and how to help others do this.

I have found such retreats a great blessing personally and a wonderful source of learning. Sometimes I have to smile when a director helps me identify in my own experience the rules that I have taught to others.

To teach the rules well, more is necessary than learning about them: we need to live them. If we do, our teaching will touch the hearts and lives of our listeners. I say this briefly because the point can be made without many words. But this—living the rules—is essential to teaching them effectively.

In part 1 of this book, we have discussed how we can prepare to present the rules. In part 2, we turn to the actual teaching of the rules. We will discuss each rule and how to teach it well.

PART TWO

Teaching the Rules

7

General Principles

Over the years, I have developed an important set of principles that guide my teaching of the rules and help me teach them effectively. Here, before turning to the individual rules, I will review these general principles.

Demystify Immediately

For most of our listeners, the term *discernment of spirits* is both inviting and mysterious. They know that discernment is important, and it awakens their interest. At the same time, *discernment of spirits* may evoke images of a Jesuit retreat director, a master of the spiritual life, off in a retreat center, and may appear remote to the "ordinary" person.

Therefore, in my teaching, before turning to Ignatius's text, I begin by immediately demystifying the term *discernment of spirits*. I explain that this phrase refers to the ordinary spiritual experience of all who love the Lord. I refer to my listeners' experience and say, "We all know that we experience times of spiritual energy when prayer is alive, God feels close, Scripture and liturgical prayer draw us, and with joy we sense our growth in the Lord. We also know that there are times when, for reasons we may not understand, that energy seems to disappear. Then we find it hard to pray, God seems distant, prayer feels dry and unfruitful, and we have little energy for spiritual things."

"These ups and downs," I continue, "are going on all the time. Often we do not know how to understand them and do not know how to respond to them. Ignatius's teaching on discernment of spirits," I explain, "is a teaching about this ordinary, ongoing experience in the spiritual life. His teaching equips us to notice, understand, and respond well to this daily experience."[1]

With this introduction, my listeners immediately perceive that *discernment of spirits* is not mysterious, remote, or abstract, and that it applies personally to them. Their attention is caught from the start.

When Time Is Short: Choices Teachers Must Make

We all will find our own rhythms regarding how much time we need to teach the rules. I find that I can teach all fourteen in ten forty-five minute sessions. These are sessions in which I speak, presenting the material. If my listeners raise questions, I answer them. These ten sessions do not include time for personal reflection or group discussion. This is valuable where possible, but it does require additional time.

I do not claim that my ten-session rhythm is absolute! We all have our own rhythms and will find the time we need to teach the rules, and with what approach. I share my own framework simply as one model. It may be varied in many ways, according to what you find helpful.

Whatever rhythm we adopt to present all fourteen rules, what of situations in which that number of sessions is not possible? In one-day seminars, for example, or weekend retreats, that full time may not be available. We then face a choice: Is it better to still cover all fourteen rules, even though less fully, or to focus in depth on some rules without attempting to cover all?

When time is limited, I prefer the second approach. I believe that my listeners benefit more from an in-depth presentation of some key rules than from a hurried presentation of all fourteen. In this approach, I still speak of all fourteen rules, but in the following manner.

I focus in detail on the title statement (be aware, understand, take action) and the first four rules (how the good spirit and enemy work when a person moves away from or toward God, spiritual consolation, spiritual desolation). This is the foundational part of the text, and I believe it is important that my listeners assimilate it well.

If time allows, I present rules 5 and 6 in the same thorough way, and if time further allows, rules 12 and 13. This does not mean that the remaining rules are not important! It simply means that when time does not allow a full treatment of all fourteen rules, I must make a choice.

Before concluding, I provide a quick overview of the remaining rules and supply means by which my listeners can complete the teaching.[2] Because we have covered the foundational rules in depth, my listeners are equipped to do so. And because we have covered several rules in depth, my listeners perceive the richness of the rules as a whole and are motivated to complete the teaching.

When time is limited, therefore, I believe that we should not feel obliged to sprint through the material at a pace that renders assimilation difficult. We all will find our own ways to adapt the teaching to the time available.

The rules touch deep places in our listeners' hearts. Our listeners are not only absorbing new content but also applying it to their own experience. They are working interiorly as the presentation unfolds, as spaces in their hearts and memories are being touched. We need to respect this fact and give our listeners the breaks they need. For this reason, I never speak longer than forty-five minutes. Again, teaching styles differ; you will choose the rhythms that work best for you. I find that the breaks between talks are valuable not only for a renewal of energies but also often as fruitful times of discussion among my listeners.

Emphasize Grace

Emphasizing grace is key to a fruitful presentation of the rules, and I cannot emphasize it enough. When I teach the rules, I continually emphasize God's grace, the gift of redemption, and the call to freedom—"setting captives free" (see Lk 4:18). I tell my listeners that this entire set of rules is *a spirituality of redemption*. God's love, redemption, grace, and the call to freedom dominate throughout the rules.

This is absolutely true! It is the reason for which Ignatius gave us the rules: to help us find freedom from the enemy's spiritual desolations and temptations. If Ignatius focuses throughout the rules on the enemy's tactics—his discouraging desolations and his deceptive temptations—it is only to show us the way to freedom from them. When we maintain this focus as we present the rules, the presentation will not be heavy; it will uplift and encourage our listeners. I have witnessed this constantly through the years: over and over, people tell me of the hope the rules inspire in them.

Thus, for example, in rules 1 and 2, Ignatius describes first the tactics of the enemy, but in both rules the final word is the action of the good spirit. God's grace, redemption, setting captives free—this is the primary reality, and I note this explicitly for my listeners. At some point, usually around rules 5 or 6, I also observe that the enemy and good spirit, both real and both actors in this spiritual drama, are not equal. The first is a fallen creature—yes, of a higher order of being than we, but still only a fallen creature; the second is the eternal, almighty, and infinitely loving God. This truth dispels any sense of heaviness in discussing the tactics of the enemy.

In rule 12 I highlight the weakness of the enemy as Ignatius describes it: if we are willing, with God's help, to stand firm in the beginning of the temptation, then "it is proper to the enemy to weaken and lose heart, fleeing and ceasing his temptations." I explain that the enemy is weak, not compared to us but to the power of Christ that is in us (Lk 11:21–22).

Throughout the presentation I consistently emphasize the positive. Thus in teaching rules 12, 13, and 14, having explained the enemy's tactics, I focus above all on the response that negates these tactics: standing firm in the beginning (rule 12), breaking the spiritual silence (rule 13), and strengthening the weak point (rule 14). The presentation remains hope-filled and centered on grace and the path to freedom. My listeners absorb this hope, and new spiritual energy is released.

The contrary—a presentation that primarily emphasizes the enemy's desolations and temptations—will have the opposite effect. My listeners will find the presentation heavy and will be little inclined to apply the rules in their lives. A door will be shut—precisely the door to freedom Ignatius wishes to open. Long experience has taught me that if grace is emphasized in presenting the rules, captives will know that freedom is possible and so will pursue it.

Reverence

Reverence is another important point. The fourteen rules touch deeply sensitive places in our listeners' hearts: places of joy and closeness to God, but also places of discouragement, shame, anxiety, and, at times, long-standing burdens. When we watch Jesus respond to the suffering people who approach him, we find that he is always sensitive to their burdens. He never "bulldozes" into human hearts, but is always gentle and reverent toward human pain (Mt 11:28–30; 12:18–21). I think, for example, of how sensitively Jesus responds to the shattered woman at his feet in Luke 7, of how gently he heals Peter's heart at the lakeside in John 21, or of how he turns Mary Magdalene's pain into joy so lovingly by pronouncing her name in John 20. We need to imitate Jesus when we present the rules.

We need to know that our words, as we present Ignatius's teaching, resonate not only in the minds but also in the hearts of our listeners. Our listeners remember times when they have experienced the tactics of the good spirit and the enemy, as Ignatius describes them. They constantly link what they hear to their own lives. Deep places are being touched. We, like Jesus, must recognize and reverence these spaces of the heart.

I express this reverence explicitly when I teach the rules. When, for example, we read an experience from St. Ignatius, St. Augustine, St. Elizabeth Seton, or others, after the reading and before I apply the example to the rule under consideration, I say, "We are on holy ground here in this person's relationship with God. We will approach it with reverence, for the sake of the learning we can find here." There is nothing artificial about these words. This is not a formula that I feel must be said. I say this out of conviction: these experiences *are* holy places in these persons' lives and *must* be approached with reverence.

My listeners appreciate this. Over and over, personally and in written evaluations, people tell me how much they appreciate this reverence. No one has ever criticized me for using the word *reverence* too much! And many, very many, have expressed their gratitude. My listeners learn from me that their experience, too, is holy ground, and that God looks upon it with reverence. Something in them relaxes spiritually, and they receive the teaching with new openness. They know that they are not being criticized but understood, held in reverence, and helped.

The reverse is also true. As we explain the tactics of the enemy, if our listeners feel accused, that their struggles are laid bare, that they are admonished, and the like, they will be slow to accept the rules. If this tone is too marked, they will not hear a message of "captives set free" and of hope. The rules will lose their power to help them.

No Shame in Experiencing Spiritual Desolation

I tell my listeners that *there is no shame* in experiencing the discouragement, lack of desire for prayer, movement to low and earthly things, absence of fervor, and all the other qualities of spiritual desolation (rule 4). I say this often when presenting the rules, and it is liberating for people who so often *do* feel shame when they experience desolation.

I say it in words like these: "There is no shame in experiencing spiritual desolation. This is simply what happens in living the spiritual life in a fallen, redeemed, and loved world. What *does* matter is this: to *be aware* of this experience, to work with it until you can *name it* for the spiritual desolation that it is, and to *take action*—use the tools that Ignatius and our tradition supply to reject it."

I find that this message of "no shame" is important and helpful to people. Many tell me how much it means for them to hear this and how freeing it is for them. Again, these rules touch places of desolation in which people often do feel shame.

All of us experience times of spiritual desolation. To know that *all* do is likewise liberating. People often feel that "I am the only one. No one else seems to have these hidden, dark, discouraging times in the spiritual life. It's just me." To learn that all undergo such times lifts a burden and sets our listeners free to resist desolation.

In part, this sense that "I am the only one" is due to the absence of a language to describe desolation. When we have no vocabulary for it, we have no way to talk about it, understand it, and respond to it. Thus the experience remains hidden: people feel the burden of desolation but have no means even to speak about it. They suffer desolation in silence and, in all too frequent cases, at great length, even for years or decades. In providing a language for spiritual desolation, Ignatius renders us an enormous service. I see this in people repeatedly when I present the rules: "Oh, that's what I've been experiencing! That's what it is! I see now how to describe it, understand it, and make choices to reject it. There is a path to freedom!"

I also add that if there is no shame in experiencing spiritual desolation, there is likewise no shame in not always experiencing spiritual consolation.[3] Some do feel shame about this, that is, "If I were what I should be in my spiritual life, I would always feel

God's closeness and love, always feel a desire for prayer, always feel energy for spiritual growth. But I do not always feel this. So something must be wrong with me. Something must be lacking in my life of faith." Obviously, a heaviness accompanies such thoughts. To learn that spiritual consolation is not a continuous experience in this life—it will be in the eternal life that awaits us—that it is a gift that God gives in the times that his loving providence knows best for us, also sets hearts free.

When we reach rule 14, I further add that there is no shame in having a weakest point. We all do. This arises from our family upbringing, temperament, experiences in life, and the like. I tell my listeners that this too is simply what it means to live in a fallen, redeemed, and loved world; what matters is to know what this weakest point is and to work to strengthen it—Ignatius's point in rule 14. When I say this, my listeners are once more set free and can absorb the wisdom of rule 14 without self-accusation.

Respect for Questions

My listeners' questions are generally valuable, and I affirm them when they are: "That's a good question, and I'm glad you've asked it." This creates confidence in asking questions. When this climate is established, the teacher will get a number of questions!

When a question is confused, if I judge that the person can clarify it, I ask for clarification: "Can you help me understand that more?" If I judge that people would be embarrassed if I asked for further clarification—maybe they do not grasp the material sufficiently, they're shy in front of a group, or for any other reason—I do not press for more clarity. I choose something in the question on which I can comment in a way that is useful for the group: "Your question is helpful because it touches on something important for our discussion." In this way the time spent answering is valuable for the group. The others in the group also note and appreciate this respect for questioners.

Often enough, questioners raise personal issues as general questions: "What should people do if they find themselves in this situation?" The question is posed in general terms, but lightly behind it I may hear, "I am in this situation. What should I do?" In this case, I reply that there is an individual level that I reverence too much to try to address in a group setting. If it seems appropriate, I add that if the person desires, I would be happy to speak one-on-one outside the group setting. I then say that although I cannot address the individual level in a group setting, I can speak about the general principles involved in such situations, and then I proceed to do so.

This approach is always well received, usually with gratitude for the reverence shown to the personal experience that underlies the question. I believe it very important that we never allow ourselves to be caught answering a deeply personal question in front of the group. We will most likely embarrass ourselves and our listeners.

If the question is off topic, I do not get involved in it. Usually there is some way I can reply that is on topic. My listeners appreciate the fact that we do not digress from the teaching that brought us together. If I do not know the answer to a question, I simply say so. My listeners also welcome this honesty, and it gains their respect.

Respect for Ignatius's Pedagogical Choices

I mentioned this point briefly in chapter 3 and return to it here because of its importance. In his rules, both what Ignatius says and *what he does not say* are important. By respecting both pedagogical choices, we can present the rules in depth and with clarity.

Ignatius wishes to convey a content in the rules and does so succinctly. In the original, the text comprises only 1,239 words, or three and a half pages of double-spaced typed text—a remarkably brief document for so deep a topic.

This detail alone tells us that Ignatius is not concerned to answer every question that might be raised about the material covered in the rules. In fact, in his title statement Ignatius explicitly affirms that these are "rules for becoming aware and understanding *to some extent* the different movements that are caused in the soul" (*SpirEx* 313).[4]

Because Ignatius's teaching on discernment and the categories he employs (spiritual consolation, spiritual desolation) are so telling, a tendency, even a sense of need, can arise to extend them beyond the content of the rules and erect them into a complete explanation of spiritual experience. In so doing, with goodwill, one moves beyond Ignatius's own pedagogical choices. I believe that in the pastoral setting presumed in this book—differently than in academic settings and the explorations proper to them—this attempt is fraught with danger: Ignatius's simplicity and clarity will be lost or at best diminished.

The teaching is much more effective when we simply present Ignatius's rules as he wrote them, neither adding nor subtracting. Then Ignatius's essential and clear presentation allows the rules to be grasped well and applied accurately in experience—precisely the goal for which he composed them.

The rules may be compared to a lighted path through a dark forest.[5] Only the path itself is lit; it does not light up the depths of the forest. Travelers on the path encounter many side paths leading into the wide spaces of the forest. Exploration of these side paths could lead to a fuller understanding of the forest—but it would also take the travelers off the path. In this case, the travelers would arrive only later or not at all, should they lose their way. Yet the goal of the path is to arrive.

In a similar way, Ignatius's text provides a clear path for discernment in daily living and that is its single goal. By remaining firmly on this path and declining further discussions not required for this path, Ignatius—and teachers who respect his pedagogical choices—guides listeners solidly along the way of daily discernment.

Reinforce the Teaching

When we have presented the title statement and first four rules, we have given our listeners all the essential categories. Our listeners know that discernment means to be aware, understand, and take action (title statement); they know how the enemy and good spirit work in persons heading away from or toward God (rules 1 and 2); and they know the meaning of the key spiritual movements, spiritual consolation and spiritual desolation (rules 3 and 4).

I find that my listeners benefit from continual reinforcement of these categories as we explore the remaining rules. I do this through frequent questions to the group when we consider examples of rules 5 through 14.

If, for example, I speak of a man whose day at work did not go well and who arrives home tired and discouraged, I ask the group, "What is this man now experiencing?" They answer, "Nonspiritual desolation." I pursue the example further and describe how, that evening, the man has no desire to pray in his usual way, does not feel God's closeness, and is drawn mindlessly to surf websites on his phone in a way that he knows can harm him. I stop and ask, "What is this man now experiencing?" They answer, "Spiritual desolation." I refer then to a teaching we saw in rule 4 and ask, "Can you see how the nonspiritual desolation has become the space into which the enemy has brought the further trap of spiritual desolation?" In this way, Ignatius's teaching on spiritual desolation in rule 4 is reinforced, and my listeners grow in confidence that they can recognize it in their own experience.

In another example, I may speak of a woman who experiences a time of peace-filled closeness to God in prayer, and ask, "What is this woman experiencing?" They answer, "Spiritual consolation." In yet another example, I may speak of a man who is in spiritual desolation and decides not to pray on his lunch hour as he usually does. I ask, "Which rule is involved here?" My listeners answer, "Rule 5" (do not make changes in desolation). Through constant reinforcing of this kind, my listeners learn to identify the key categories and apply the rules in daily experience.

The "Enemy"

I employ the word *enemy* by conscious choice, and find that it serves the teaching well. Years ago, when I began presenting the rules, I used the term *evil one* and spoke, for example, of "the evil one's" tactics. On one occasion, a woman told me that the constant repetition of the word *evil* was unsettling for her. Her observation prompted me to examine Ignatius's text more closely in this regard.

I found that Ignatius most often uses not "evil one" but "enemy" to describe our foe in the spiritual life. In the fourteen rules, Ignatius employs the phrase *evil spirit (el mal espíritu)* twice, and in these same rules the word *enemy (enemigo)* seven times.[6] Since then, I have used the word *enemy* when teaching the rules, both because it is Ignatius's preferred word and because it resolves difficulties such as those the woman mentioned.

When I present rule 1, the first in which Ignatius speaks of the "enemy," I explain the term with some care. I indicate that it refers to the evil one, the personal angelic being whom Scripture describes as the adversary (1 Pt 5:8), tempter (Mt 4:3), accuser (Rev 12:10), and liar (Jn 8:44). I further indicate that the word *enemy* also includes the remaining two elements of the classic triad: the "flesh" (Gal 5:17)—that is, our own weakness (concupiscence) as a legacy of original sin—and any spiritually harmful influences in the "world" (Jn 17:14) around us.[7] These are the enemies of—they are inimical to, opposed to—our progress toward God.

This presentation accomplishes two ends. It solidly roots the word *enemy* in the Church's tradition and so sets my listeners at ease: they know that we are on firm ground in this exposition.

It also clearly recognizes the reality of our spiritual enemy while avoiding both of two possible extremes: simply ignoring or unduly overemphasizing this influence.[8] It is no small merit of Ignatius to have found a realistic and balanced way to present our "enemy" in the spiritual life.

Teaching the Individual Rules

Having reviewed these principles about teaching the rules, I turn now to the individual rules. In the next chapters, I will share the approach I have found helpful in presenting the title statement (*SpirEx* 313) and each of the fourteen rules that follow (*SpirEx* 314–327).

I have treated this material in two earlier books, *The Discernment of Spirits: An Ignatian Guide to Everyday Living* and *Setting Captives Free: Personal Reflections on Ignatian Discernment of Spirits*. In those books, my focus is the content of the title and the rules. My focus here is the teacher's role in presenting these rules. Therefore, for the content of the title and rules I refer the reader to those earlier books. In the following chapters, our question is, "What will help us present effectively the title and the rules?"

8

Start with the Basics—the Title Statement

Ignatius's brief title statement answers this most fundamental question, "What is discernment of spirits?" Ignatius—who offers in this a guideline for teachers—begins his entire exposition by addressing this question. The title statement reads:

> Rules for becoming aware and understanding to some extent the different movements which are caused in the soul, the good, to receive them, and the bad to reject them. And these rules are more proper for the first week.

I find the following approach effective in presenting this title statement.

Introducing Discernment of Spirits

As mentioned, I try immediately to demystify discernment of spirits. I speak of the ups and downs, the ebb and flow of spiritual energy that we all experience in daily life: times when God feels close, prayer is alive, and we have energy for the spiritual life; and times when we feel far from God, with little desire to pray and little energy for the spiritual life in general. I explain that Ignatius's rules for discernment are directed to help us understand this experience and know how to respond to it. I add that Ignatius is not the only one in our tradition who describes this experience, but that he addresses it with unmatched clarity, practicality, and usability.

I then ask why a group of fifty, one hundred, two hundred or more people, of whom few or (more often) none are Jesuits,

Start with the Basics—the Title Statement 51

would spend time learning a teaching of St. Ignatius of Loyola, founder of the Jesuits. Is not this Ignatian teaching for Jesuits? Why would people who are not Jesuits seek to learn it? In some settings it may not be necessary to raise this question. In others, where some or many of the listeners follow other schools of spirituality—Franciscan, Carmelite, Dominican, Benedictine, and so forth—it is important to address this question.

I answer with parallels in our spiritual tradition.[1] St. Francis of Assisi, for example, with his love of evangelical poverty and simplicity of life, assists not only his Franciscans but also all in the Church who seek the poverty in spirit that gives entrance to the kingdom (Mt 5:3). Likewise, the teachings of the saints John of the Cross and Teresa of Avila on the higher states of prayer guide not only Carmelites but also all in the Church who seek to understand mystical prayer. Again, St. Benedict's love for the liturgy not only blesses his Benedictines but also, through them, strengthens the liturgical life of the entire Church. In the same way, St. Ignatius of Loyola's teaching on discernment offers wisdom not only for Jesuits but also for all in the Church who seek to discern.

None of these spiritual paths is exclusive. One may seek poverty in spirit without reference to Francis, deeper contemplation without John and Teresa, more nourishing liturgy without Benedict, or discernment without Ignatius. In each case, however, these figures stand in a special way as resources for the entire Church. They do so because so many over the centuries have found them helpful in their respective spiritual competencies. The clarity and practicality of Ignatius's teaching on discernment is a gift offered to all who love Christ.

Ignatius's Conversion Experience

I find that Ignatius's conversion experience effectively introduces the title statement. The story is fascinating and immediately engages my listeners. It also prepares my listeners well to grasp the content of the title statement. Ignatius tells this story in his autobiography.[2]

I describe Ignatius's morally wayward life prior to the age of thirty, centered on worldly honor and glory, feats of arms, womanizing, and gambling. Then, in battle, a cannonball shatters his legs. A first surgery is performed on the battlefield and a second after Ignatius's return home. A protruding piece of bone leads Ignatius to demand a third surgery. After this, a long convalescence begins. To pass the time, Ignatius requests reading and is given the only reading available in the house: a life of Christ and a volume on the lives of the saints. Reluctantly he begins to read.

Two contrasting sets of thoughts now arise for him: one of pursuing a woman who, in Ignatius's aristocratically stratified culture, is in practice unattainable for him; the other of imitating the heroism of the saints whom he is now encountering through his reading. The decisive moment arrives when one day "his eyes were opened a little" and Ignatius realizes that though both sets of thoughts delight him while he thinks of them, what happens afterward is very different.[3] After pursuing the unattainable woman in his thoughts, his heart consistently remains "dry and discontented"; after pursuing the heroism of the saints in his thoughts, his heart consistently remains "content and happy."

Once Ignatius is aware of these patterns, he works with this experience until he understands that a set of thoughts that consistently leaves him empty does not have the feel of where God is leading, whereas another set of thoughts that always leaves him happy does have the feel of God's leading in his life. Understanding this, Ignatius takes action accordingly. He abandons the worldly project and begins, with great decision, to imitate the saints. We know the sequel.

The three basic categories that underlie the title statement are now introduced: *be aware*, *understand*, and *take action*; that is, we reject what we now know is not of God and accept, adhere to, follow what we now know to be of God. This example also powerfully illustrates the difference that discerning attention to the spiritual experience of our thoughts and hearts can make in our lives.

The Title Statement: Exploring the Text

At this point, I turn to the text of the title statement. With my listeners, I examine its various parts, following the flow of the text.

"Rules"

Rule for Ignatius signifies a practical guideline about a spiritual reality. The rule instructs about this reality and, above all, gives concrete guidance on how to respond to it. I comment that this first word tells us that Ignatius is not writing a developed treatise on the spiritual life as, for example, St. Francis de Sales's *Introduction to the Devout Life* or St. Teresa of Avila's *Interior Castle*, but rather a set of fourteen short, essential guidelines for how to understand discernment of spirits and especially for how act in its regard.

This clarification is also useful because, culturally, we tend not to like "rules." When the word is explained as Ignatius understands it, any cultural resistance listeners may feel diminishes significantly.

"For Becoming Aware"

This is the first step in discernment: simply to notice, become aware of, this interior spiritual experience in our hearts and thoughts. For Ignatius, this is the moment when "his eyes were opened a little" and he first realizes that this interior experience exists and has significance for the spiritual life.

This step is key. I indicate to my listeners that if we *do not even notice* the spiritual experience in our hearts and thoughts—popular language for our affective and cognitive experience—the rest of discernment (understand, take action) will never follow. I ask my listeners, "What was in our hearts and thoughts as we rose this morning? *Did we even notice?* What was in our hearts and thoughts yesterday? Last week? This past year? How much did we notice?" Such questions engage my listeners, and Ignatius's text quickly ceases to be abstract for them.

"And Understanding"

The second step in discernment is to work with the experience in our hearts and thoughts that we have now noticed, using the tools supplied by our tradition and formulated by Ignatius, until we understand what is of God and what is not of God in it: these stirrings of my heart, inclinations, resistances, thoughts of choosing or acting in this way or that, are of God and these others are not.

I provide examples: In the past six months, one of us carried a burden in her heart. Something troubled her in her relationship with God and weighed on her prayer and service of the Lord. She could not understand what was happening, and the burden persisted. Then a day comes when she grasps what is happening and now *understands* the spiritual meaning of this burden. This understanding sets her free to act appropriately. Another has experienced warm joy in the Lord in recent weeks, and now he *understands* what the Lord is saying to him through the joy in his heart and its related thoughts. He sees where the Lord is leading and is set free to follow that leading. My listeners, who themselves have had such experiences, readily perceive the power in this second step.

"To Some Extent"

As mentioned, Ignatius will not attempt to say all that could be said about discernment of spirits but only what is needed for his purpose: to help us be aware of, understand, and take action in response to the spiritual experience he envisages in these fourteen rules. This "to some extent" is a humble phrase! No one ever, and with such economy of words, shed more light on this experience and how to respond to it.

"The Different Movements That Are Caused in the Soul"

Referring to Ignatius's conversion experience, I can already begin to exemplify these "movements": *delight, dryness, discontent, consolation, happiness*—all words that Ignatius uses in his account—and their related thoughts. I expand a little: such movements also might include joy, sadness, hope, discouragement, peace, anxiety, and the like, again with their related thoughts.

I explain to my listeners that these interior movements are the stuff of discernment of spirits. These are what we seek to become aware of, understand, and take action in response to.

"The Good, to Receive Them, and the Bad to Reject Them"

This is the third step in discernment of spirits: to *take action*. If the movements are good, of God, then the appropriate action is to receive, to *accept* them, to drink them in, be guided by them, to put them into effect so that they will lead us toward God. If the movements are bad, not of God, then the appropriate action is to *reject* them, firmly set them aside, so that they can never harm us.

"And These Rules Are More Proper for the First Week"

I do not comment on this line other than to say that here Ignatius situates these rules within the context of his Spiritual Exercises.[4] This completes our exploration of the text.

Discernment of Spirits: A Basic Paradigm

When our review of the text is complete, I tell my listeners that Ignatius has already said the most important thing about discernment of spirits. I continue, "If you and I are asked, 'What is discernment of spirits?'" we answer, "Discernment of spirits is a spiritual action, a spiritual operation, or, to use Ignatius's own word, a spiritual exercise that asks us:

- to *be aware* of the spiritual movements in our hearts and thoughts
- to work with them until we *understand* what is of God and not of God in them
- and to *take action* accordingly, *accepting* what is of God, acting on it, putting it into practice, and *rejecting* what is not of God, firmly setting it aside so that it can never harm us.

This is discernment of spirits. This answer, which is the heart of the title statement, provides my listeners with a fundamental clarity about discernment: they now know what it is. I tell them that in the rules that follow, Ignatius will put "flesh" on this basic understanding and apply it concretely.

Throughout the entire teaching, I keep this paradigm before my listeners' eyes:

> **BE AWARE**
> **UNDERSTAND**
> **TAKE ACTION**
>   **(ACCEPT/REJECT)**

I refer constantly to this paradigm and, as I teach the successive rules, I repeatedly invite my listeners to identify it in the examples we explore. As the teaching unfolds, my listeners assimilate it well.

I learned years ago the power of this paradigm and the value of reinforcing it in my listeners. It gives them a fundamental grasp of discernment. From this time forward, discernment of spirits is no longer mysterious. At times, with a smile I tell my listeners that this paradigm will be put on my tombstone; it would not be a bad epitaph!

"Be Aware"

Be aware, understand, take action: in the fourteen rules that follow, Ignatius will focus on the second step and, above all, on the third. He will give further instruction (second step: understand) regarding discernment of spirits and, above all, will show us how to respond to this spiritual experience (third step: take action). Obviously, however, awareness is the constant presupposition of the second and third steps; without this key first step, the second and the third will never occur. Ignatius explicitly refers to this awareness only in the title statement. Therefore, once we have explored the complete text of the title statement, I return to his initial words—"rules for *becoming aware*"—and guide my listeners through a reflection on this awareness. If attention to such awareness is important in any age, it is more so today: culturally we are not well equipped to notice spiritual experience.

I introduce this reflection with a short quotation from St. Augustine. In his *Confessions,* Augustine reviews the years when he was far from God, and says to God, "You were within, and I was without. You called, you shouted, and you broke through my deafness. You flashed, you shone, and you dispelled my blindness."[5] *Within* and *without.* Augustine's text provides a striking image of God powerfully at work "within," in the human heart, calling, shouting, flashing, shining. But the human heart is focused "without," engaged in a thousand plans, activities, concerns, and pastimes, and so does not hear or see—is not aware of—God's action "within."

I ask my listeners, "In terms of Augustine's words *within* and *without,* does our culture today live more habitually within or without?" A chorus from the group immediately replies, "Without." I offer examples of our culture's absorption in phones, tablets, earbuds, screens, bustle, noise, and activity, and then continue. "If it is true that our culture—and we are part of it!—lives more habitually without than within, then let's ask a deeper question: 'Why is that so? What is at work in this? Why does our culture live more habitually without than within?'"

I invite my listeners to propose answers to this question. The response is always lively: because of the cultural pressure to produce, because we put our worth in material things, because life has become so busy, because it is not easy to be within, because—and here we get to the roots of the issue—we are afraid to stop and look within. Time usually requires that I conclude the discussion before my listeners have finished suggesting answers.

By now, the key factors have generally emerged: our need for instruction to help us know what to look for within, the effort required to be within and notice, our fear of what we will encounter within, and a number of similar factors.[6] To my mind, the deepest is that identified by Blaise Pascal in his *Pensées*: We live without because we fear to face our limitations—illness, eventual death, emotional pain, failures to live Christ's Word fully, and the like. This fear leads us to divert our awareness without into ceaseless and ultimately unsatisfying activity.[7] Such is the dynamic of *diversion* that Pascal describes so well.

I comment that if we wish to live the discerning life, we will need *the courage to be spiritually aware*.[8] Further, that this flight from within will continue until the human heart discovers that a "light shines in the darkness and the darkness has not overcome it (Jn 1:5 NABRE), and that to be within, far more than to meet our limitations, is to encounter the deep, personal, warm, faithful, and eternal love of the Savior.

A consequence follows. Discernment is never the first reality in the spiritual life. *Evangelization*, just to know that there is a Savior who loves us, and then *catechesis* (discipleship), learning more about and growing in the life of faith, must precede it.

When people know Jesus as the Savior and are living the life of faith, then they will recognize in their own experience everything Ignatius describes in these rules. He simply puts words to that experience and so helps them—an invaluable service!—be aware of it, understand it, and know what action to take in response to it.

I conclude this discussion by affirming that awareness, with all the importance just described, is not an end to itself. This *awareness* is important because it permits *understanding*, and that understanding is important because it permits us to *take action*—the action (*accept* or *reject*) that is the goal of these rules. At this point, we are ready to turn to rule 1.

9

The Spirits in Persons Far from God
Clarity for Your Listeners
Rule 1

Rules 1 and 2 form a pair. In them, Ignatius clarifies a basic criterion for discerning whether the good spirit or the enemy is at work; that is, the person's *fundamental spiritual orientation* as either heading away from (rule 1) or toward God (rule 2). Only when we see this orientation can we discern which spirit is at work. Here we will discuss how to teach rule 1. The text reads:

> **First Rule.** The first rule: in persons who are going from mortal sin to mortal sin, the enemy is ordinarily accustomed to propose apparent pleasures to them, leading them to imagine sensual delights and pleasures in order to hold them more and make them grow in their vices and sins. In these persons the good spirit uses a contrary method, stinging and biting their consciences through their rational power of moral judgment.

Leading with an Example: St. Augustine's Conversion

When I present rule 1, I begin with an example. Because the rules arose from experience—Ignatius's own and that of people who sought his spiritual aid—they are best taught through experience. From concrete experience to the text—this approach gives life to the text and clarifies how it applies in daily living.

Augustine's Experience

To introduce rules 1 and 2, I describe the spiritual experience that immediately precedes Augustine's dramatic conversion in the garden.[1] I provide a larger context by referring to Augustine's experience as a young man when his imagination is filled with images of sensual pleasures: "In my youth, I burned to fill myself with evil things." I cite also those "fruitless seedings of sorrow" and that "weariness without rest" that burden Augustine's heart throughout those twenty years of serious sin.[2]

We read Augustine's account of how his friend Ponticianus tells him of two young men who decisively and without delay dedicate their lives to Christ. As Augustine listens, the burden in his heart becomes anguish as he cannot but compare his own helplessness, year after year, to turn back to God with these two young men who no sooner hear God's call than they answer it. Augustine writes, "I was in torment, reproaching myself more bitterly than ever as I twisted and turned in my chain. . . . O Lord . . . in your stern mercy you lashed me with the twin scourge of fear and shame in case I should give way once more."[3]

When Augustine would turn to God, "all my old attachments . . . plucked at my garment of flesh and whispered, 'Are you going to dismiss us? From this moment we shall never be with you again, for ever and ever. From this moment you will never be allowed to do this thing or that for evermore.'" I amplify Augustine's words for my listeners and note that lightly behind these whisperings are discouraging thoughts such as these: "You are too weak. You cannot do it. How many times have you tried? How long has it ever lasted? What makes you think it will be any different this time? Why make an effort that is bound to fail?" I ask, "Have any of us ever heard such whisperings when we desired to eliminate harmful habits or take new steps in God's service?" Many heads nod affirmatively; my listeners recognize the relevance to their lives of the experience described.

But Augustine also hears more encouraging promptings. Imagining God as the personified virtue of continence—because his struggles involve this virtue—Augustine continues, "I could see the chaste beauty of Continence in all her serene, unsullied joy, as she modestly beckoned me to . . . hesitate no more. . . . She smiled at me to give me courage, as though she were saying . . . 'Why do you try to stand in your own strength and fail? Cast yourself upon God and have no fear.'" The encouraging promptings continue: So many others, no stronger than you, with the same humanity, have broken these chains and lived holy lives. Trust in God's strength and love, for "he will welcome you and cure you of all your ills."

The decisive moment of conversion follows. Augustine flings himself on the ground beneath the fig tree. With tears he pours out an anguished prayer for liberation; he hears the voice of the child beyond the garden chanting, "Take and read, take and read." He opens the Scriptures to Romans 13 and reads, "The night is advanced, the day is at hand. Let us throw off the works of darkness [and] put on the armor of light" (Rom 13:12),[4] and his heart is changed. From that moment, a life of holiness begins.

Applying the Experience

When we have read Augustine's account, I ask my listeners, "Now, how do we make spiritual sense out of all the different threads interwoven in this experience: The young Augustine's imagination filled with images of sensual pleasures, images that awaken a burning desire to fill himself with evil things and hold him bound to sin for twenty years? That interior weariness and sorrow, becoming even bitterness and anguish, that never leaves him in peace throughout those twenty years? And when he would turn toward God, the voices stealthily plucking at his back, whispering that he is too weak to change, that it is useless to hope for such change? Finally, the encouraging and loving voice of Continence, assuring him that change is possible, that the chain can be broken, that God can accomplish this in him?"

My listeners are now well prepared to approach both rules 1 and 2. The tactics of the enemy and good spirit described in these two rules are already illustrated. In the person *heading away from God* (rule 1), like the young Augustine of those twenty years of sin:

- The *enemy* fills the *imagination* with *images of sensual pleasures* in order to conserve the person in this sinful life.
- The *good spirit stings and bites* in the person's *conscience*, troubling the person, never leaving the person in peace, so that the person will turn away from sin and toward God, the only true source of happiness.

When the person does turn away from sin and *heads toward God* (rule 2), like the later Augustine who seeks freedom from sin and communion with God:

- The *enemy* attempts to *sadden and discourage* the person so that the person will desist from this effort.
- The *good spirit* seeks to *encourage and give hope* so that the person will go forward toward God.

Rule 1: Exploring the Text

I turn then to the text of rule 1. We read it as a whole, and then I comment on its several parts. My commentary follows the unfolding of the text.

"In Persons Who Are Going from Mortal Sin to Mortal Sin"

Ignatius begins by specifying the persons to whom the rule applies. In whom do the enemy and good spirit work in the ways Ignatius will describe in this rule? These are "persons who *are going from mortal sin to mortal sin*," persons who have turned from God and who, in a determined way, are living lives of serious sin.[5]

The Augustine of those twenty sinful years aptly illustrates this spiritual situation.

I ask the group, "Is this spiritual situation real today?" My listeners readily answer, "Yes." I provide concrete examples. Here is a college sophomore who stopped going to church when he left home. He is leading a life of unrestrained promiscuity, with all that accompanies it: certain kinds of partying, harmful use of the internet, substance abuse, association with groups and places that foster this lifestyle, and all the rest. Again, here is a forty-one-year-old married businessman. He has not been to church for twenty years. He is not always faithful to his wife. He is willing to engage in seriously dishonest business practices when it serves his purpose. When these persons or any like them are living lives of persistent serious sin, then, Ignatius says, the enemy and good spirit will act in the ways he describes in rule 1.

"The Enemy"

I have already commented on Ignatius's use of the term *enemy*. I will simply note that here in rule 1, where Ignatius first uses this term, I make the observations given above (chapter 7).

"Is Ordinarily Accustomed"

This is what Ignatius wishes to teach us: how the enemy and good spirit *ordinarily act* in *given spiritual situations*. Such clarity is obviously an enormous gift for the spiritual life. I point out to my listeners that if we already know, even before a situation arises, how the enemy and good spirit will ordinarily act in it, we will all the more quickly identify the tactics of these two spirits in that situation. We will reach the second of the three steps in discernment—be aware, *understand*, take action—more readily, thus freeing us to take the appropriate action.

I also take this opportunity to highlight God's mercy. That Ignatius formulated rule 1, which has blessed countless disciples of the Lord, from the experience of his own wayward years powerfully indicates that there is nowhere we can have been in our lives, nothing we can have done, that God cannot turn to good when we give our lives to Christ. This reflection heartens those among my listeners who themselves have been far from God at some point.

"To Propose Apparent Pleasures to Them, Leading Them to Imagine Sensual Delights and Pleasures in Order to Hold Them More and Make Them Grow in Their Vices and Sins"

I ask my listeners, "In what part of our humanity does Ignatius say the enemy is ordinarily accustomed to act when a person is living far from God and in persistent serious sin?" In the text we find the answer, "leading them to *imagine.*" The enemy works in the *imagination* of such persons, filling it with images of "sensual delights and pleasures" so as to "hold them more and make them grow in their vices and sins." The effectiveness of this tactic is evident in the twenty years that it held Augustine captive.

I give examples, including the college sophomore who is alone in his room at 10:00 p.m. His cell phone rings. It is one of his "buddies": "Look, a group of us is planning to go to the Caribbean for winter break. Do you want to come?" "What goes through his imagination?" I ask. "Which spirit is at work?"

I comment that we speak today of our culture as a "culture of the image." Screens with images are everywhere—in our homes, workplaces, cars, pockets, and hands. Images can work great good. If, for example, we see an uplifting movie with a good message, we are inspired to want what is good.

But images can also serve this tactic of the enemy in persons heading away from God. The college sophomore puts down the smartphone at 11:30 p.m. after an hour and a half of surfing the web. What kind of images fill his imagination? Which spirit is at work? The forty-one-year-old businessman shuts off the television at 1:00 a.m. after two hours of watching various channels. What kind of images fill his imagination? Which spirit is at work? If these images serve "to hold them more and make them grow in their vices and sins," the answer is evident.

"In These Persons the Good Spirit"

When we turn to the second part of rule 1, I emphasize that for Ignatius, grace always has the final word, that these rules provide *a spirituality of redemption* that engenders great hope. In the second part the rule, Ignatius answers the question, "How will the good spirit work in those who have turned from God and are living lives of serious sin?" God never abandons anyone! God works in such persons, and Ignatius will clarify how God does this.

In the first part of the rule, as mentioned, I explore the term *enemy* with my listeners. We understand the word as comprising the personal angelic being who is inimical to our spiritual progress, our own weakness as a legacy of original sin, and harmful influences around us in the world. At this point, I propose a similar exploration of "good spirit," the other actor in this spiritual drama. What does Ignatius mean by "good spirit"? I invite my listeners to suggest answers.

"Good spirit," obviously, above all signifies the *Holy Spirit*, God who works in the hearts of his children whom he loves. It also indicates the *good angels* that Scripture shows us as God's agents on our behalf, accompanying, enlightening, bearing God's Word to us, strengthening us for the journey. Ignatius shares the Church's faith in the reality of the good angels' role in our lives.

"Good spirit" also designates the whole reality of grace implanted in us through baptism, which the spiritual writers term *the supernatural organism*. I tell my listeners that if there is a wound (concupiscence) in us as a legacy of original sin, much more is there a saving power in us through the manifold gifts of baptism: the indwelling of the Trinity, sanctifying grace, actual grace, the infused theological and moral virtues, the gifts of the Holy Spirit, and individual charisms.

I also add that if there are harmful influences around us in the world from which we must defend ourselves, much more in a fallen, redeemed, and loved world are there *influences for good*, which, if we open ourselves to them, will lead us toward God. I offer examples: Ignatius's sister-in-law, who gives him the two books about the life of Christ and the lives of the saints, is an instrument of the good spirit for Ignatius. The two books themselves are instruments of the good spirit for him. Ponticianus, who tells Augustine of the two young men who decisively follow Christ, is an instrument of the good spirit for Augustine. The example of the two young men is a further instrument of the good spirit for him.

I conclude that all those influences that either are God or are from God and directed toward God are comprised in the phrase "good spirit." I tell my listeners that henceforth we will use the words *good spirit* in this comprehensive sense.

"Uses a Contrary Method"

Ignatius expresses another key element here: in the spiritual experience these rules describe, if the enemy does one thing, the good spirit will do *exactly the opposite*.[6] This contrariety is a great aid toward discerning which spirit is at work. Thus in rule 1, if the *enemy* attempts to *facilitate* the movement away from God and toward serious sin, we may expect that the *good spirit* will attempt to *hinder* that movement. Such, as Ignatius immediately explains, is in fact the case.

"Stinging and Biting"

The action of the enemy in these persons is "sleep-inducing," presenting sensual pleasures in order to draw these persons further down the path of sin. The action of the good spirit is precisely the contrary, "stinging and biting," causing a sense of trouble, of burden, of disquiet, so that these persons will awaken from their dangerous situation and turn to God, the only true source of peace. The trouble that constantly fills Augustine's heart during his years of sin and the anguish he feels at hearing of the two who turn decisively to Christ is the action of the good spirit in him, "stinging and biting," never leaving him in peace, ever calling him back to God. In the end, this action of the good spirit is decisive and awakens a great desire for conversion in Augustine.

I ask my listeners, "Is this 'stinging and biting' action of the good spirit in those heading away from God real today?" I answer with the examples already given. The college sophomore is alone in his room this evening. No one has called, no one has come to visit. He sits alone with his thoughts—and his heart is troubled, uneasy. He knows that something is not right with his life. The good spirit is "stinging and biting." If the sophomore is open to this action of the good spirit, he may find himself thinking, "Why do I live like this? I'm not even happy. I used to be happier before I began living this way. I can't go on like this." If so, he is already on the path that leads back to God. But . . . he may also choose to call a companion, put in the earbuds, go online, or leave his room to be with others. Something similar may be said of the forty-one-year-old businessman in a time when he, too, is alone.

I also add, speaking with reverence for my listeners' experience, that some present, at some point in their lives, may have experienced this stinging and biting action of the good spirit. If so, at this point in their lives they are grateful for it: that very stinging and biting brought them back to God.

"Their Consciences through Their Rational Power of Moral Judgment"

If the enemy works in the *imagination* of those "going from mortal sin to mortal sin," the good spirit works in their *conscience*. The good spirit stings and bites in their conscience "through their *rational power of moral judgment.*"

As an example, I refer once more to the forty-one-year-old businessman. The time has come when his young son is taking catechism lessons in preparation for his first Communion. Catechism is taught at 9:00 a.m., before the 10:00 a.m. family Mass. The man drives his son to church at 9:00 a.m. and returns home. His wife meets their son at 10:00 a.m. and attends Mass with him.

As the months pass, occasionally the man finds himself wondering, "What will I say if at some point my son asks me why he and his mother go to Mass, and I never do?" And again, "What will I do on the day of my son's first Communion? What if he expects me to be there? And if I go, what will I do when he and my wife go up to receive Communion?" Such thoughts arise from time to time, but life is busy and pursues its habitual course.

Today he is driving home from work. He is on a highway, traffic is light, and his thoughts roam freely. By God's grace, the phone is off and the radio as well. For perhaps the first time in many months, this man is—to use Augustine's term—within and aware of the stirrings in his heart.

He finds questions such as these arising: "What will you say if your son asks why you never go to Mass with him and his mother? And what will you do on the day of his first Communion? Why have you caused such terrible suffering to your wife with your infidelities? Why have you done such great harm to your marriage? Are you proud of yourself when you see yourself betraying the trust of a client for your own advantage? When you look in the mirror in the morning, are you proud of what you see? When you look back ten or twenty years from now at the way you are living, will you be proud of what you see?"

At this point, I tell my listeners that this man has a choice. If he chooses, it is as simple as reaching down and turning on the radio. To employ once more Augustine's words, "You [God] were within and I was without." But if he is willing to accept this stinging and biting of the good spirit in his conscience "through his rational power of moral judgment," we can also see that *he is only a hair's breadth away* from making the one change that can give true peace to his heart—he is only a hair's breadth away from a return to God.

I add, "We say that our God is a God of peace, and it is true. But our God is a God who loves his children too much ever to let them go, and who is willing to sting and bite in their hearts in the hope of bringing them back to him, their only true source of peace."

I cite Francis Thompson's lovely poem, "The Hound of Heaven," as, to my mind, the most beautiful literary representation of this stinging and biting action of the good spirit that calls human hearts back to God: "I fled Him, down the nights and down the days. . . . Halts by me that footfall: Is my gloom, after all, Shade of His hand, outstretched caressingly?"[7] Shade, yes, because this action of the good spirit stings and bites, but shade "of His hand, outstretched caressingly," lovingly calling his children back to him.

I share with my listeners my own experience of times when people like this forty-one-year-old man do accept the stinging and biting action of the good spirit and begin to return to God. Let us say that this man calls his parish priest and asks to speak. When they meet, the man pours out his story of the bitterness, emptiness, and heaviness of heart he has experienced, which for him are the clearest signs that God has abandoned him. When his parish priest shows him that, on the contrary, that very emptiness that never left him in peace is the clearest sign that God has always loved him too much to let him go, it melts something within him.

A Brief Note about Examples

In this chapter I have shared the examples that I use to present this rule, and I will do the same for the subsequent rules. My hope is that this sharing illustrates the key role that examples have in teaching the rules.

I have developed this set of examples over the years and find it helpful. Obviously these are not the only examples that can serve the teaching! As your own presentation develops, you will find your own path in the choice of examples.

The Transition to Rule 2

Having presented rule 1, I conclude by asking, "What will happen when this man or any like him *do* turn away from sin and toward God?" I answer, "Then, according to the law of contrariety that holds throughout these rules, the actions of the enemy and good spirit will reverse. When people head *away from* God, the *enemy* attempts to *facilitate* this movement and the *good spirit* to *hinder* it. Now, when people head *toward God*, the *enemy* will attempt to *hinder* this movement and the *good spirit* to *facilitate* it. Ignatius addresses this spiritual situation in rule 2."

10

The Spirits in Persons Growing Toward God
Addressing Your Listeners' Experience
Rule 2

The text of rule 2 is the following:

> Second Rule. **The second:** in persons who are going on intensely purifying their sins and rising from good to better in the service of God our Lord, the method is contrary to that in the first rule. For then it is proper to the evil spirit to bite, sadden, and place obstacles, disquieting with false reasons, so that the person may not go forward. And it is proper to the good spirit to give courage and strength, consolations, tears, inspirations and quiet, easing and taking away all obstacles, so that the person may go forward in doing good.

As with rule 1, Ignatius first clarifies the *persons* to whom the rule applies and then the *tactics* of the enemy and good spirit in such persons. When teaching rule 2, I simply follow Ignatius's lead.

The Persons of Rule 2

To whom does rule 2 apply? In whom do the enemy and good spirit work in the ways Ignatius describes in this rule? Clearly, this is a key question for any accurate application of the rule!

Ignatius tells us that these two spirits employ the tactics described "in persons who are going on *intensely purifying their sins* and *rising from good to better in the service of God our Lord.*" These persons, then, are identified by two complementary qualities: they are energetically *striving to overcome sin* and simultaneously *growing in God's service*.

I provide an example for my listeners.[1] Peter is a fifty-three-year-old married man. He was raised Catholic and has always practiced his faith. For Peter, this means attending Sunday Mass, seeing that his children receive the sacraments, and praying on occasion.

Today Peter is attending Sunday Mass. After the Mass, the pastor announces a forthcoming parish retreat and warmly invites his parishioners to attend. The retreat will be held in a local retreat house during the approaching Lent. Peter has never made a retreat, and something about the thought of a weekend with talks on the faith, times of prayer, and space for quiet appeals to him. His wife supports his interest and encourages him to attend. Peter registers for the retreat.

When the weekend arrives, Peter finds the talks engaging and the times of prayer fruitful. On Saturday evening, a Penance service is held with preparation in common and individual confession after. Peter decides to receive the sacrament and approaches one of the priests, who receives him with goodness and understanding. Peter usually went to Confession before Christmas and Easter, but this was different. The talks, the quiet, and the prayer have prepared him for a deeper experience of the sacrament.

Peter shares with the priest his new insight into habits that are not spiritually good for him: ways of using the internet and television that diminish his spiritual energy; kinds of conversation into which he has drifted and now sees as harmful; practices at work that skirt moral boundaries regarding honesty; a slowness to assist his wife and children when this conflicts with his own interests.

Peter speaks openly of all this to the priest and finds the priest's response helpful. The priest's words lift his heart and help him experience God's love, mercy, and forgiveness. As he leaves the confessional, Peter feels a deep peace he has long sought.

That evening, Peter walks on the grounds of the retreat house. His heart is filled with a quiet joy. He finds himself desiring to begin a new spiritual journey. He resolves that he will go to Confession regularly, and after the retreat does so. He changes his use of the internet and television, eliminating the harmful practices. Unobtrusively, Peter distances himself from the unhealthy conversations and questionable business practices. He also seeks to overcome the self-centeredness that has limited his love for his wife and children. In Ignatius's terms, Peter is now a person who, with humble trust in God and diligent effort, is *going on intensely purifying his sins*.

As Peter does this, something else happens. He grows more patient with his children and more present to his wife when she needs him. He is more cheerful at work and more ready to assist his fellow workers, who appreciate his new attentiveness to them.

During the retreat, Peter learned of a men's group in the parish that meets before work on Wednesday mornings. He joins the group and enjoys the sharing and the talks. Some of the men attend daily Mass, and a few months later, Peter also begins attending Mass occasionally during the week. As the weeks pass, this practice grows more frequent. Peter's new interest in his faith encourages similar steps in his wife, and a new spirit of faith and harmony develops in their home. In Ignatius's terms, Peter is now a person who is *rising from good to better in the service of God our Lord*.

In Peter and in any like him, Ignatius tells us, the enemy and good spirit will work in the ways he describes in rule 2. I tell my listeners that, in all likelihood, Ignatius is speaking directly to them in rule 2: "You would not be here today if you did not seek a growing freedom from sin and to rise in God's love and service." At this point, I have their engaged attention.

The Tactics of the Enemy

Ignatius names four tactics of the enemy in such progressing persons. If we focus on and provide examples of each, our listeners will grasp them well and begin to identify them in their own experience.

"For Then It Is Proper to the Evil Spirit to Bite"

When Peter or anyone who is progressing toward God experiences the joy of this growth, the enemy, Ignatius says, will "bite" (*morder*). He will gnaw at that joy, try to induce a sense of trouble, a breath of anxiety that will diminish that joy "so that the person may not go forward." So, for example, Peter may find at a certain point that the new spiritual energy he has been feeling has lessened and that now there are times when he feels more troubled than happy about this new spiritual journey.

I cite a letter of Ignatius to Sister Teresa Rejadell, a person solidly progressing toward God: "The enemy is leading you into error . . . but not in any way to make you fall into a sin that would separate you from God our Lord. He tries rather to *upset* you and to *interfere with* your service of God and *your peace of mind*."[2] With such persons, the enemy does not begin by tempting them to sin—the last thing people like Peter desire in such times of joy-filled spiritual growth—but rather by "biting," striving to upset the person and strip away the new peace.

A further example is found in Ignatius's own experience at Manresa, some months after his life-changing confession in which he repudiated thirty years of sin. Now, growing rapidly toward God, a thought comes to him: "How do you know that you said everything you should have said in that confession?" Ignatius tells us that the thought troubled him: "Even though the general confession he had made in Montserrat had been made with great diligence and completely in writing, as has been said, nonetheless it seemed to him at times that he had not confessed some things, and this *caused him much affliction.*"³ The enemy does not attempt here to move Ignatius to sin—the last thing Ignatius now desires—but simply to diminish his joy. You will find the examples that best help you illustrate this tactic of the enemy.

"Sadden"

I indicate to my listeners that this is not the natural and healthy sadness the heart feels at the loss, for example, of a loved one or when called to leave a loved place or occupation. Such sadness is simply the expression of a heart that can love. This sadness does need healthy remedies: prayer, the support of others, and the like.

The sadness that is a tactic of the enemy in those progressing toward God is, on the other hand, a heaviness, a burden as regards one's spiritual life, one's relationship with God, prayer, and love and service of God in general. There is nothing healthy about this sadness and, unless resisted, it will only harm the person. Ignatius writes to Sister Teresa Rejadell, "We find ourselves sad without knowing why. We cannot pray with devotion, nor contemplate, nor even speak or hear of the things of God with any interior taste or relish."⁴ I read this text with my listeners and then ask, "Have any of us ever experienced this?" They respond with many affirmative nods, and I add, "You have, and I have. There is no shame in this. It is simply a tactic of the enemy. What matters is to be *discerning*—to be aware of this tactic, understand it for the tactic of the enemy that it is, and reject it."

"Place Obstacles"

The enemy will also, Ignatius says, *place obstacles* in the way of one progressing toward God. Again I quote Ignatius's letter to Sister Rejadell:

> The enemy as a rule follows this course. He *places obstacles and impediments* in the way of those who love and

begin to serve God our Lord, and this is the first weapon he uses in his efforts to wound them. He asks, for instance: *"How can you continue* a life of such great penance, deprived of all satisfaction from friends, relatives, possessions? How can you lead so lonely a life, with no rest, when you can save your soul in other ways and without such dangers?" He tries to bring us to understand that we must lead a life that is longer than it will actually be, by reason of *the trials he places before us* and which no one ever underwent.[5]

This quote illustrates well the enemy's tactic of presenting obstacles to those progressing toward God: "It will be so difficult, your life will be so heavy, the trials will be harder than you can bear, they will go on and on . . . and *you don't have to do all this* to save your soul. You can love God without all these new steps you've been undertaking. Why don't you just let all this go? You know you won't persevere anyway." Then I ask, "Have any of us ever felt such thoughts and heard such questions when we have taken new steps to love and serve God?" Again, many heads nod affirmatively.

I return to Augustine and to the "voices stealthily plucking at his back" when he wants to go forward toward God: "You can't do it. You're too weak. You know you can't live without these things. How many times have you tried? How long has it ever lasted? What makes you think it will be any different this time?" *Obstacles, obstacles, obstacles, obstacles* . . . in the way of one who would progress toward God, a classic tactic of the enemy and effective if we are not aware, do not understand, and do not take action to reject it.

I add a further example, returning to Gerald, the forty-one-year-old married businessman.[6] Now, after twenty years away from the Church, he has returned to the sacraments. For six months he has faithfully attended Sunday Mass with his family and is making sincere efforts to overcome earlier patterns of sinfulness. Gerald rejoices at the new peace he experiences and the new harmony in his family and at work.

Today Gerald is attending Sunday Mass. The Gospel is Luke 11:1–13, "Lord, teach us to pray" (v.1).[7] The priest gives a simple but heartfelt homily on prayer, and invites his parishioners to consider spending ten minutes a day in prayer with the readings of the Mass for that day. As Gerald listens, he feels God's closeness, and his heart is warmed with gratitude to God for the goodness of what is happening in his life. A thought comes to him: "If praying once a week at Sunday Mass is already making this difference, what would happen if I did what Father suggests and prayed daily?" Further thoughts arise: "I could arrange my morning to set aside ten minutes each day. And, actually, all I have to do is ask my wife for help because she has been doing this for several years. She will be happy to show me how to find the readings and get started." Gerald resolves that he will speak with his wife that evening and will begin this practice the next morning.

Sunday morning and afternoon unfold with their various activities. At supper, a tension arises between Gerald and his teenage son, and it does not resolve well. This tension burdens Gerald's heart after supper. Now the children are asleep, and Gerald is in his study, preparing for work the next morning. He then remembers that he had planned to speak with his wife this evening about the ten minutes each day with Scripture.

But now the thoughts are different: "Who are you kidding? You've been away from the Church for twenty years, and look at the way you've lived. You've never even read Scripture. What makes you think you'll understand anything you'll read there? Why approach your wife about a practice that is bound to fail? You'll just embarrass yourself and her. You had a nice experience at Mass this morning, but that doesn't change anything, and it is not going to last." *Obstacles, obstacles, obstacles* . . . in the way of one who is seeking to rise from good to better in God's service.

I now ask, "Can we see that this matters? That what Gerald decides this evening matters? What if Gerald is not aware of, does not understand, and does not reject this obstacle-placing action of the enemy this evening, does not speak with his wife, and does not begin the ten minutes with Scripture the next morning? What will his prayer life look like a week later, six months, a year, five years? But what if, by God's grace, Gerald is aware of, understands, and rejects this tactic of the enemy; he speaks with his wife this evening and begins the ten minutes with Scripture the next morning? Now what will his prayer life look like a week later, six months, a year, five years?"

I ask again, "*Can we see that this matters?*" And I comment: "Right here, in daily life, is where most of the spiritual life is lived. Peak moments a few times in the spiritual life—our vocational decision, a time of conversion, significant choices regarding family or career, and so on. Most of the spiritual life, however, is lived precisely on this daily, often hidden level, and *right here* is where Ignatius wishes to help us." Such observations indicate to my listeners that this Ignatian teaching can assist them greatly in their spiritual lives. Their interest grows.

My listeners now understand this "biting" tactic of the enemy and can begin to identify it in their own experience; captives are beginning to be set free. Generally they are excited to understand, often for the first time, these tactics of the enemy.

"Disquieting with False Reasons"

Finally, Ignatius affirms, the enemy will attempt to *disquiet* the hearts of progressing persons with *reasons* that—in keeping with his nature as the "liar" (Jn 8:44)—are *false*. I return to Gerald, who desires to begin praying with Scripture for ten minutes each morning. In addition to the enemy's other tactics, Gerald may also find thoughts such as these arise: "You want to begin daily prayer with Scripture. You know what this is really about? You've been getting nice feedback on your new spiritual journey, and you like the compliments. You want more of them. And you know what else is at work in this desire? You won't admit it, but you are competing with your wife. You want to be as spiritual as she is, and maybe begin to get more respect from your in-laws. And if you're really honest, you'll admit that you'd like the children to see you as even a little more spiritual than she is." No! None of this was present in that grace-filled Sunday morning Mass, only a sincere desire to grow in prayer. But if Gerald is not aware, does not understand, and does not take action to reject these false and disquieting "reasons" of the enemy, they will harm him; if he is discerning, the enemy's attempt will be undone.

The Tactics of the Good Spirit

I turn now to the second part of the rule and present the tactics of the good spirit in these progressing persons. When I begin this presentation, I once again emphasize Ignatius's spirituality of grace and redemption: if the tactics of the enemy are real, all the more real are those of the good spirit. Grace always has the final word.

"And It Is Proper to the Good Spirit to Give Courage and Strength"

I return to Augustine's experience of Continence—that is, the good spirit—smiling at him to give him courage, stretching out loving hands to welcome him. The good spirit gives Augustine "courage and strength" when he seeks to progress toward God.

I add a further example. A woman who loves the Lord rises one morning and walks down the hallway to put on coffee and begin the day. This afternoon she will meet with the doctor to get the results of the biopsy, and, understandably, she is afraid. As she walks along the hallway, her eye catches a placard she has placed on the wall with the parable of the footprints in the sand.[8] Just for a moment, as she passes, the meaning of the parable speaks to her heart: in our times of burden, God is close, carrying us safely through our trials. Her heart lifts, and she knows that the Lord will be with her this day in all that may happen. The good spirit, in a thousand creative ways, gives courage and strength to those who love the Lord.

I share yet another example. A woman, active in the Church in her own country, immigrated to a new nation. She joined the local parish and sought her customary involvement in it. Parish life there, however, was so culturally different that she found this increasingly difficult. Finally, at Mass one Sunday, she could bear it no longer. As the readings were beginning, she rose, walked down the aisle, and started down the front steps of the church; she was leaving and would never return. At that moment, in God's providence, a woman who had arrived late for Mass walked up the steps. As they passed, the woman entering smiled at the woman leaving. The woman leaving stopped, turned around, and went back into the church. When she shared this story, she had been a leader in that parish for forty years. Again, in endlessly creative ways, the good spirit gives courage and strength to those who love and seek God.[9]

In these and similar examples, this action of the good spirit becomes concrete and understandable to my listeners. You will find the examples that best help you present the good spirit who gives courage and strength to those progressing toward God.

"Consolations"

I tell my listeners that in the next rule (rule 3) we will explore spiritual consolation in depth. As a result, here I only mention that *consolation* signifies those times when our hearts are warmed with a sense of God's love and closeness, a warmth of love that strengthens our hope and encourages us to progress further toward God.

"Tears"

Again, because in the next rule Ignatius will refer to tears in depth, I simply comment that tears may be the body's expression of the warmth of God's love. I tell my listeners that we will return to this in the next rule.

"Inspirations and Quiet"

The enemy brings *false reasons* that *disquiet*; the good spirit brings *inspirations* and *quiet*—that is, peace—of heart. Inspirations: this is *when we see it*—when we now perceive how to respond to a situation in our spiritual lives, deal with a burden, or take the next step in our prayer or service of God. Such inspirations are the intellectual component of the good spirit's action, clarifying the way, revealing the path forward.

Again, examples render this tactic concrete. When Peter hears the announcement of the forthcoming retreat, he thinks, "I could do that. And I would like to do that." After his fruitful confession during the retreat, he thinks, "I would like to begin regular Confession after the retreat." Later he thinks, "Why not join the men's group in the parish." When Gerald hears the priest invite the people to pray daily with Scripture, he thinks, "I could do that. All I have to do is ask my wife's help, and she will be glad to give it. I can start tomorrow."

Through events in our lives, conversations with others, clarity in a time of prayer, spiritual reading, a homily . . . in a thousand ways, the good spirit gives inspirations that reveal the next step forward. I comment that we have all experienced this tactic of the good spirit, and again my listeners nod affirmatively.

"Easing and Taking Away All Obstacles"

The enemy *places obstacles*; the good spirit *eases and takes away all obstacles* "so that the person may go forward in doing good." I highlight that hope-filled *all*.

Thus when Augustine hesitates, when he is unable to break the chain, when the voices stealthily plucking at his back tell him that he is too weak, that he will never change, that the obstacles are too great . . . the voice of Continence assures Augustine that the opposite is true, that many others, with his same humanity, have done it, that it is God's love for him and God's strength, and not his own weakness, that will be decisive . . . easing and taking away all obstacles. This "easing" action of the good spirit assists Augustine finally to overcome the obstacles and break the chain.

At Sunday Mass that morning, Gerald has decided to pray daily with Scripture for ten minutes. As mentioned, at supper his conversation with his teenage son is tense and leaves him discouraged. Gerald is now in his study, preparing for work the next day. Disheartened and burdened, Gerald feels no desire to speak with his wife about prayer with Scripture and is on the verge of relinquishing this new step. Then his young daughter comes to say good night. She hugs him and tells him that she loves him. Gerald returns the hug and says, "I love you too." She leaves the room. Something in Gerald now says, "I will begin the prayer with Scripture tomorrow as I planned!" The good spirit, with endless creativity, has eased and taken away the obstacles so that Gerald may go forward in doing good.

Through this exposition of rules 1 and 2, my listeners grasp the tactics of the two spirits in accord with the direction of the person's life, moving either away from or toward God. We are now ready to explore rules 3 and 4 in which Ignatius will describe the two basic spiritual movements, spiritual consolation (rule 3) and spiritual desolation (rule 4).

11

Helping Your Listeners Recognize Spiritual Consolation
Rule 3

The goal in presenting rule 3 is to give our listeners a clear understanding of spiritual consolation, helping them recognize and respond to it in their own experience. I follow the same pedagogy—from example to text—and begin with an example.

I quote from the spiritual journal of Raïssa Maritain, wife of the philosopher Jacques Maritain. Raïssa describes a joyful experience of prayer:

> At the first invocation [of the Litany of the Sacred Heart], *Kyrie eleison*, obliged to absorb myself, my mind arrested on the Person of the Father. Impossible to change the object. Sweetness, attraction, *eternal youth* of the heavenly Father. Suddenly, keen sense of his nearness, of his tenderness, of his incomprehensible love which impels him to demand our love, our thought. Greatly moved, I wept very sweet tears. . . . Joy of being able to call him Father with a great tenderness, to feel him so kind and so close to me.[1]

Without much comment, I indicate that Ignatius terms joyful experiences of this kind *spiritual consolation*.

We then turn to the text. Ignatius writes:

> Third Rule. **The third is of spiritual consolation. I call it consolation when some interior movement is caused in**

the soul, through which the soul comes to be inflamed with love of its Creator and Lord, and, consequently when it can love no created thing on the face of the earth in itself, but only in the Creator of them all. Likewise when it sheds tears that move to love of its Lord, whether out of sorrow for one's sins, or for the passion of Christ our Lord, or because of other things directly ordered to his service and praise. Finally, I call consolation every increase of hope, faith and charity, and all interior joy that calls and attracts to heavenly things and to the salvation of one's soul, quieting it and giving it peace in its Creator and Lord.

Two Words: Spiritual *and* Consolation

After reading the text with the group, I return to the introductory sentence: "The third is of spiritual consolation." We focus on both words: *spiritual* and *consolation*.

I explain to my listeners that in terms of head and heart, *consolation* is a word on the level of the *heart*. It indicates an *uplifting movement of the heart*. Said more formally—though with most groups I do not use this vocabulary—consolation is an uplifting affective movement. I invite my listeners to suggest examples of uplifting movements of the heart. Generally, many respond. They mention joy, peace, hope, love, and similar uplifting affective movements. The point is made clearly: consolation is an *uplifting* movement of the *heart*.

I then turn to Ignatius's adjective *spiritual*. I note how Ignatius explicitly states that the consolation (uplifting movements of the heart) he intends is on the level *of our spiritual lives*, of *faith*, of *our relationship with God*. This is evident, for example, in Raïssa's experience: "Sweetness, attraction, eternal youth of *the heavenly Father*. Suddenly, keen sense of *his nearness*, of *his tenderness*, of *his incomprehensible love* which impels him to demand our love, our thought. . . . *Joy of being able to call him Father* with a great tenderness, to feel him *so kind and so close to me.*" Raïssa experiences *consolation*—a great joy—and this consolation is clearly on the *spiritual level*: what gives her joy is her happy experience of the tenderness and love of God as Father.

Next, I observe that if there is *spiritual* consolation, there is also another kind of consolation. This may be described with various words, and I invite my listeners to suggest these: "If there is *spiritual* consolation, then there is also what other kind of consolation?" Various answers emerge: "natural" consolation, "human" consolation, "psychological" consolation, and the like. I then say that we will use the word *nonspiritual* for such movements on the natural level. *Nonspiritual consolation*, therefore, is an uplifting movement of the heart (*consolation*) on the natural level (*nonspiritual*).

Nonspiritual, I continue, does not necessarily mean "bad." There are many healthy nonspiritual consolations. I ask my listeners to propose examples of healthy nonspiritual consolation. We generally have fun with this even as we learn. My listeners will propose various examples: the uplift of heart in viewing the beauties of nature—the ocean, mountains, stars, and the like; the good feeling that follows healthy exercise; the satisfaction of a job well done; the joy of friendship; the delight in chaste and Christ-centered love between a man and a woman; the enjoyment of good music; the pleasure of a good meal with family or friends, and similar experiences. When I judge that enough experiences of this kind have been expressed, I comment that all of these are good, given by God, intended for our enjoyment, and made richer in Christ. I likewise indicate that Ignatius does not speak of such consolations in rule 3—these are *nonspiritual*, natural consolations. In rule 3, Ignatius speaks of *spiritual* consolations that, like Raïssa's, are on the spiritual level, the level of faith, of our relationship with God.[2] Everything in these rules, I add, is—as we would expect in rules about discernment of *spirits*—on the spiritual level.

Here another point must be made. Though the distinction between spiritual and nonspiritual consolation is important, it need not be overstressed. Very often, in God's providence, *healthy nonspiritual consolation* is the space into which God infuses the further gift of *spiritual consolation.*

I provide an example. On June 7, 1897, in the final summer of her life, St. Thérèse of Lisieux visited with her older sister Pauline in the garden of their Carmelite monastery. Pauline recounts the following incident:

> Descending the steps leading into the garden, she saw a little white hen under a tree, protecting her little chicks under her wings; some were peeping out from under. Thérèse stopped, looking at them thoughtfully; after a while, I made a sign that we should go inside. I noticed her eyes were filled with tears, and I said: "You're crying!" She put her hand over her eyes and cried even more.
>
> "I can't explain it just now; I'm too deeply touched."
>
> That evening, in her cell, she told me the following, and there was a heavenly expression on her face:
>
> "I cried when I thought how God used this image in order to teach us his tenderness toward us. All through my life, this is what he has done for me! He has hidden me totally under his wings! Earlier in the day, when I was leaving you, I was crying when going upstairs; I was unable to control myself any longer, and I hastened to our cell. My heart was overflowing with love and gratitude.[3]

After we have read this text, I guide my listeners through the steps in this experience. Thérèse goes into the garden, sees a charming scene from nature—a mother hen protecting her chicks under her wings; she stops and enjoys looking at this scene. I ask mylisteners, "At this point, is Thérèse experiencing *nonspiritual* or *spiritual* consolation?" All readily answer, "Nonspiritual."

I continue. As Thérèse gazes at this scene, it dawns on her that this is the image God uses in Scripture to reveal his protecting love for his people: "How many times I yearned to gather your children together, as a hen gathers her young under her wings" (Mt 23:37).[4] Again, in the psalms, "You indeed are my savior, and in the shadow of your wings I shout for joy" (Ps 63:8).[5] As the image before her evokes this rich scriptural truth, Thérèse's heart turns to God in joy and her tears begin to fall: "I cried when I thought how God used this image in order to teach us his tenderness toward us."

I ask my listeners, "Is Thérèse now experiencing *nonspiritual* or *spiritual* consolation?" All answer, "Spiritual." I ask, "Can you see how God has infused the grace of spiritual consolation into an experience of healthy nonspiritual consolation?" All nod affirmatively, and the point is made.

I proceed further in exploring Thérèse's experience. The scene before her in the garden has led her to a *general* teaching in Scripture: God's protecting love for his people. Now she progresses from this general teaching to an awareness of how that teaching illuminates her *personal* life: "All through my life, this is what he has done *for me*! He has hidden me totally under his wings." At this point, Thérèse is too affected even to speak and her tears fall, silently revealing the deep and joyful gratitude that fills her heart before God—rich and overflowing spiritual consolation. This example always engages my listeners' attention and serves well to make the point.

I take this opportunity to add a further consideration regarding nonspiritual consolation: Even though Ignatius does not speak of nonspiritual consolation in his rules—everything in the rules is on the spiritual level—healthy nonspiritual consolation may exercise a positive role in the spiritual life. If God may and often does infuse the gift of *spiritual* consolation into experiences of *healthy nonspiritual* consolation, then a certain amount of healthy nonspiritual consolation may bless the spiritual life. This point, too, generally engages my listeners.

Examples of Spiritual Consolation

I turn then to the remainder of rule 3. I introduce the text by observing that Ignatius does not give a definition of spiritual consolation: his text is not a treatise of speculative, abstract theology but rather a set of spiritual *exercises*, a wisdom for spiritual practice. I note that Ignatius simply gives a list of experiences of spiritual consolation—this is an experience of spiritual consolation, this is another, this yet another, and so through the entire text: "I call it consolation when . . . and, consequently when. . . . Likewise when. . . . Finally, I call consolation every increase of . . . and all interior joy." His goal is to familiarize us with spiritual consolation and thereby equip us to recognize (be aware, *understand*, take action) it in our own experience. That recognition sets us free to take the appropriate action in response to it.

After this general observation on the text, I turn to the individual experiences of spiritual consolation.[6] Here, too, I simply follow Ignatius's text.

"Inflamed with Love of Its Creator and Lord"

Ignatius refers to those times when our hearts are enkindled, warmed, even "inflamed" with love of God. We feel this warmth and welcome it with joy. It strengthens us to love and serve our "Creator and Lord."

I provide an example. A woman prays daily with Scripture, and today her text is the healing of the woman with the hemorrhage (Mk 5:25–34). She reads through the text attentively a first time, but nothing strikes her in any particular way. She rereads the text slowly. She notes how this woman hopes for healing but only as an anonymous brush of a finger in a crowd. The woman does touch Jesus's garments and is healed. But now Jesus asks who touched him. The disciples make the obvious answer about the press of the crowd, but Jesus knows, and the woman knows.

As the woman prays with this scene, she sees this woman, now healed, come with great courage, fall down before Jesus, and tell him the whole truth. As she prays, she hears Jesus's first word of response, "Daughter." That word alone tells the woman that she is far more in his heart than an anonymous brush of a finger in a crowd, and that a deep and beautiful relationship is established between them. As the woman praying perceives Jesus's response, her heart is warmed with an awareness that Jesus calls her "Daughter" as well, and that he loves her, too, with all the richness this word signifies. Her heart is, in Ignatius's words, "inflamed with love of her Creator and Lord." She is experiencing a gentle, warm, and rich spiritual consolation.

You may also wish to refer to the examples of Raïssa and Thérèse that I just shared. In both, this enkindling of the heart is abundantly present. In both, the intensity of this enkindling can only be described as an "inflaming" of the heart.

I comment that all of us, with our individual nuances, have had such experiences, perhaps at Mass, while reading Scripture, in times of quiet prayer, in moments when we perceive God's loving action in our lives, or in many other circumstances. This enkindling of the heart may, as with the woman praying with Mark 5, be gentle. At other times, it may be stronger or even very strong, so that our hearts are truly "inflamed" with love of our God. These are beautiful experiences of spiritual consolation, and we are rightly grateful for them. As I say this, my listeners are remembering experiences of this kind, and Ignatius's text comes alive for them. They *know* what he means by "the soul is inflamed with love of its Creator and Lord."

"Love of Created Things in Their Creator"

I note the link between the first experience of spiritual consolation ("when the soul is inflamed with love") and this second, "and *consequently* when." When the heart is warmed with God's love, a further gift, a second experience of spiritual consolation may also be given, "and consequently when it [the soul] can love no created thing on the face of the earth in itself but only in the Creator of them all."

I explain that by "created things" Ignatius intends all that surrounds us in our lives: places, possessions, relationships, occupations, and the like (*SpirEx* 23). In the gift of this second experience of spiritual consolation, when the heart is enkindled with God's love, any tension between attachments to these "created things" and where God is leading in our lives simply vanishes. Our hearts are set free to love created things not less but more, because we love them in harmony with God's love and leading in our lives. This is a great gift.

Again I supply examples. A priest faces a decision in his ministry and struggles to be open to what he perceives the Lord wills. He makes a retreat to seek the Lord's light and strength in this matter. Today he prays with the annunciation of the angel Gabriel to Mary (Lk 1:26–38). He describes his experience of prayer:

> I prayed with the annunciation to Mary and the incarnation of Jesus. I focused simply on Mary. Very strong consolation, with tears. Love for Mary, with a sense of her deep beauty, a great sense of reverence, of hope, of melting of barriers to do God's will in this matter of how I am facing my ministry.
>
> A sense of Mary's total openness, totally flexible, with no resistance, no "my way of programming things": simple openness, with beauty, depth, and love. As I see this in Mary, something in my own encrusted adherence to "my way" seems to give way.[7]

The first experience of spiritual consolation is evident here. As he prays, this priest's heart is inflamed with love of God—"Very strong consolation, with tears." In the warmth of this love, something else happens. The struggle he has been experiencing between where the Lord is leading and other attachments in ministry now disappears, and he is totally open to God—"a great sense of . . . melting of barriers to do God's will in this matter of how I am facing my ministry. . . . As I see this in Mary, something in my own encrusted adherence to 'my way' seems to give way." Again, the richness and beauty of this grace are evident.

Such availability to God is a second experience of spiritual consolation that may be given when the first is present. Because of this grace, the earlier tension between love for "created things" and God's leading in his life dissolves, and the priest is free to love the people, places, and occupations of his ministry in the richest and most fruitful way—as Ignatius says, "in the Creator of them all."

A young woman is praying in church. She is discerning between a call to marriage and to religious life. She knows that her heart is not free simply to hear and follow the Lord's leading. She prays for the gift of availability, but still she struggles. Today she lifts her gaze to the Blessed Sacrament in the tabernacle behind the altar. As she does so, her heart is warmed with a deep sense of Jesus's presence to her and love for her. Her tears begin to fall. In the joy of this experience, she finds herself saying very easily to the Lord, "Jesus, whatever you want. If you want me to be married, I'll be married. If you want me to be a religious, I'll be a religious. Just show me, and I will say yes." Such is the second experience of spiritual consolation. You will find the examples that best help you illustrate this second experience.

"Tears for the Love of the Lord"

Here I note that the body, too, may share the experience of spiritual consolation. Tears may "manifest, accompany, and complete" the heart's experience of God's love.[8] We are not simply spirits, but incarnate spirits: through tears, the whole person may share in the spiritual consolation.

I note that tears may express many things: bitterness, anger, the tearing of a heart, or pain. Ignatius refers here to one kind of tears, tears that "move to love of the Lord," that is, that physically express the heart's awareness of being loved deeply by God. These are warm and happy tears.

I offer examples. A man rises and goes to church this morning. He arrives thirty minutes before Mass and dedicates the time, according to his habitual practice, to praying with the day's Gospel. He is tired and discouraged because of problems that have arisen at work. The church is large and cold, and few others fill its emptiness at this hour.

This day's Gospel is the encounter of Jesus with the disciples on the way to Emmaus (Lk 24:13–35). As the man reads this text, he sees these two disciples, whose hearts are sad and who have lost hope, quietly leave the community. He sees how Jesus approaches them, listens to them, and speaks with them. He watches their "slow" hearts become "burning" hearts (Lk 24:25, 32). Then he reaches the moment when they arrive at the village, and Jesus appears to be traveling further. He hears the prayer of these two disciples, a prayer this man, too, has often made to the Lord, "Stay with us! Darkness is falling" (see Lk 24:29). The man sees how Jesus welcomes that prayer, goes in with them, and their lives are changed. As he reads this, the beginning of a tear comes to his eye: "Lord, you are with me, too, in my tiredness and discouragement. You hear my prayer when I call out to you." This, too, is a beautiful experience of spiritual consolation, of "tears that move to love of his Lord."

The woman who enters the Pharisee's house never says a word, but expresses everything with her tears (Lk 7:36–50). Her tears are tears of spiritual consolation, "out of sorrow for one's sins," as Ignatius writes in rule 3. These are blessed and healing tears that express her heart's awareness that, perhaps for the first time in her life, she is welcomed, respected, understood, loved, and set free for a new life.

I tell my listeners that all of us will recognize tears of spiritual consolation in our own experience, and we rightly treasure such times of grace. The room is generally silent at this point as my listeners recall personal experiences of such tears. Something joyful fills the room.

"Every Increase of Hope, Faith, and Charity"

I note that the "increase of hope, faith, and charity" to which Ignatius refers is concrete, felt, and perceptible. It is accompanied by uplifting movements of the heart—warm, happy, and encouraging stirrings.

A man is praying with Scripture one morning. Prayer has been dry for the past two weeks, and everything in him expects it to be equally dry today. Still he faithful and fully intends to dedicate his customary time to prayer. His text this day is Luke 5:1–11, Peter and the catch of fish. The first minutes of his prayer, as he reads through the text, are as dry as he expected. He reads the text again, and this time notices Peter's response when, through the sign of the fish, he recognizes that the Divine has come close to him in Jesus. The man sees Peter fall on his knees before Jesus and say, "Depart from me, Lord, for I am a sinful man" (Lk 5:8)[9]—"I am not holy enough, I am too sinful to be this close to you, and so, depart from me, leave me, let me be farther from you." His attention is then caught by how Jesus responds to Peter. Jesus does not argue with him; he simply confirms Peter's belonging with him and Peter's place in his mission (Lk 5:10–11).

As this man perceives Jesus's response to Peter, something in his own heart gently lifts: "Lord, you respond to me in the same way when I sense my limitations and failures." Now he finds that he is glad to be at prayer: "Lord, you may have more yet to give me in my prayer this morning." This man is experiencing the *increase of hope* that Ignatius describes as spiritual consolation. This is a perceptible, felt experience, with an uplift of heart.[10]

A woman is at daily Mass. She loves the Mass and is present with goodwill. Her attention wanders a little at times, and when it does, she brings herself back to the flow of the prayers.

The Mass reaches the consecration. The priest takes the bread, pronounces the words "This is my Body," and elevates the now consecrated Bread. As the woman gazes toward the altar, a warm and lively awareness fills her heart, "This is really you. You are truly present before me in the consecrated Bread." She is experiencing the *increase of faith* of which Ignatius speaks in rule 3. She always believed the truth of the Real Presence in the consecrated Bread and Wine, but in this moment, by God's gift, she experiences this truth more deeply with a happy uplift of heart.

The same might occur, for example, when listening to or reading Scripture. As we listen and read, the Word comes alive: with joy we sense that Jesus is speaking to us now through that text. We always believed that Jesus speaks to us through his Word; in this moment, however, we *experience* this truth in a lively fashion and with a warm, happy movement of the heart. Similar experiences may occur with regard to many truths of our faith: the mystery of the Holy Trinity, God as Creator of the world around us, Jesus's death and resurrection, his abiding closeness as our Savior, his providence in our lives, his presence in our neighbor (Mt 25:40), and other tenets of the faith.

The woman at daily Mass receives Communion and remains after Mass to pray for a few minutes. She feels herself deeply loved by the Lord, and her heart rests gladly in that love. She senses that this love prepares her for the day and that she is now more ready, in Jesus, to love the others at work. She is experiencing the *increase of charity* that Ignatius describes as spiritual consolation. I add that, again, we can all remember times when we have felt something similar, whether in prayer or in the activity of the day.

"Joy That Calls and Attracts to Heavenly Things"

Finally, Ignatius speaks of "all *interior joy* that *calls and attracts to heavenly things* and to *the salvation of one's soul*, quieting it and giving it peace in its Creator and Lord." *Interior* here, for Ignatius, is synonymous with "spiritual." This spiritual joy moves the heart in a specific direction: in it, the heart is *called* and *attracted* "upward" as it were, toward what Ignatius calls *heavenly things* and the *things of salvation.*

When it seems appropriate for the group, I may invite my listeners to remember times of joyful consolation in their lives: a period of prayer, a blessed weekend of retreat, a time of new steps in the spiritual life and the joy of growth, weeks or perhaps months of consolation in the Lord. I ask them to recall what they felt drawn toward in such spiritually joyful times. I receive answers such as these: "I wanted to pray." "I loved reading Scripture." "I wanted to be in church before the Blessed Sacrament." "I wanted to love my husband and children in a new way and found joy in this effort." "I looked forward to activities in the parish." "I wanted to serve the Lord in new ways." At this point, my listeners grasp clearly what Ignatius means by an "interior joy that *calls* and *attracts* to *heavenly things* and to the *salvation of one's soul.*"

I offer an example from author Evelyn Waugh's biography of Monsignor Ronald Knox. Waugh describes Knox's prayer after his entrance into the Catholic Church:

> He told a friend that in his first months as a Catholic he received the "consolations" he needed and *often ran to church* in his *impatience to begin his prayers.* He *looked forward to his meditations* as periods of pure joy. And at St. Edmund's it was his radiant devotion which most impressed his more discerning colleagues.
>
> The present Bishop of Lancaster, Dr. Flynn, writes: "My most outstanding memory of him [at St. Edmund's] is his absorption in prayer before the Blessed Sacrament. That made so profound an impression on me that one day, years after, preaching in the North on the love of God as an act of the will, which would not involve the

emotions, I said: 'Don't tell me that this is all the love of God means. I have *seen* people in love with God.'"[11]

In his spiritual joy, Knox's heart is *called* and *attracted* to heavenly things and the things of salvation: he is so strongly drawn to the presence of the Blessed Sacrament that he often runs to church; he is so drawn to prayer that he is impatient to begin and looks forward to his meditations as times of pure joy.

Such experiences exemplify the spiritual joy that Ignatius highlights in rule 3. When our hearts are filled, gently or more strongly, with joy in the Lord, then we are "called and attracted" to the things of faith and of the spiritual life in general. I add for my listeners that we need only think of past—or present—times of spiritual consolation to see this blessed dynamic at work in our lives.

Intensity and Duration

Finally, I discuss the varying *intensity* and *duration* of experiences of spiritual consolation. The examples already given render this point easy to illustrate.

Experiences of spiritual consolation may differ in *intensity*; they may be gentle, stronger, or very strong. As the woman prays with Mark 5 and the woman with the hemorrhage, she hears Jesus say "Daughter," and her heart is gently warmed. Raïssa is "greatly moved." Thérèse's heart is so filled with love and gratitude and her tears fall so abundantly that she cannot speak of her experience until later, still deeply moved.

Experiences of spiritual consolation also vary in *duration*. The experience may last a minute or a few minutes during a time of prayer (like the woman praying with Mark 5); it may encompass a morning, a day (like that of Thérèse), a week, a month or several months (like that of Monsignor Knox). In every case, with their varying intensities and durations, these spiritual consolations bless us as God's loving providence intends in giving them.

Transition to Rule 4

The group is now ready to turn to rule 4. I introduce rule 4 by asking, "According to the law of contrariety that holds throughout these rules, if there is spiritual *consolation*—with the accent on the noun *consolation*—there is also spiritual . . . ?" All immediately reply, "Desolation." I then say, "We'll turn now to rule 4 in which Ignatius describes spiritual desolation."

12

Helping Your Listeners Recognize Spiritual Desolation
Rule 4

I begin the presentation of spiritual desolation by saying, "This is obviously not the most pleasant topic in the spiritual life! At the same time, after thirty-five years of learning and presenting Ignatius's spiritual teaching, I believe that his teaching on spiritual desolation may be the most valuable part of all that he offers. I believe that for most faithful people, for most of the way on the spiritual journey, the real obstacle is spiritual desolation: the times when we grow discouraged and lose heart in the spiritual life and find ourselves inclined to diminish or simply relinquish the effort to grow. A teaching that equips us to understand these 'lows' in the spiritual life, and to navigate them not only without harm but even with growth, is among the most valuable services that Ignatius can render us."

I find it valuable to begin rule 4 with this observation. It removes something of the burden of discussing spiritual desolation and immediately presents rule 4 in its true light: a treatment of spiritual desolation only in order to show the path to freedom from it.

I introduce the rule through examples. Alice is a dedicated woman of faith, active for years in her parish. Sharing the life of the parish is a source of spiritual strength for her and brings her joy in the Lord. (I ask my listeners to identify this as spiritual consolation, one more exercise in learning rule 3.) More recently she has moved to a new town and joined the local parish. Here, too,

Alice has sought involvement in the parish community but in her new setting has found this involvement more difficult to achieve. A year passes amid struggles, and she begins to question the value of her efforts. A point comes when,

> Alice sees herself as a pretty complete failure and feels altogether discouraged.... Recently, even in her own personal prayer, she has experienced feelings of emptiness, of being abandoned by God. She feels that God is no longer near and she becomes overwhelmed with frustration. She wonders if she isn't altogether losing her faith in God's loving care. She does continue to be faithful to community worship and to her personal times for prayer, but it all seems hopeless and meaningless.[1]

I supply a second example. Jane is a dedicated woman in her late thirties. She has come to a retreat center to make a retreat with the assistance of her spiritual director. During the first days of her retreat, Jane has experienced great peace and a happy sense of God's closeness to her. (Again I invite my listeners to identify this as spiritual consolation.) On the third day, the joy she feels in God's loving presence moves her to increase her time of prayer. The following then occurs:

> *Day 4:* Jane gets up with a bad headache, feeling exhausted and under strain. She cannot pray well. All joy has evaporated. She is tired and sad and moody. Finally, in the evening she tells the director about her action of the previous day and its results. The director advises cutting down on prayer time and resting more.
>
> *Day 5:* She follows the advice, prays less but still has no enthusiasm and is filled with gloom.
>
> *Day 6:* At her morning prayer she becomes very much disturbed. She begins to doubt the Lord's presence to

her even in the opening days of the retreat. Probably, she thinks, she should attribute everything to her overactive imagination. Who is she to be given a taste of the sweetness of the Lord? She begins to grow discouraged at the thought that she is not meant for a deep prayer life. Her desire for God is just an illusion. The rest of the day is one of disquietude, confusion, and a sense of discouragement.[2]

I tell my listeners that experiences like that of Alice and Jane are the subject of Ignatius's fourth rule. At this point, we read the text of rule 4:

> Fourth Rule. **The fourth is of spiritual desolation. I call desolation all the contrary of the third rule, such as darkness of soul, disturbance in it, movement to low and earthly things, disquiet from various agitations and temptations, moving to lack of confidence, without hope, without love, finding oneself totally slothful, tepid, sad and, as if separated from one's Creator and Lord. For just as consolation is contrary to desolation, in the same way the thoughts that come from consolation are contrary to the thoughts that come from desolation.**

Two Words: Spiritual *and* Desolation

As with rule 3, I turn first to the initial sentence of rule 4, "The fourth is of spiritual desolation." I focus on both words: *spiritual* and *desolation*.

I explain to my listeners that in terms of head and heart, *desolation* is a word on the level of the *heart*. It indicates a *heavy movement of the heart*. Said more formally—though I do not generally use this vocabulary with the group—desolation is a heavy affective movement. I invite my listeners to suggest examples of heavy movements of the heart. Various responses follow:

sadness, discouragement, hopelessness, anxiety, and similar heavy affective movements.

I will interject one general comment here. I employ this interactive style throughout the entire presentation; in it, as just indicated, I pose questions to my listeners. These questions may reinforce teaching already covered or invite my listeners to reflect on the current point I am presenting. Such questions are generally welcome and help keep them engaged and active in the presentation. As they respond to questions of this kind, my listeners learn the material more deeply.

Having identified the meaning of *desolation*, I turn to Ignatius's adjective *spiritual*. I note how Ignatius explicitly states that the desolation (heavy movements of the heart) he intends is on the level *of our spiritual lives*, of *faith*, of *our relationship with God*. This is evident, for example, in Alice's experience: "She feels that *God is no longer near*. . . . She wonders if she isn't altogether *losing her faith in God's loving care*. She does continue to be faithful to . . . *prayer*, but it all *seems hopeless and meaningless*." The specifically *spiritual* level is also evident in Jane's experience: "She begins to *doubt the Lord's presence* to her. . . . She begins to grow discouraged at the thought that she is *not meant for a deep prayer life*. Her *desire for God* is just an *illusion*."

I then comment that if there is *spiritual* desolation, there is also another kind of desolation. This—as with consolation—can be described with various words, and I invite my listeners to suggest these. Again, various replies follow: "natural" desolation, "human" desolation, "psychological" desolation, and the like. As they now expect, I tell them that we will use the word *nonspiritual* for such movements on the natural level. *Nonspiritual desolation*, therefore, is a heavy movement of the heart on the natural level.

I ask my listeners if they can identify the word our culture most commonly uses for what we have called nonspiritual desolation. The answer readily comes: *depression*. I observe that the whole discussion of depression in the culture around us is in the vocabulary of discernment, a discussion of nonspiritual desolation.[3]

I explain that nonspiritual desolation may be caused by a depletion of physical or emotional energy or a combination of both. I give examples. In order to accomplish more in his work, a man stays up late, night after night, while continuing to rise early. A heaviness eventually enters his life: he is experiencing a *nonspiritual desolation* arising from a depletion of *physical* energy. A woman's day at work is going well, and she is cheerful. In midmorning, however, she meets a colleague who makes disparaging remarks about a project this woman has just completed. The woman is discouraged, and a film of grayness now enters her day. She is experiencing a *nonspiritual desolation* arising from a depletion of *emotional* energy.

I emphasize that in rule 4, Ignatius speaks specifically of *spiritual* and not nonspiritual desolation. This does not mean, I continue, that nonspiritual desolation—the times when, in varying degrees, we are tired or depressed—has no importance for the spiritual life. Just as *nonspiritual consolation* is often the space into which God infuses the further gift of *spiritual consolation*, in like manner, *nonspiritual desolation* (tiredness or depression) is often the space into which the enemy brings the further trap of *spiritual desolation*. I note that the enemy willingly works in our vulnerabilities.

Some important considerations about nonspiritual desolation follow. Usually, as I discuss these, I have the full attention of my listeners; as I speak, they are applying these points to their own experience.[4]

I observe that a certain amount of nonspiritual desolation is normal in a well-lived life. The mother, for example, who is up for several nights with an ill child, grows physically and perhaps emotionally weary. There is, however, something even holy about this weariness: the mother accepts it out of love for her child and fidelity to her vocation as a mother. Again, the pastor who guides his parish through Holy Week or is called to the hospital in the early morning grows tired. Here, too, there is something holy about this weariness: the pastor accepts it out of love for his parishioners and fidelity to his vocation as a priest. I note that evidently, both the mother and the priest will need to find healthy ways to recover their energy.

But if there is too much and too persistent nonspiritual desolation—a person says, "I always feel tired" or "I always feel depressed"—then not only as good stewards of our humanity, which God calls us to be, but also *for the sake of our spiritual lives*, we need to do something about this. Many problems that we consider spiritual resolve when we pay wise attention to the needs of our humanity on the nonspiritual level.

I offer an example. Most of us have a daily routine of prayer. We esteem it, know that it helps us, and try to be faithful to it. Then I note for my listeners that that I am not likely alone in experiencing days when I feel that "Today I just can't do it!" I ask, "You know what often resolves that for me?" I pause, and then answer, "Exercise. I go and get some exercise, and then I am ready to pray. The problem never was that I did not want to pray. I do want to pray. The problem was that I had not paid wise attention to a *nonspiritual* need of my humanity." The example resonates with my listeners and makes the point. You will find your own examples.

I conclude that one of the best things we can do for our spiritual lives is to take wise care of our humanity on the nonspiritual (natural) level. Applying this principle to rule 4, I affirm that many struggles with *spiritual desolation* will resolve when we address opportunely our experiences of *nonspiritual desolation*.

What we have just said indicates that, again by exact parallel with *spiritual* and *nonspiritual consolation*, the distinction between *spiritual* and *nonspiritual desolation* is both important and, at the same time, must not be overstressed. It is important because spiritual and nonspiritual desolation are distinct realities, calling for spiritual or nonspiritual remedies respectively. When both are used wisely—the person, for example, with appropriate psychological help, gradually overcomes the depression, and with appropriate spiritual help, grows in prayer and love of God—then wonderful progress occurs.

The distinction, therefore, between spiritual and nonspiritual desolation is important for a proper understanding and application of rule 4. Nevertheless, the distinction must not be overstressed. As we have seen, *nonspiritual* desolation is often the space into which the enemy brings the trap of *spiritual* desolation. When the whole person is integrated into the spiritual journey, the enemy's spiritual desolations significantly lose their power to wound.

Examples of Spiritual Desolation

I turn now to the remainder of rule 4. I observe that, as with rule 3, Ignatius does not give a definition of spiritual desolation but rather a list of experiences of spiritual desolation. His goal is to familiarize us with spiritual desolation and so equip us to recognize it in our own experience. That recognition sets us free to take the appropriate action in response to it.

"Darkness of Soul"

People in spiritual desolation may experience *darkness of soul*. They feel a burden in their spiritual lives, do not understand what is happening, and go forward with a heavy sense that things are bad and likely to get worse. I illustrate this simply: "One of us lived the past six months or year with a vague sense that something was not right spiritually, that a weight, a burden, colored everything, and without being able to see it clearly. That burden colored everything in prayer, participation in church, and God's service, diminishing his or her joy and spiritual energy to love the Lord. Everything has seemed confusing and heavy. This person, I affirm, has experienced the *darkness of soul* that is spiritual desolation."[5]

"Disturbance in the Soul"

People may also experience a *disturbance* in their hearts, a lack of serenity, a sense of turmoil and restlessness in their lives of faith. Troubled, anxious thoughts flit through their minds, and there is little peace, little serenity, as they relate to God.

"Movement to Low and Earthly Things"

I generally dedicate a little time to this experience of spiritual desolation. In spiritual consolation, I comment that people feel an "upward" call and attraction toward heavenly things and the things of salvation (rule 3); in spiritual desolation, they feel exactly the opposite pull. Now these people experience a *movement to low and earthly things*: material comforts, gratification of the body in various ways, memories of such things from the past, immersion in the empty trivia of the surrounding society, diversion through the media, the internet, busyness, superficial conversation, and similar occupations.[6]

Again, an example. Philip is a man who loves the Lord. He usually ends his day at 10:00 p.m. with some minutes of reading Scripture and the examen prayer.[7] This has been a day of spiritual desolation, however, and this evening Philip feels no inclination to pray. As he sits at his desk, a few inches in front of one hand is the Bible, and a few inches in front of the other is the smartphone. Nothing in Philip now wants to reach out for the Bible, and everything in him wants to reach out for the smartphone—and one touch of the screen will become fifty, then a hundred . . . and more. Philip is experiencing the *movement to low and earthly things* that characterizes spiritual desolation.

I add with some emphasis that *there is no shame* in experiencing this pull, that this is simply what happens in living the spiritual life in a fallen, redeemed, and loved world. What matters critically is that Philip be aware, understand what is happening, and reject the pull toward low and earthly things—that is, that he live the discerning life.

"Disquiet from Various Agitations and Temptations"

In spiritual desolation, people further experience *disquiet* from various *agitations* and *temptations*. Their hearts are troubled, disquieted, and various temptations float in and out of the desolation. I exemplify, "Why don't you let your prayer go till later?" "You can let yourself see that. It doesn't have to get too far out of hand . . . " and similar deceptive suggestions of the enemy.

I note Ignatius's pairing of *spiritual desolation* (heaviness of heart in our spiritual lives) and *temptation* (deceptive suggestions of the enemy). I tell my listeners that we may expect that temptations will generally accompany the affective heaviness of spiritual desolation. But, again, there is no shame in experiencing this disquiet and these temptations. What matters is discernment: awareness, understanding, and action.

"Lack of Confidence, without Hope, without Love"

In spiritual consolation, people experience an increase of hope, faith, and charity; in spiritual desolation, they feel exactly the contrary: a movement toward *lack of confidence* and a sense of being *without hope* and *without love*. As Philip, for example, sits at his desk at 10:00 p.m. in desolation, he finds himself thinking, "Look at you! You'll never be a man of prayer. You'll never really love the Lord. All your efforts to grow spiritually will never lead to much [lack of confidence]. Why pray tonight? Nothing is going to come from it. And what is the point of getting up early to go to the men's breakfast in the parish? Nothing will change [without hope]." As Philip sits at his desk, he feels no warmth of God's love and of love for others in God [without love].

Once more, *there is no shame* in this . . . and what matters is discernment. As I said earlier, no one ever tells me that I repeat this—there is no shame in experiencing this—too often!

"Totally Slothful, Tepid, Sad"

People in desolation experience themselves as *totally*—a powerful adverb—*slothful* (without energy for spiritual things), *tepid* (without fervor), and *sad* (without joy). They may be faithful to prayer, to involvement in the parish, and to the effort to love, but all is heavy and joyless.

Ruth, for example, has been experiencing spiritual desolation for the past week and has found her desolation deepening in the past few days.[8] For several years, she has participated in a Bible study group and has always found in these meetings rich nourishment for personal prayer and an encouraging sense of communion with others who share her love of God. Ruth consistently looks forward to these meetings and participates willingly. This week, however, she feels no energy for the study of Scripture and for sharing with the others. In this time of desolation, she has almost to force herself to attend the Bible study. Ruth feels, in Ignatius's sense here, wholly *slothful* with regard to an activity that brings her closer to God: she feels completely *without spiritual energy* with respect to the meeting.

Ruth does attend the Bible study in spite of her lack of attraction for it. The meeting is tasteless for her. The Scriptures do not come alive for her this time as they have in the past. She joins in the common prayer and contributes to the sharing but without affective involvement. She does her best "to get through it" as the group expects, but her heart is distant and unengaged. Ruth feels, again in Ignatius' sense here, totally *tepid* in carrying out a habitual practice of her spiritual life. Though she is faithful, she feels *no fervor* as she participates in the Bible study.

As the burdensome days of desolation continue, Ruth increasingly feels a sense of sadness. There is little "interior joy that calls and attracts to heavenly things" now in her life of faith. Often God seems far away and her spiritual life, formerly Ruth's greatest cause of happiness, is now a source of heaviness. She fears that she has regressed spiritually and that her spiritual condition may continue to worsen; in her time of spiritual desolation, Ruth feels *sad in her life of faith*. This is one experience of spiritual desolation in which a person feels "totally slothful, tepid, and sad." You will find the examples that best help you illustrate Ignatius's words.

People seeking God may recognize these or similar experiences in their own spiritual journey. It is important to observe that none of these three attitudes—*slothfulness, tepidity*, and *sadness*—is an indication that Ruth's love of God has diminished. They do not signify that Ruth has ceased to be a dedicated woman of faith. All three are, rather, experiences of the trial of spiritual desolation. If Ruth is aware of and understands this, she will find it easier to resist the feelings of slothfulness, tepidity, and sadness and persevere faithfully until they pass and peace returns. If she is not spiritually aware and does not understand this, the harm these three attitudes can cause is all too evident.

"As If Separated from One's Creator and Lord"

Finally, Ignatius writes, people in spiritual desolation feel "as if separated from [their] Creator and Lord." The words *as if* unmask the lie of desolation: God is Emmanuel (Mt 1:23), ever with us to the close of the age (Mt 28:20), providing even in the smallest details of our lives (Lk 12:6–7). The feeling, however, in spiritual desolation is that "I am here, and you, God, are a million miles away. I am alone." As Philip, for example, sits at his desk at 10:00 p.m., he may well feel "as if separated from his Creator and Lord," alone in the heaviness of his heart and exposed to temptation. Here, too, my listeners apply the example to their own experience.

As I conclude this section, I observe that, as with spiritual consolations, spiritual desolations will also vary in intensity and duration. They may be slightly discouraging, more heavily disheartening, or seemingly overwhelmingly dark (variation in intensity). They may also last for just a moment—perhaps a minute or five minutes of an otherwise peaceful time of prayer—for an hour, a morning, a day, weeks, months, and, sadly, even for years (variation in duration). Here I affirm with much emphasis that such long-enduring periods of desolation *need not happen*, that Jesus did not come that we might be captives to the enemy's discouraging lies, that he came to *set captives free*.

Often this affirmation touches my listeners deeply. Some, at least, have experienced or are experiencing long periods of spiritual desolation in which they have felt or are feeling helpless, simply constrained to live with the burden. When they learn the truth, hope begins to dawn.

"The One of Them He Gives, the Other He Permits"

At this point, I find it useful to quote and comment on a section from the letter of Ignatius to Sister Teresa Rejadell. I cite here the text, highlighting the words on which I wish especially to comment:

> I will call your attention briefly to *two lessons* which our Lord usually gives, or permits. The one of them he *gives*, the other he *permits*. The first is an interior consolation which casts out all uneasiness and draws one to a complete love of our Lord. . . . In a word, when this divine consolation is present all trials are pleasant and all weariness rest. He who goes forward with this fervor, warmth, and interior consolation finds every burden light and sweetness in every penance or trial, however great. This consolation points out and opens the way we are to follow and points out the way we are to avoid. It *does not remain with us always*, but it *will always accompany us* on the way *at the times that God designates*. All this is for our progress.
>
> But when this consolation is absent the other lesson comes to light. Our ancient enemy sets up all possible obstacles to turn us aside from the way on which we have

entered. He makes use of everything to vex us, and everything in the first lesson is reversed. We find ourselves sad without knowing why. We cannot pray with devotion, nor contemplate, nor even speak or hear of the things of God with any interior taste or relish. Not only this, but if he sees that we are weak and much humbled by these harmful thoughts, *he goes on* to suggest that we are entirely forgotten by God our Lord, and leads us to think that we are totally separated from him and that *all that we have done* and *all that we desire to do* is entirely worthless. He thus endeavors to bring us to *a state of general discouragement.* . . . For this reason is it necessary for us *to be aware* of our opponent.⁹

This text permits me to make a number of key points:

- "Two *lessons*": These are, as Ignatius's next sentences indicate, spiritual consolation and spiritual desolation. That Ignatius would employ the word *lesson*—a positive word indicating that something is gained, is learned—of spiritual consolation seems evident. That he also applies it to spiritual desolation is, I note for my listeners, our first indication in the vocabulary that there is a reason why a God who loves us permits us to undergo spiritual desolation. I comment that Ignatius will address this in rule 9.

- "The one of them he *gives*, the other he *permits*": Gives or permits. I ask my listeners, "Of these two, spiritual consolation and spiritual desolation, which one does God *give*?" All immediately reply, "Spiritual consolation." I then state clearly that spiritual consolation is always and only the gift of God. I continue, "Of these two, spiritual consolation and spiritual desolation, which one does God *permit*?" All immediately reply, "Spiritual desolation." I continue, "God never gives spiritual desolation." I ask, "Spiritual desolation is always and only the work of whom?" All immediately reply, "The enemy." Further, "If spiritual desolation is always the work of the enemy, then what is the only appropriate response to it?" All reply, "To reject it." I conclude, "These are fundamental truths about spiritual consolation and spiritual desolation that we must grasp clearly."

- "It [spiritual consolation] *does not remain with us always*": I ask, "How many of us wish that we experienced more spiritual consolation than we actually do?" Smiles appear, and hands are raised. I add my hand as well! Then I ask, "When will we experience unbroken spiritual consolation?" The answer readily comes, "In eternal life." I observe that this is one way of describing eternal life: unending spiritual consolation. Then I add, "Therefore, if there is no shame in experiencing spiritual desolation, there is also no shame in not always experiencing spiritual consolation." This, too, lifts the hearts of some listeners who, however consciously, feel that "If I were a better follower of Jesus, I would experience more or less constant spiritual consolation, and certainly more consolation than I do experience." Ignatius serenely affirms that "it does not remain with us always."

- "It *will always accompany us* on the way *at the times that God designates*": This is the complement to the preceding affirmation. We will not always experience spiritual consolation in this life, but we will always experience it at the times that God, in his loving providence, knows that we need it. I comment that all of us, looking back over our lives, see the truth of this: how the felt experience of God's love strengthened us in times of difficulty and helped us find the way forward.

- "If he [the enemy] sees that we are weak and much humbled by these harmful thoughts, *he goes on*": If we allow the spiritual desolation to work in us, if we become afraid and give way to it, the enemy, Ignatius says, does not stop at the initial discouragement but *goes on* to deepen and darken the desolation. He will suggest "that we are *entirely* forgotten by God our Lord, and leads us to think that we are *totally* separated from him." Unresisted desolation will grow. Hence the importance of resisting and rejecting the desolation once we are aware of it.

- "That *all that we have done* and *all that we desire to do* is entirely worthless": I emphasize this key point for my listeners. "All that we have done": this is our entire spiritual past; "all that we desire to do": this is our entire spiritual future. If we are not aware of, do not understand, and do not reject the desolation, it will claim power to *interpret our spiritual past* and *predict our spiritual future*—and that interpretation and prediction will be dark: both will be seen as "*entirely worthless*." "Spiritual desolation," I tell my listeners, "is like wearing a pair of sunglasses. We can shade them more or less dark according to the intensity of the desolation. You look back, and all looks dark; you look forward, and all looks dark. But you *take off the sunglasses* and the lie of the darkness is revealed. If we believe the enemy's lie about our spiritual past and future, great heaviness of heart will follow. When we unmask and reject the lie, spiritual desolation loses much of its power to oppress."

- "He thus endeavors to bring us to *a state of general discouragement*": If we do not resist and reject spiritual desolation, this is where it will lead, to "a state of general discouragement." Such is precisely the enemy's intention. When we experience such general discouragement in our spiritual lives, we are prone to harmful decisions regarding prayer, God's service, and our vocation itself.

- "For this reason is it necessary for us *to be aware* of our opponent": If this is the enemy's tactic and purpose, what should be our response? The answer, I tell my listeners, is pure Ignatius: "It is necessary for us *to be aware* of our opponent." This awareness of spiritual experience is fundamental for Ignatius and, as my listeners by now are well aware, enormously beneficial in the spiritual life.

"The Thoughts That Come from Desolation"

I then turn to the final sentence in rule 4: "For just as consolation is contrary to desolation, in the same way *the thoughts that come from consolation* are contrary to *the thoughts that come from desolation.*" Another important point is made here. Spiritual consolation and spiritual desolation are heart-level (affective: feelings, emotions) experiences. They are accompanied, however, by significant head-level (cognitive: thoughts, ideas) experience. Said more simply, when our hearts experience the joy or discouragement of spiritual consolation or spiritual desolation, something corresponding happens in how we find ourselves thinking.

As we would expect, just as the heart-level experiences of spiritual consolation and spiritual desolation are contrary, so too the thoughts that arise from the one and the other are contrary. This is Ignatius's point, that the *thoughts that arise from spiritual consolation* will be exactly the contrary of the *thoughts that arise from spiritual desolation.*

Once more, an example helps grasp the point. When Gerald attends Sunday Mass and hears the homily on Luke 11:1–13 with the invitation to pray with Scripture for ten minutes each day, his heart is warmed with gratitude to God for the change that has occurred in his life. He feels God's closeness and love, and a quiet joy fills his heart. Gerald is experiencing spiritual consolation.

As his heart experiences, *thoughts arise from the spiritual consolation*: "If praying once a week at Sunday Mass already makes this difference, what would happen if I did what Father is suggesting and prayed daily?" And again: "I could arrange my morning to get ten minutes each day. And actually, all I have to do is ask my wife for help because she has been doing this for some years. She will be happy to help me, to show me how to find the readings and get started. This evening, after the children are in bed, I will ask her help and then start this prayer tomorrow morning."

At supper that evening, the conversation with his teenage son does not resolve well, and Gerald is discouraged. He is now in his study, preparing for work the next morning. Gerald remembers that he had planned to speak at this time with his wife about the ten minutes with Scripture. But now he does not feel God's closeness; there is no warmth, no peace, no attraction to new steps in prayer, only a heaviness of heart about all of this. Gerald is experiencing spiritual desolation.

As his heart experiences this, *thoughts arise from the spiritual desolation*: "Who are you kidding? You've been away from the Church for twenty years. You've never even read Scripture. What makes you think you'll understand anything written there? Why approach your wife about a practice that is bound to fail? You'll just embarrass yourself and her. You had a nice experience at Mass this morning, but that doesn't change anything, and it is not going to last."

As is evident, the thoughts that arise from spiritual consolation are *exactly the contrary* of those that arise from spiritual desolation. At this point, I ask my listeners, "In this set of rules,[10] which spirit is at work in the thoughts that arise from spiritual consolation?" All answer readily, "The good spirit." Then, "Which spirit is at work in the thoughts that arise from spiritual desolation?" All answer, "The enemy." I continue, "In this set of rules, what is the appropriate response to the thoughts that arise from spiritual consolation?" All reply, "To accept them." And again, "What is the appropriate response to the thoughts that arise from spiritual desolation?" All reply, "To reject them." I conclude with a final question: "Can you see why it is so important to know when we are in spiritual consolation or spiritual desolation?" The point is clearly made, and my listeners grasp it well.

Spiritual Desolation Presents Itself as Our Spiritual Identity

I now raise another important observation regarding spiritual desolation. I summarize it in the following sentence: "Spiritual desolation presents itself as our spiritual identity." I often repeat this sentence three times for my listeners so that they will hear it clearly and remember it.

Spiritual desolation—that is, the enemy working through his tactic of spiritual desolation—will attempt to tell us that "what you are experiencing (spiritual desolation) is *who you are* spiritually (identity)." Examples clarify the point.

A woman loves the Lord and prays faithfully. Today she is experiencing spiritual desolation and feels no desire to pray as usual. The spiritual desolation (enemy) says to her, "Do you see *who you are*? You are a person who really doesn't love prayer." A man who loves God and dedicates his life to God's service today experiences spiritual desolation and feels far from God—in Ignatius's words, "as if separated from his Creator and Lord." The spiritual desolation (enemy) says to him, "Do you see *who you are*? You are a person who is far from God." A woman has experienced trials in her life. Through them, she has grown in trust that God's love and providence will guide her through dark times. Today she experiences spiritual desolation and finds it hard to trust in God's loving care for her—in Ignatius's words, she experiences the "lack of confidence" that may typify times of spiritual desolation. The spiritual desolation (enemy) says to her, "Do you see *who you are*? You are a person who really doesn't trust God."

I tell my listeners that in every case, the answer is a resounding no! The woman is a person who loves prayer; she is simply experiencing spiritual desolation today. The man loves God and is close to God; he is simply experiencing spiritual desolation today. The woman deeply trusts God; she is simply experiencing spiritual desolation today.

If we undo the false equation between the spiritual desolation we experience and our spiritual identity, the spiritual desolation loses much of its power to burden. Again, hope rises in my listeners as the truth sets them free.

13

The Advice That Your Listeners Never Forget
Rule 5

I begin the presentation of rule 5 with these words: "If you forget everything else we say in these talks—you won't, but this is a way of making a point—I beg of you never to forget rule 5. It will get you safely through almost any darkness you may face in life." My listeners generally smile when I say, "If you forget everything else we say in these talks," but they hear the seriousness and emphasis with which I speak of rule 5. Most never do forget rule 5. When I meet them even years later, my listeners will often mention rule 5 and how it has helped them.

Then I note that with rule 5 a shift occurs in the rules. "At this point," I tell my listeners, "you possess the basic groundwork of the rules: you know what discernment is (title statement: be aware, understand, take action); how the enemy and good spirit work in persons heading away from and toward God (rules 1 and 2); and the nature of the two interior movements, spiritual consolation and spiritual desolation (rules 3 and 4). Now Ignatius will begin to apply this understanding to our concrete experience in life.

"In the remaining nine rules (rules 5 through 14)," I tell them, "Ignatius will focus primarily on the third step in discernment: be aware, understand, *take action (accept/reject)*. He will add further to our understanding of discernment (second step), but his primary focus will be step 3. Above all, Ignatius will now equip us to apply this teaching in our lives."

Ignatius will have something to say about the first term, *accept*, in rules 10 and 11. In these nine rules (rules 5 through 14), however, the almost unvarying focus is on the second term, *reject*.

I raise a question for my listeners: "Which of these two—to accept God's work in spiritual consolation or to reject the enemy's discouraging lies in spiritual desolation—is primary?" I continue, "Obviously both are important, but which is primary? What is more important? What God is doing or the ways in which the enemy attempts to attack God's work?" All answer that God's action is primary.

A further question follows: "But where are there generally more problems for us, in accepting God's consolations or rejecting the enemy's desolations?" All readily reply, "In rejecting the enemy's desolations." I draw the conclusion, "And Ignatius, who knows our experience so well and who is eminently practical in these rules, will supply help above all where we generally have the greatest need."

Here I affirm once more that for most of us—for dedicated people such as my listeners who seek Ignatius's help—for most of the way on the spiritual journey, the greatest obstacle is spiritual desolation, the times when we grow discouraged in the spiritual life and may, if we are not discerning, diminish or abandon our efforts to love and serve the Lord. A teaching, therefore, that equips us to be aware of, understand (identify), and take action wisely to reject spiritual desolation is among the greatest services Ignatius can render us.

This consideration of the points just mentioned removes much of the heaviness that discussion of spiritual desolation might otherwise engender. My listeners understand why Ignatius dedicates so many rules to helping us reject spiritual desolation. They perceive that his whole purpose is to *set captives free* from the burden of spiritual desolation. An air of hope then pervades the presentation.

Finally, I note the importance of responding rightly to spiritual desolation and therefore of the discussion to follow. If we are not aware of, do not understand (identify), and do not reject spiritual desolation, it will work great harm in our spiritual lives. If, on the other hand, we do notice, identify, and strive to reject spiritual desolation, not only will it do us no harm, but also the very effort to reject it will transform desolation into a path toward God. The rules that follow matter!

"In Time of Desolation Never Make a Change"

I now turn to the text of rule 5 and read it with my listeners. At the end of the first sentence, I note that in this first sentence Ignatius gives a *guideline* for action; in the second, he gives the *reason* for the guideline:

> Fifth Rule. The fifth: in time of desolation never make a change, but be firm and constant in the proposals and determination in which one was the day preceding such desolation, or in the determination in which one was in the preceding consolation. Because, as in consolation the good spirit guides and counsels us more, so in desolation the bad spirit, with whose counsels we cannot find the way to a right decision.

Before proceeding further, I highlight the first eight words: "In time of desolation never make a change." I tell my listeners that these eight words have blessed generations of Christians for five hundred years. I invite my listeners to repeat them with me, and all join in. We do it a further time. My listeners now know that these words contain something important.

"In Time of Desolation"

I first clarify what Ignatius means by "in time of desolation." Because rule 5 applies *in this context*, it is important that my listeners grasp well the meaning of the phrase and be able to apply it to their experience. I do this through examples:

- A man's project at work this morning did not go well, and he is discouraged. Because of his discouragement, he did not go to Mass on his lunch hour as he usually does. Normally he prays evening prayer from the Liturgy of the Hours when he returns home from work but, again because of his discouragement, he omitted this prayer. Now he is alone in his room at 10:00 p.m. He does not feel God's closeness, has no desire to pray, and simply wants to flop mindlessly in front of the television. If this man is aware and understands his experience, he can say, "I am now in a time of spiritual desolation." Whenever we can say this, rule 5 applies.

- Three days ago, things were going well for a woman at work until a fellow worker made a cutting remark that touched an emotionally vulnerable space. The woman found herself sad and discouraged, and that heaviness has now accompanied her for three days. In these days, prayer has slipped, and she did not go to the evening Bible study as she usually does. Today, in late afternoon, she sits alone in the kitchen, sad, disheartened, feeling far from God and with no energy for spiritual things. If this woman is aware and understands her experience, she can say, "I am now in a time of spiritual desolation." Whenever we can say this, rule 5 applies.

Examples of this nature prepare my listeners to grasp when rule 5 applies in their lives.

"Never Make a Change"

In time of spiritual desolation, Ignatius writes, "*never make a change*, but *be firm and constant* in the *proposals and determination* in which one was the *day preceding such desolation*, or in the determination in which one was *in the preceding consolation*." I restate Ignatius's guideline for my listeners: "In time of spiritual desolation, never make a change to any spiritual proposal that you had in place before the desolation began, but remain firm in such proposals."

In rule 5, as throughout the rules, everything is on the spiritual level. I specify that Ignatius speaks here of *spiritual* desolation and *spiritual* proposals—decisions, plans, ways of proceeding in our spiritual lives that we had decided to adopt before the present spiritual desolation began.

I observe for my listeners, however, that this guideline will generally apply on the nonspiritual level as well. A woman, for example, is struggling with significant depression. She meets regularly with her counselor. Today she tells the counselor that she has decided to quit her job and move to another city. Most likely, the counselor will say something like this: "You know, this may not be the best time for you to make changes like these. Why don't we work through the depression first, and once you are through it, we can look at these changes again." Though the guideline applies on the nonspiritual level as well as the spiritual, Ignatius has the spiritual level specifically in mind here.

I next give examples of what Ignatius means by "never make a change" in time of spiritual desolation. I give a number of these so that the point is made clearly.

- A woman had a difficult phone conversation with her college-age daughter last evening. The conversation did not resolve well, and the woman senses anew the tension between her and her daughter. The day ended in discouragement. She rises this morning. Normally she attends morning Mass before work. This morning she feels disheartened and far from God, with little energy for prayer and little desire to "get herself to church" for Mass. She finds herself thinking, "I don't know. I just don't feel like going to Mass this morning. In any case, the way I'm feeling I wouldn't get much out of it. I think I'll just let it go for today."

Now I ask my listeners two questions: "Is this woman in a time of spiritual desolation?" All readily answer yes. "Is this woman, in a time of spiritual desolation, thinking of changing a spiritual proposal that she had in place before this desolation began?" Again the group readily answers yes—her proposal to attend daily Mass each morning before work was in place before the desolation began. Then I draw the conclusion: "Whenever the answer to these two questions is yes, what does Ignatius tell us in rule 5?" The answer is evident, and my listeners express it, but I also say it clearly for my listeners: "We should never make such changes but remain firm in what we had proposed to do before the desolation began." Finally, I ask my listeners, "What should this woman do this morning?" With the group, I answer, "Get herself to Mass exactly as she had planned to do before the desolation began."

- A man planned to go to Confession next Saturday afternoon when Confessions are heard in the parish from 3:00 to 4:00 p.m. The Tuesday before, a painful disagreement arises with fellow office members and leaves him doubting his ability to accomplish the tasks given him. A heaviness of heart fills his week. Disheartened, he lets his prayer slip and finds himself spending time online in a way that is not spiritually good. Now it is Saturday morning, and the man remembers his plan to go to Confession that afternoon. But now he finds himself thinking, "What's the point? It's not going to change anything about this situation at work. Besides, if I try to go to Confession feeling the way I am, I'll just embarrass myself and the priest. I think I should wait for Saturday of next week when I'll be better able to profit from Confession."

Once more, I guide my listeners through the drill with the two questions: "Is this man in a time of spiritual desolation?"

All readily answer yes. "Is this man, in a time of spiritual desolation, thinking of changing a spiritual proposal that he had in place before this desolation began?" Again the group readily answers yes—his proposal to go to Confession on this Saturday was in place before the desolation began. I draw the conclusion: "Whenever the answer to these two questions is yes, what does Ignatius tell us in rule 5?" As a group, we answer, "We should never make such changes but remain firm in what we had proposed to do before the desolation began." I ask my listeners, "What should this man do this Saturday afternoon?" Together we answer, "Get himself to Confession exactly as he had planned to do before the desolation began."

- A college student has long felt a troubling burden in her relationship with God. She has gotten to know the chaplain, appreciates his goodness and wisdom, and knows that she could speak openly with him about this burden. She asks to meet with him, and they set an appointment for Friday at 2:00 p.m. Earlier in the week, however, her "friends" ignore her in planning an outing for the coming weekend. This rejection touches a vulnerable place in her heart, and she is deeply hurt. The days are filled with this burden. Her life of prayer slips, her energy for spiritual things declines, and God no longer feels close. Now it is Friday morning, and she remembers her meeting with the chaplain. But now her thoughts are different: "You are in no condition to talk about such sensitive things as this burden you've carried for so long. If you try, feeling as you do now, you won't be able to speak openly and clearly enough for the chaplain to be of any help. This is not a good time for you to raise such issues. You should text the chaplain, explain that you can't make it today, and tell him that you'll be in touch to reschedule."

Again, I take my listeners through the drill with the two questions.

If I feel it helpful for the group, I may add a further example:

- A man planned, as he does every year, to attend a weekend retreat in early June. In January, when registration opens, he reserves a place in the retreat house for that weekend. As May unfolds, however, tensions in the family and at work disturb him, and his energy for spiritual things wanes. Prayer is slipping, and he no longer feels joy in the Lord. June begins, and the retreat is only days away. He finds himself thinking, "The way I'm feeling, a weekend retreat will only be a long and miserable experience. I think I'll call and cancel my registration. I can reschedule for the fall when I'll be in better shape to profit from a retreat."

The same drill follows. By this time, my listeners have grasped well what Ignatius means when he counsels that in time of spiritual desolation we should never make a change to any spiritual proposal that we had in place before the desolation began. They are already applying it to their own experience in the past, looking back over their lives, and in the present.

I use the examples given here or others like them according to the group I have before me. You will find the examples that best help you present rule 5.

"Never"

I now highlight the adverb in Ignatius's words, "in time of desolation *never* make a change." *Never*. This is an absolute imperative that admits of no exceptions. Because it is absolute, rule 5 is eminently *usable*.

In time of spiritual desolation, the desolation (enemy) may urge with great force that "you got it wrong before! What you planned—that decision about prayer, that commitment in the Church, that service to the poor, even your vocational decision—and what seemed so clear to you then was all wrong. Now you are seeing things more clearly. You need to change this! And you shouldn't wait! You need to change it now!" In the face of promptings that, in the darkness of the spiritual desolation may appear so reasonable, so *right*, and so *urgent*, Ignatius's calm "never" stands like a rock of strength. Two questions: "Am I in a time of spiritual desolation?" and "Am I, in a time of spiritual desolation, thinking of changing a spiritual proposal that I had in place before this desolation began?" Whenever the answer to these two questions is yes, I know that I should *never* make the change the desolation (enemy) is suggesting but remain "firm and constant" in what I had planned before the desolation began. Through such considerations, my listeners are increasingly readied to apply rule 5 in their lives.

Experiences of Rule 5

I share with my listeners my deep gratitude for rule 5 in my own life.[1] I tell them that many times, it has made all the difference, helping me avoid decisions that often only a short time later I could see would have been harmful.

I share an experience that repeated several times in my early years of priesthood. The work of my religious community includes giving retreats, and shortly after my ordination I began to do this. Many of these were weekend retreats for groups in a retreat house. I would arrive on Friday afternoon, get settled, share supper with the people, and then around 7:00 p.m. I would gather with the people in the chapel to begin the retreat.

I would give them the schedule I had prepared for the weekend, with the various times of talks, personal prayer, Mass, meals, and prayer together in chapel. Then I would give the first talk, about thirty minutes. When I finished, we would enter into silence. Some would remain in chapel to pray; others would go quietly to their rooms.

Then I would be alone in my room, with all the vulnerabilities of a new priest beginning a new ministry. Obviously there was no feedback yet. I would sit in my room wondering, "How did this beginning go? Is the schedule right? Am I packing too much into the weekend and demanding too much of them? Did they like the first talk? Did I say anything helpful? Did they not like it? Will some decide this retreat is not worth their time? Will I find cars missing from the parking lot in the morning? Maybe I need to lighten the schedule . . ." There I would be, anxious, worried, uncertain, struggling.

At this point, I ask my listeners if they can name what I am describing—inviting them to identify my experience. We specify that this is nonspiritual desolation arising from the vulnerabilities of a new priest who has not yet received feedback on his efforts. I add that this nonspiritual desolation could easily become spiritual since, in this vulnerable space, I might find it harder to pray and trust in the Lord's love for me in this ministry.

I resume the narrative. In the midst of all this anxiety and confusion, I would remember rule 5. I would say to myself, "No, this is no time for you to make any changes to what you planned for this retreat. You stay exactly with what you planned." And it would always work out well.

I find that sharing of this kind, provided that it is appropriate, fosters the bond between presenter and listeners—"This presenter, too, experiences what we do!" You will decide whether such sharing seems helpful in your own presentations.

Literary references may also help. For example, if I find it opportune for the group, I may cite a moment from J. R. R. Tolkien's *The Lord of the Rings*. When Frodo is on the verge of the darkest part of his journey, he encounters Lady Galadriel. She is a figure of great wisdom, goodness, and nobility. Lady Galadriel gives Frodo a small crystal phial filled with white light, and tells him that it will be a light for him in the dark when every other light goes out.² *A light in the dark when every other light goes out*—that, I say to my listeners, is what rule 5 can be for us. In time of spiritual desolation, when everything in us cries out that the spiritual proposals we thought were right were in fact mistaken and must be changed, then rule 5 can be for us a light in the dark; it can keep us safely on the path toward God.

I reinforce this point with the more sober consideration of changes that have been made in time of spiritual desolation. I ask, "How many times have we seen people make, or made ourselves, changes in time of spiritual desolation, from the 'smallest' things such as letting prayer go or withdrawing from a church activity, to the largest—even vocational changes? They are always," I affirm, "harmful changes." I conclude, "In his rule 5 it is precisely from such harm that Ignatius would save us."

If time allows, I explore an example from St. Ignatius himself.³ When time does permit and we are so inclined, this text provides an opportunity to illustrate rule 5 and to reinforce much of the preceding teaching with our listeners.

I explain the background to the text. Ignatius is writing the Constitutions for his Jesuits and is seeking to determine the manner of gospel poverty they will embrace. He sets aside forty days to pursue clarity regarding whether, as was the current practice, the Jesuits should accept fixed revenues for the churches it administered, or whether this constituted a departure from the complete poverty that God willed for them. Ignatius decides to celebrate Mass on each of these forty days, seeking light from the Lord.

During the forty days, in fact, Ignatius perceives clearly that the Lord does not want this exception to the Jesuits' practice of full gospel poverty. He has received the answer he sought. Now Ignatius has reached the last of these forty days and is about to celebrate the final Mass. He is hoping to receive a spiritual consolation that will confirm the decision he has reached.

The text follows. I have added italics to highlight examples of spiritual consolation and spiritual desolation with their respective qualities. At these points, I invite my listeners to identify the experience. By now, they respond with increasing ease. I have also included brackets to supply further details and explanations. Ignatius writes:

> In the customary prayer [upon rising in the morning], *I felt great devotion* and from midway on there was much of it, *clear, lucid,* and as it were *warm* [experience of spiritual consolation]. . . .
>
> During a part of the Mass I felt *great devotion*, sometimes with *movements to tears* [further experience of spiritual consolation]. During the other part, I struggled many times with what I would do to finish because I was not finding what I was seeking. . . .
>
> When the Mass was finished, and afterward in my room, I found myself *totally alone* and *without help of any kind, without power to relish any of my mediators or any of the Divine Persons*, but *so remote and so separated from them*, as if I had *never felt anything* of them, or *never would feel anything again*. [This is the experience of spiritual desolation. Many qualities of spiritual desolation are expressed here. Note the claim of power over Ignatius's spiritual past ("as if I had never felt anything of them") and future ("or never would feel anything again")—this man who has had deep, mystical experiences of God!]
>
> Rather, thoughts came to me, sometimes against Jesus, sometimes against another [Divine] Person, being so confused with different thoughts [note the thoughts that arise from spiritual desolation], such as . . . to begin the Masses over again. . . . [Rule 5 has now come into play: in time of spiritual desolation, a thought has arisen of changing

the proposal of forty days for the discernment about poverty, "Look at the way that these forty days are ending in confusion! This discernment has not worked! You need to renounce the clarity that you thought you had—that God does not want the mitigation of Jesuit poverty for the sake of their churches—and start the forty days of Masses all over again."] In nothing could I find peace.[4]

Having read and explored the text with my listeners, I then focus on this thought that arises in time of spiritual desolation, that is, that Ignatius should "begin the Masses over again." On this fortieth day, Ignatius has completed the sequence of Masses seeking God's will and has received his answer clearly. Now, on the verge of concluding this process as planned, and in a time of spiritual desolation, a thought arises suggesting that the entire process has been a failure and should be redone.

In light of rule 5, I ask my listeners how Ignatius should act with respect to the change suggested by this thought. Should he set aside his preceding clarity regarding God's will and begin the forty Masses over again? The answer of rule 5 is unmistakable: "In time of desolation *never* make a change," but rather remain "firm and constant" in the determination chosen before the desolation began. In fact, already by midday Ignatius perceives the enemy's action, rejects it, and is confirmed in the clear discernment of the preceding days.

This example helps my listeners realize how plausible the enemy's urging to make changes may appear in the darkness of spiritual desolation. Also, Ignatius's clear perception of his experiences of spiritual consolation, spiritual desolation, and the thoughts arising from them illustrates for my listeners the spiritual awareness (*be aware*, understand, take action) that permits discernment of spirits. As this text reveals, Ignatius is profoundly aware of these spiritual movements and their related thoughts. I remind my listeners that Ignatius did not begin with such refined awareness! We witness here how discernment may grow as a person lives the discerning life over the years.

When Helpful Changes May Be Considered

I conclude rule 5 with a final observation regarding changes.[5] When may changes that will truly prove helpful—new steps for growth in prayer, new initiatives to serve Christ in the needy, new ways of loving in the family, and the like—be considered? *Never in time of spiritual desolation!* This is the emphatic counsel of rule 5. Rule 5 does not say, however, that helpful changes in our spiritual proposals—changes that will truly lead to spiritual progress—may never be considered.

Such changes may be considered in time of spiritual consolation, when "the good spirit guides and counsels us more," or simply in a time of spiritual calm. Ignatius speaks of this last as the "tranquil time" (*SpirEx* 177), when we are neither in the joy of spiritual consolation nor in the heaviness of spiritual desolation, but are calm and able to use our "natural powers freely and tranquilly" (*SpirEx* 177).

This reflection allows me to address a further question that some listeners have, that is, "Are we always either in spiritual consolation or spiritual desolation?" Ignatius's answer is no, that there is also a third spiritual space, the "tranquil time." These are the times when, if we are within, we may find ourselves saying, "I do not seem to feel the joy of spiritual consolation, but neither do I seem to feel the heaviness of spiritual desolation. Things seem to be calm in my spiritual life." This calm, even-keel tranquil time is a time when we can richly love and serve the Lord. Ignatius does not exclude the possibility of helpful changes in our spiritual lives in such times of calm and tranquility.

Returning to rule 5, I add that those changes that seemed so necessary and urgent in time of spiritual desolation often no longer appear so when the desolation has passed. If we adhere to rule 5 and never make such changes in time of spiritual desolation, and wait until spiritual consolation or at least calm have returned, all will be clearer and simpler. We will avoid harm and will follow God's leading without swerving.

14

Liberating Your Listeners
Never Be Passive in Desolation
Rule 6

I begin the presentation of rule 6 by reading the rule together with my listeners:

> Sixth Rule. The sixth: although in desolation we should not change our first proposals, it is very advantageous to change ourselves intensely against the desolation itself, as by insisting more upon prayer, meditation, upon much examination, and upon extending ourselves in some suitable way of doing penance.

In this first approach to the rule, I interrupt the reading after the first line—"although in desolation we should not change our first proposals"—and ask, "This line sums up what?" All readily answer, "Rule 5." When the reading is finished, I observe for my listeners that, through this first line, Ignatius explicitly links rules 5 and 6 as a pair. Each rule has meaning in its own right, but each is also the counterpart of the other. Rule 5 tells us what we should *not* change in time of spiritual desolation (our former proposals); rule 6 tells us what we *should* change in spiritual desolation (ourselves, and how we respond to the desolation). Each rule complements the other; taken together, their meaning is complete.

Respond Actively to Spiritual Desolation!

I now focus on the key point that underlies all of rule 6. This point engenders new hope in my listeners, at times in life-changing ways. Ignatius firmly teaches that we are *never* called passively to endure spiritual desolation. The call, in time of spiritual desolation, is *always* actively to resist and reject it, and to do this with energy, hope, and the spiritual tools Ignatius supplies in this and the subsequent rules. In time of spiritual desolation, Ignatius writes, "it is very advantageous to *change ourselves intensely against the desolation* itself."

I examine these words more closely with my listeners. We are not to change our proposals in time of spiritual desolation, but we *are* called to another kind of change in desolation—"it is very advantageous to change *ourselves.*" We are to change ourselves precisely "*against the desolation itself*," that is, actively to employ the spiritual tools that help us reject it. This active resistance to spiritual desolation is, Ignatius tells us, not only *advantageous* but *very* advantageous. When we experience spiritual desolation, therefore, this active effort to reject it will bring great benefits to our spiritual lives.

Then I apply this truth to the experience of my listeners. Here I speak with sensitivity and reverence, knowing that what I say may touch deep places in their hearts. I tell them that at times, good people, in good faith, may think in the way I will describe. Such thoughts are seldom voiced explicitly, but if they were, they might be expressed something like this: "I know that some people experience joy in the Lord. I almost never do. It seems that my lot is to serve the Lord as faithfully as I can, but always with this heaviness of heart. I have felt this heaviness for months and years, and it is hard to believe that this will change. I do hope to experience joy in God in the next life, but it seems that here my part is to serve God with this burden in my heart and to bear it as best I can."

With a certain energy I repeat Ignatius's basic point in rule 6, that God *never* calls on us passively to bear spiritual desolation, and that the call is always actively to resist and reject it. At times, I almost literally see a light dawn in some listeners' eyes as they realize that they are called to freedom from the enemy's desolations.

I add a further important consideration. I affirm that there are other kinds of burdens that we may be called to bear. Some may be inherent in the vocation to which God has called us: parents, for example, who assist their children through the various difficulties they face, or a pastor who guides his parish through a time of struggle. Others may concern health—physical burdens that remain even as we do all we can to take proper care of our health—or finances or work. We have a word in our Christian tradition for such situations. I ask my listeners what that word is, and they readily respond, "The Cross." I comment that Jesus told us that the Cross would be a daily part of discipleship (Lk 9:23). We also have his assurance that when our crosses are carried with him, our Good Fridays, like his, lead to an Easter Sunday—a blessing of grace and new life in us and through us for others.

We *are* called to carry the Cross with Jesus in this life, in whatever form God's loving providence may ask of us. But we are *never* called passively to endure the enemy's discouraging spiritual desolations. Here the call is always to resist and reject the desolation. Such is the basic message of rule 6. Once again, Ignatius's teaching is revealed as a spirituality of hope.

Four Spiritual Means

We turn then to the four spiritual means that Ignatius supplies for resisting desolation, "by insisting more upon *prayer, meditation*, upon *much examination*, and upon extending ourselves in some *suitable way of doing penance*." I note that these four means may be employed in many spiritual contexts; in rule 6, Ignatius directs them specifically to the person now experiencing spiritual desolation. Practiced in *this* situation and in the manner Ignatius describes, each will be, as he indicates, "very advantageous" to the one in desolation.

Ignatius asks people in desolation to *"insist more"* upon these four means. Those who apply rule 6 will most likely have an ongoing spiritual life in which they dedicate time to prayer and other spiritual practices.[1] In time of desolation, these people are consciously to increase their exercise of four such spiritual means. Each of the four provides a movement directly contrary to the spiritual desolation.

Prayer

The first means Ignatius supplies to resist spiritual desolation is simply *to ask God's help*. I explain that this is prayer of petition.[2] I exemplify this in concrete ways: "Jesus, be with me." "Holy Spirit, show me how to resist this." "Father, love me and guide me in this struggle." In the communion of saints, we may ask the aid of the "cloud of witnesses" (Hb 12:1), the Virgin Mary, or any of the saints to whose intercession we wish to turn. More formal prayers may also help—the psalms, for example, or any prayer we love.

I apply the examples already used: the man in desolation at 10:00 p.m., poised between the Bible and the smartphone, or the woman in desolation alone in her apartment in late afternoon, poised between her usual prayer and mindless soap operas. To these or any like them, Ignatius's first counsel is to *pray*, to ask for help of the God who promises that when we ask, we will receive (Mt 7:7; Jn 14:13–14).

I then ask, "Is this too evident to say? Do we think to do this when we are in the darkness of desolation?" My listeners realize that often we may not think to do this, and a resolution to remember this in time of spiritual desolation begins to form. I note that it will not always be easy to pray in this way when the darkness and loneliness of desolation weigh upon us. I explain that it also will be enormously helpful, and add that it may be that Ignatius consciously placed this means first: our first and most effective resource against desolation is to turn to the all-powerful God whose love is always ready to respond when we call.

I share with my listeners my experience of the power of such petitionary prayer.[3] I tell them that in the residence of my community, my office stands at the end of a corridor of offices. Behind it is the back stairwell, little frequented during the day. My own room is directly above my office. When I am at home, I often walk the flight of stairs—eight steps up, a landing, then eight steps more—between my office and my room. Over the years, the short time of that walk, in the quiet of that stairwell, has become a place of prayer for help in desolation.

The following has repeated often. As the day unfolds, I will be vaguely aware that something is weighing on me. In the brief moments as I walk those stairs, I will recognize that I am in desolation, and I will make a short, simple prayer for help. A few hours later, with an uplift of heart, I will realize that I am no longer in desolation. Something has intervened—an encouraging email, a phone call, a conversation, a time of prayer—and the desolation has passed. Then I remember the prayer on the stairwell. Each time this happens, I am further confirmed in the power of simply *asking God's help* in time of desolation. You will find your own ways to speak of the power of this prayer.

Meditation

I explain that Ignatius is not speaking here of meditation simply as a generally good practice in the spiritual life—it obviously is. Here Ignatius is addressing the person who is, right now, in spiritual desolation and in need of spiritual means to resist it. This meditation might include a conscious calling to mind of the *truths of faith* that can sustain us in the struggle. Such truths might include reflection on God's ever-present and loving providence, on the power of Jesus's redemption, on his unceasing intercession for us (Hb 7:25), on our identity as beloved sons and daughters of the Father in Jesus, and on similar truths.

In this meditation, we might also turn to *biblical passages* that assure us of God's faithful love in times of struggle. Again, I provide examples to make this concrete for my listeners: well-loved texts such as Psalm 23 or 27, or Jesus's words in John 14:1, or similar passages may greatly encourage us in the battle.

I note that this meditation might also embrace *memories of God's fidelity in past struggles*, those times when darkness weighed on us and we saw how faithfully God brought us through them. Such memories, called to mind in time of desolation, assure us that God will guide us safely though the present darkness.

I mention further examples.[4] One man told me that in desolation he reflects on Psalm 46:10, "Be still, and know that I am God."[5] A woman has her "anti-desolation" hymn and sings it in time of desolation. Its refrain especially, as she sings it, assures her of God's faithful love. Another woman has a favorite poem with a similar message and recites it in time of desolation. These people have found personal ways of meditating to help counteract the discouraging lies of desolation: they are doing precisely what Ignatius recommends in rule 6.

I think of finding personal ways for this meditation as filling our spiritual quiver with spiritual arrows and having these ready for times of desolation. If we have prepared these in advance, we can employ these meditative "arrows" all the more quickly against desolation when we experience it.

If it seems helpful for the group, I share a personal experience. I had been stationed outside the country for several years and was then called back to work with our seminarians. The move involved not only a cultural readjustment but also work for which I did not feel prepared. Other factors, too, rendered the situation difficult. As the months passed, the burden grew.

One winter's evening I stepped off the subway and began walking toward our house, about a quarter mile away. I remember the dark of that evening, the cold, the headlights and noise of rush-hour traffic on the street alongside, and the snow piled by the sidewalk. Each step took me closer to a task that had become very heavy. I found myself saying to the Lord, "Lord, why is this happening? I'm just trying to do the best I can." Then I found these words in my heart, "I have been here before." *I have been here before*, that is, "Lord, there have been other times in my life when I have felt what I am feeling now, and I can now look back on them and see more clearly how you blessed me through them. I trust that someday I will look back on this time also and see what you, Lord, were giving me through it." The burden did not lift completely, but something did change. My heart grew just a little lighter because I could believe that this experience, too, was within God's providence in my life, and that someday, at least in some measure, I would understand why.

Those words—*I have been here before*—are one of my points of meditation in time of desolation. They remind me that God has seen me faithfully through former times of desolation and even made them channels of growth. When I recall these words, I feel a beginning of hope, and the desolation gets a little easier to bear. This is one personal way in which I find Ignatius's invitation to "insist more" upon meditation a great help in time of desolation. We will all find our personal ways.

Some years ago I met a wonderful woman religious then in her seventies and now with the Lord. She told me that when she got into a "low"—in Ignatian terms, a time of desolation—she would turn to the Lord and say, "You've carried me for fifty-five years of religious life. You won't drop me in this little thing either." It was a perfect application of rule 6: a reflection, in time of desolation, on God's past fidelity that strengthens the person to resist present desolation.

By this time, my listeners understand well what Ignatius means by meditation in time of spiritual desolation. As always, you will find your own ways to exemplify Ignatius's counsel.

Much Examination

I ask my listeners, "Why would Ignatius counsel much examination to one burdened by spiritual desolation?" I further ask, "What is the undiscerning, unreflective, unaware response to the desolation?" The answer readily emerges: flight into some form of diversion—food, a novel, a movie, the internet, simple busyness, or the like. Then I ask, "What lies on the other side of the diversion, when we rise from the television two hours later, close the refrigerator for the final time, or finally put down the smartphone?" I answer, "The 'aspirin' has worn off, and the symptoms (desolation) are still there, perhaps even a little heavier because we know that we have given in to the desolation."

Instead of this, Ignatius tells us that we should do exactly the contrary of this flight into diversion, and we should stand our ground. Instead of running from the desolation, we should *look at it and examine it carefully*.[6] I propose two questions for this examination: "What am I feeling?" and "How did this begin?"

As regards the first, I note that simply to recognize that "I'm in desolation" is very freeing. This recognition changes the experience from a feeling of "overwhelming, all-encompassing burden" to a spiritual experience that we can name and to which we can respond. The difference is enormous: we cannot deal with an overwhelming burden, but we can deal with a specific spiritual experience. Just to examine what we are feeling to the point in which we can name it as spiritual desolation is already a beginning of liberation.[7]

Then I propose the second question, "How did this begin?" When we can pinpoint this beginning, the sense of liberation grows stronger. Again, we cannot deal with a confusing, dark cloud of heaviness. But we *can* deal with a situation that, for example, began when we received that email or phone message at 10:00 a.m. this morning, when we got the results of the test from the doctor, or felt discouraged to see ourselves react again in a way we had hoped to have overcome. Once we perceive when and how the desolation began, we can make decisions regarding how to reject it: I'll call that person, I'll make a follow-up appointment with the doctor to discuss remedies, I'll prepare for that situation so that I am not caught off guard next time, I'll take this to further prayer, I'll talk with this person who can help me, and the like. The desolation continues to lose its grip.

As always, I supply examples. I read and comment on the following experience. The text in brackets indicates my commentary on the text.

> Ray has long placed faith at the center of his life, and in recent years, especially, has grown closer to the Lord. He rejoices in seeing that, as a result of this spiritual growth, his love for his wife and children has deepened, and their family bond is now stronger. Each day, as he rides the commuter train to work, Ray dedicates a few minutes to reading from Scripture. [This is the portrait of a person who is growing toward God.]
>
> Today, on his way to work, Ray finds himself distracted and unable to read with attention or to reflect fruitfully. He arrives at work, and the busyness of the morning envelops him, but he is also vaguely aware of a certain interior malaise. While his fellow workers have no direct awareness of his deepening faith in the Lord, they have noticed a change in Ray recently and appreciate his ready smile and willingness to help. Today, however, Ray struggles even to be patient with them and only wishes the working hours to end.
>
> The lunch hour arrives. As the hour begins, Ray normally takes a few minutes alone in his office to lift his heart to God in prayer. Today he feels no desire to pray and does not. [Here I ask my listeners, "Good decision? Bad decision?" All answer, "Bad decision." I ask further,

"Which rule is involved here?" They answer readily, "Rule 5." I confirm the answer: in a time of at least nonspiritual desolation and in all likelihood spiritual desolation as well, Ray changes a proposal to pray that he had in place before the desolation began. This exercise confirms my listeners further in applying rule 5.]

Instead, Ray finds himself considering taking his meal in a place nearby where he knows the surroundings and the conversation are not conducive to his life of faith. [Here I ask if anyone can identify in the rules what Ray is experiencing at this moment. This question is a little more difficult, but generally a listener will identify this as the "movement toward low and earthly things" that Ignatius lists in rule 4 as one of the experiences of spiritual desolation. We continue to exercise the application of the rules.]

Ray is on the point of leaving the office with this intention when suddenly he stops. He is aware that his heart is troubled. [Ray now notices the signs that something is not right.] His distracted prayer on the train, his lack of willingness to assist his companions in the office, his omission of habitual prayer as his lunch hour began—all these signal that something is spiritually amiss. Ray senses that he must address this. [Here I ask my listeners, "In terms of the three steps in discernment—be aware, understand, take action—where is Ray at this point?" My listeners easily answer, "The first step." I confirm the answer: "Yes, Ray has crossed the blessed threshold from being unaware of his interior experience and simply swept along by it, to a point in which he is now *aware* of his interior experience. He has begun the process of discernment." I ask further, "Does Ray as yet *understand* his interior experience?" My listeners answer that he does not. This question prepares them to identify the second step in discernment when it appears.]

Liberating Your Listeners

Ray sits down at his desk in the silence of his office and asks the Lord's help to understand what is occurring within him. He remembers how only the day before he was happy and energetic in his service of the Lord, of the others at work, and of his family. As he reflects, Ray is able to pinpoint the moment when the change took place. Before leaving home this morning, preoccupied with his preparations for work, Ray unthinkingly brushed aside a request for attention from his little son. His wife was present, and Ray saw the hurt in her eyes, mirroring the hurt in those of his son. Rushed and impatient, he responded to neither and left for work.

Ray perceives that this was the moment when he lost his peace; this was the origin of the malaise he has felt since and that has burdened everything thus far in the day: prayer, relationships at work, even his present decision regarding where he will take lunch. [Now I ask, "In terms of the three steps in discernment, where is Ray at this point?" The group quickly responds, "The second." I confirm the answer: "Yes, Ray now understands what is going on, how it got started—to see this is, as we have said, a great help—and how it developed." If it seems appropriate, I may highlight how, as so often is true, Ray's desolation begins as a nonspiritual desolation—disappointment at how he disregarded his son's need and so hurt both his son and his wife—that creates a vulnerable space into which the enemy brings the trap of spiritual desolation as well—Ray feels no desire to pray and is inclined to low and earthly things.]

This new sense of clarity lightens Ray's heart, and he grasps clearly what he must do. [Again I ask, "In terms of the three steps in discernment, where is Ray at this point?" All reply, "The third." I continue, "At the risk of being a little too analytical, but for the sake of the learning we are pursuing, let's look at the three choices Ray makes to reject the desolation."]

Ray calls his wife and expresses his sorrow for his impatience that morning and for the hurt he caused her and his son [Ray's first choice]. Her joy in their conversation lifts his heart further.

He prays as usual in his office. [Ray's second choice. Ray undoes the harmful change he made earlier in violation of rule 5. I observe that even when we have made harmful changes in time of spiritual desolation, the story is not over! We can always take positive steps after the harmful change or even to reverse it, as Ray does here. Redemption is not blocked by our harmful choices!]

Ray rejects the thought of taking lunch in the inappropriate place and eats with his office companions as usual. [Ray's third choice. Here he rejects the movement to low and earthly things described in rule 4.]

Now he finds that his smile again comes easily and that his habitual willingness to assist others has returned.[8]

As we conclude our exploration of Ray's experience, I ask, "Can you see why Ignatius counsels much examination in time of spiritual desolation?" My listeners do see this clearly.

If time allows, I add two more experiences. One is personal, a practice I have developed over the years. When, like Ray, I sense that something is not right in my heart, and I do not know what the issue is, I take the first opportunity I have—between phone calls, before a meeting, driving, or even walking through the building to my next appointment—to examine it briefly with the Lord. At times, I see the origin of the burden quickly and know what I must do to address it. At other times I am less able to understand the situation and know that I will need to examine it again. In every case, however, the simple exercise of stopping to examine my interior experience begins to lift the burden.

The second is that of a woman who is a nurse. She told me that at times she senses that something is not right in her heart. Because the busyness of her hospital day does not permit her to stop and examine it then, she "parks" it, as it were, near her heart. When she rides the commuter train home from work, she examines the heaviness with the Lord. This is a beautiful and practical application of Ignatius's "much examination" in time of desolation.

Finally, I cite two phrases from an author on discernment: "myself-in-desolation" and "myself-reflecting-on-myself-in-desolation."[9] I ask, "Before Ray stops in his office at lunchtime to examine his interior experience, is Ray 'myself-in-desolation' or 'myself-reflecting-on-myself-in-desolation'?" All reply, "myself-in-desolation." I then ask, "When Ray sits down in his office at lunchtime to examine his interior malaise, is Ray now 'myself-in-desolation' or 'myself-reflecting-on-myself-in-desolation'?" All answer, "Myself-reflecting-on-myself-in-desolation." I draw the conclusion: "Can you see the great difference between the two, and how the transition from the first to the second—that is, from unawareness to the examination of which Ignatius speaks—powerfully reduces the burden of spiritual desolation?" The point is made, and we have introduced two phrases that will assist us again as we explore further rules.

If I judge it helpful for the group, I may add one or both of two further observations on Ignatius's "much examination." First, that Ignatius speaks of such examination in the context of spiritual desolation, an experience that all share at times. This, therefore, is a review of "ordinary" spiritual experience. Ignatius does not speak here of the different reality of deep psychological trauma and the wounds this may cause. Here, too, deeper understanding will help the person heal, but this should be done with competent professional accompaniment. To advise a person, in the name of rule 6, to examine unaided such deep nonspiritual pain is to misread the rule and most likely to increase the person's pain. In our presentations, if we judge that our listeners may understand Ignatius's "much examination" as applying to deep psychological pain, we would do well to clarify this point.

Second, what if a person examines spiritual desolation and does not find clarity, rather, the examination results in deeper confusion and anxiety? What then should be done? Having raised this question—or responding to a listener who has raised it—I answer that a person should never persist in an examination that only leads to deeper pain. For Ignatius, the discerning life is never lived alone. If the examination does result in confusion and anxiety, the person needs to speak with a wise and competent spiritual person who can help find clarity and growth. Ignatius will speak of sharing spiritual burdens with a competent spiritual person in rule 13. If we judge that some of our listeners have this concern—that is, if they think, "If I examine my interior experience I risk further confusion and pain"—we would do well to address it here.

Suitable Penance

Finally, Ignatius writes that people in spiritual desolation should extend themselves "in some suitable way of doing penance." I tell my listeners that I will alter the vocabulary slightly and speak of "suitable gestures of penitential courage."

I ask my listeners, "Why would Ignatius counsel some form of suitable penance to a person burdened by the discouraging lies of spiritual desolation?" I ask further, "What is the undiscerning, unreflective, unaware response to the desolation?" The answer is again some form of flight into gratification: "This desolation is painful. Let me find something more gratifying to escape the heaviness." Spiritual desolation, if not resisted, may lead to self-indulgence in unnecessary eating, unwise use of the internet, and in other ways—the "movement to low and earthly things" of which Ignatius speaks.

I tell my listeners once more that Ignatius counsels us to act directly contrary to the spiritual desolation. Instead of fleeing into a debilitating self-indulgence, we stand our ground with suitable gestures of penitential courage. The penance is to be *suitable*—not unsuitable, that is, not excessive, ill-advised, more harmful than helpful. It is also suitable when it helps us resist the spiritual desolation we are experiencing in the moment. Thus, for example, if the "movement to low and earthly things" involves a temptation to use the internet in spiritually harmful ways, the suitable penance might consist in waiting a half hour before going on the internet or simply avoiding the internet entirely at the time. Such gestures may require courage; they will also assist us greatly to reject the desolation.

I observe that no such gesture of penitential courage is too small! I remark that I have become "shameless" in this; that is, if the best I can do is a very small penitential gesture, I try to do it, knowing the power of such choices. I offer examples: a person waits ten minutes to head to the refrigerator again, waits fifteen minutes before going online, smiles at another when disinclined to do so, performs a simple service for another, undertakes that little task that has been waiting for several days, chooses to exercise rather than watch television, and many similar "suitable" gestures of penitential courage. These "small" gestures have great power to break the discouraging sense of helplessness that desolation insinuates. When we take even one small step with the Spirit, the Spirit prepares the next and the next . . . and the downward trajectory of desolation collapses.[10]

I further illustrate such suitable gestures of penitential courage by citing a counsel that Ignatius gives elsewhere in the *Spiritual Exercises*. I include my commentary in brackets:

> We should note that, just as in time of consolation it is easy and requires little effort to remain in the contemplation for a full hour [we all know this experience—these

are the times when prayer is alive, God feels close, and the time passes quickly; we look at our watch and can hardly believe that forty-five minutes or an hour have already passed], so in time of desolation it is very difficult to complete the hour. [We all know this experience as well! Ignatius does not exaggerate when he says that it is "very difficult" to remain the full time in prayer when we are in desolation. We look at our watch—for the third time—and only ten minutes have passed. When I say this, my listeners often smile; they know by experience what Ignatius is saying.]

Consequently, the person who is praying, in order to fight against the desolation [this is always the call in time of spiritual desolation: to *fight against* the desolation] and to conquer the temptation [here the temptation is to shorten the hour of prayer because it is desolate and therefore hard to stay the full hour], must always remain a little more than the full hour. [Not a second hour, an extra half hour, or even fifteen minutes: a "little more," that is, perhaps an extra minute or two. I comment that those who have done this know how difficult—and how helpful—it can be at such times to stay even an extra minute.] In this way, he accustoms himself not only to resist [always the call in desolation] the adversary, but even to overthrow him (*SpirEx* 13).

When, in time of desolation, the temptation is to shorten the planned time of prayer, the "suitable gesture of penitential courage" is to lengthen it slightly. This penitential gesture is small, but it significantly aids the effort to resist and reject the spiritual desolation. The difference between such gestures of penitential courage and helpless flight into gratification is great. The person thereby grows accustomed, as Ignatius says, to resist and even to overthrow the enemy.

A Brief Application of the Four Means Together

I conclude the presentation of rule 6 by bringing together the four means in a final example. "What will happen," I ask, "if the man in his room at 10:00 p.m. or the woman in her kitchen in late afternoon, both in spiritual desolation, turn to Jesus and ask his help (prayer); recall the words, for example, of Psalm 23 or remember how God has never abandoned them in previous dark times and actually gave them growth through such times (meditation); stop and examine when and how this desolation began and how it has unfolded (much examination); and rather than fleeing to the internet or television choose in small ways to stand their spiritual ground against the desolation (suitable penance)? What is likely to happen to the spiritual desolation?"

"What is *unlikely* to happen," I answer, "is that the desolation will simply continue and deepen. And, as God gives grace, what is much more likely to happen is that the desolation will not last as long or grow as dark. The desolation may not disappear immediately, and the man and woman may need to continue to resist it for a time, but the struggle is likely to be easier and to conclude sooner."

"Such," I conclude, "is the gift that Ignatius offers in rule 6." At this point, my listeners grasp the richness of Ignatius's counsel in this rule.

15

Understanding Desolation
A Trial, Its Reason, and Its Fruit
Rule 7

In rule 7, Ignatius continues what he has begun in rules 5 and 6: he supplies further resources for taking action to reject spiritual desolation. I introduce this rule with an experience of St. Angela of Foligno (1248–1309), a figure of holiness in the Franciscan tradition. In the following passage, she shares a time of spiritual struggle. I read and comment on this text in the usual way. Before we read the text, I invite my listeners to note in it the dynamic of *what is taken away* and *what remains*:

> During this period, I was in a state of great stress, for it seemed to me that I felt nothing of God, and I also had the impression that I was abandoned by him. . . . [Here I ask, "What is Angela experiencing?" All reply, "Spiritual desolation." I note that *what has been taken away* from Angela is all felt sense of fervor, of God's closeness, of joy in the Lord, that is, all spiritual consolation. If I judge it helpful, I may add, "Can you see once again why I can say so confidently that there is no shame in experiencing spiritual desolation? Here is another saint who shares our own experience."]
>
> It seemed to me that all that was left of God in me [this is *what remains*, what has not been taken away] was . . . that I did not want to fall away from his grace by sinning for all the good or evil or sufferings that the world

has to offer, nor did I want to assent to any evil. [This is *what remains*: something deeper in Angela than the spiritual desolation, a rock-solid adherence to God, a grace at work that strengthens her sufficiently to get through the desolation safely, without spiritual harm.]

I was in this intense and terrible state of torment for more than four weeks. [This is prolonged and deep spiritual desolation.][1]

I highlight for my listeners these three qualities of Angela's experience: spiritual consolation has been taken away; she is in spiritual desolation; and a grace deeper than the spiritual desolation, a grace that is not taken away, that remains, is at work strengthening Angela sufficiently to get through the desolation without harm. I ask my listeners if, as we read the text, they can "feel"—that is, in some way sense—the deep grace in Angela that is untouched by the spiritual desolation. If they can, I tell them, then they have already grasped the core of rule 7.

We then turn to the text of rule 7. I read it with limited introductory commentary:

> Seventh Rule. **The seventh: let one who is in desolation** [again, as in rules 5 and 6, we have a rule for the person in spiritual desolation; Ignatius continues to equip people in desolation to resist and reject it] **consider** [this is the key word in rule 7; the "tool" Ignatius offers is the call to *consider*, think about, reflect on, certain truths that will sustain the person in the struggle with spiritual desolation] **how the Lord has left him in trial in his natural powers** [first truth to consider], **so that he may resist the various agitations and temptations of the enemy** [second truth to consider]; **since he can resist with the divine help, which always remains with him** [third truth to consider; this divine help is *what remains* in time of spiritual desolation], **though he does not clearly feel it; for the Lord has**

taken away from him his great fervor, abundant love and intense grace [this is what is taken away, that is, the experience of spiritual consolation], **leaving him, however, sufficient grace for eternal salvation.** ["Sufficient grace" is another description of the divine help that *remains* with us in time of spiritual desolation, that is, all the grace we need to stay solidly on track toward eternal salvation in time of spiritual desolation, to come safely through the desolation without harm.]

"Consider"

Now we explore and apply the text in more detail. In rule 5, Ignatius counseled us never to change our spiritual proposals in time of spiritual desolation. In rule 6, he supplied four spiritual tools to be used energetically in time of spiritual desolation. In rule 7, Ignatius highlights *three interrelated thoughts* that we are to *consider*—call to mind, reflect on—in time of spiritual desolation. If we do, we will find spiritual desolation easier to resist. I indicate that rule 7 underlines the importance for discernment *of how we think*.

First Thought: "The Lord Has Left Him in Trial"

The first thought to consider in time of spiritual desolation is that this desolation is not useless pain, a cruel trick of a meaningless fate. On the contrary, it is a *trial* in which *the Lord* has left us. Ignatius invites us, I observe, to consider the spiritual desolation on the level of *faith*, as an experience that God, in his providence, permits us to undergo for reasons of a love that Ignatius will describe in rule 9.

I explain that if the man at 10:00 p.m. and the woman in midafternoon can *consider* this thought—that this experience is not just meaningless pain but rather a *trial* permitted by the

Understanding Desolation

Lord—they will be greatly heartened to resist the enemy's discouraging lies.[2] Suffering that has no meaning quickly becomes unendurable. If the man and the woman perceive their desolation as such meaningless pain, the man will likely reach for the smartphone and the woman for the remote control. If, on the other hand, they understand the desolation as a trial permitted by the Lord—if, that is, they *find meaning* in this difficult experience—they will be greatly strengthened to resist it and will emerge from it without harm, even with growth.

I cite another application of this principle. From his experiences in the concentration camps of Nazi Germany, psychiatrist Viktor Frankl wrote his classic book, *Man's Search for Meaning*. Observing with a professional eye, Frankl perceived the difference between those who survived and those who did not. Those who found meaning in their suffering—wives and children whom they were determined to see again, a life's work to be completed, and the like—survived; those who found no meaning in their pain, succumbed. When spiritual desolation appears to us as empty pain, we are likely to succumb; when we consider its meaning—that this is a trial in which God has left us for reasons of love—we are much more likely to escape harm and grow through it. Many of my listeners are familiar with *Man's Search for Meaning*, and mention of it helps to reinforce the dynamic of rule 7: meaning that gives courage to endure.

Second Thought: "So That He May Resist"

The first thought tells us that this spiritual desolation is a trial. The second tells us the *purpose* of this trial: *so that we may resist* the spiritual desolation and, by resisting, grow in the ability to resist it.

I ask my listeners, "How do we grow in patience?" They readily answer, "By being in situations that require patience and being patient." I continue, "How do we grow in the ability to pray?"

My listeners answer, "By praying faithfully, day after day." Again, "How do we grow in charity toward our neighbor?" They respond, "By being in situations that require charity and being charitable toward others." Then I ask, "How do we grow in the ability to resist spiritual desolation?" They now readily answer, "By being in spiritual desolation and resisting it."

Spiritual desolation, therefore, is not fruitless, wasted time in the spiritual life. God permits it, Ignatius tells us, so that by resisting it we may grow in one of the most helpful strengths for the spiritual life: the ability to resist spiritual desolation. I add that if it is true that for most of us, for most of the way on the spiritual journey, spiritual desolation is the principal obstacle, then this ability is one of the most valuable that God can give us. If the man at 10:00 p.m. and the woman in midafternoon *consider* this second thought, they will find new courage to resist their desolation.

At this point, I often cite a personal experience.[3] Early in my priesthood, for two consecutive years I made my annual eight-day retreat without a director. This was certainly unwise. Both years, the same thing happened: by the fourth day I found myself struggling with spiritual desolation.

At the time, a retired Jesuit whom I knew, Fr. William Reed, was living in this retreat house. He had been a professor all his life, and he was a good religious and a fine priest. Both years, on that fourth day, I called his room and asked if we could meet. Each time, the same thing happened. Fr. Reed set a time, and at that time, I knocked on his door. When I did, I heard his voice from within say, "Come in." When I opened the door and saw him, instantly I began to feel peace.

He was very much the professor! His room and desk overflowed with books and papers. Amid them all, he sat in his rocking chair with his pipe. What immediately calmed me was Fr. Reed's deep sense of serenity. I had the feeling, looking at him, that this was a man who knew life's struggles, had experienced them, and had reached a state in which he would no longer be easily shaken by them. For me, as a young priest burdened by desolation, simply to see him brought peace. An hour later, after our conversation, I left strengthened in that peace and ready to resume the retreat.

I imagine that most of us know people like this. Generally, though not always, they are people in the latter decades of life. Such people are pillars of strength for the rest of us, and we willingly converse with them. How did they get there? How did they reach this point? How do people attain this seemingly unshakable state of peace and wisdom? Most often, I believe, this occurs through undergoing trials over the years and faithfully enduring them. Having witnessed God's faithful love in their struggles, such people's peace deepens as they face life and all it brings.

This, I conclude, is the second thought Ignatius counsels us to consider in the trial of desolation: that God has left us in this trial *so that we may resist* the desolation and, by resisting, grow in the ability to resist it. Each time we resist an experience of desolation, two things happen: we are freed from the discouraging lies of that desolation, and we grow in the ability to resist future desolation. This thought, considered in time of desolation, strengthens us to resist that desolation.

Third Thought: "Since He Can Resist"

"Since he can resist"—I tell my listeners that this is one of the most hope-filled lines in the whole set of rules. It is, and this statement also gets their attention!

I return to the final part of the text, and we review its content. The person in desolation *can resist* it—can emerge from it without succumbing—because of "the divine help, which always remains with him." This person "does not clearly feel" this divine help "for the Lord has taken away from him his great fervor, abundant love and intense grace," that is, the experience of spiritual consolation in which we *do* clearly feel the divine help. The Lord has left this person, however, *sufficient grace*, that is, all the grace the person needs to resist the spiritual desolation and remain firmly on the path toward eternal salvation.

This is the grace, for example, that keeps Angela solidly rooted in the Lord even in a dark and prolonged desolation. This grace is deeper than the desolation, a grace the desolation can never touch, a grace that is *sufficient*—it provides all the help the person needs. Because of it, the person—all of us—can always resist spiritual desolation. I note that Ignatius asks us to *consider* what we *cannot clearly feel* in time of desolation: that God's grace is always with us and that it always supplies all we need for the struggle. The strength this consideration provides is evident.

I explain that there is what I call the Litany of Spiritual Desolation.[4] This litany is the following: "I can't, I can't, I can't, I can't, I can't. . . . I can't go to prayer today, I can't finish this time of prayer, I can't take part in the Bible study this evening, I can't spend a day longer with these people, I can't go on in this vocation. . . . I can't, I can't, I can't . . ." There are usually smiles at this point as my listeners remember their own experiences of this kind! When in desolation everything in us cries out *that we can't*, Ignatius urges us to consider *that we can*, because though we do not clearly feel it—the warmth of spiritual consolation has been taken away—God is giving us sufficient grace to resist the desolation. If we *consider* this truth in time of desolation, the desolation's power to harm us will greatly diminish.

If time allows and it seems opportune, I specify further that there *are* situations of *nonspiritual* desolation that surpass our strength and in which we truly *cannot*. There may be situations of physical tiredness or emotional exhaustion such that we cannot go further without first restoring our physical or emotional energy. But this is *never true of spiritual desolation*. Always, in every experience of spiritual desolation, Ignatius urges us to

Understanding Desolation

consider the truth: that God is giving us all the grace we need to resist the desolation.[5]

I use the following example to illustrate the difference this perception makes. Two young boys are learning to ride a bicycle. The first is convinced that he can learn to ride. The second is convinced that he cannot. The outcome is already largely determined: the first will likely learn to ride and the second is unlikely to do so. In the first case, difficulties will not dishearten the young boy but will be accepted as part of the learning. In the second, the same difficulties will further convince the boy that he cannot learn to ride.

If the man at 10:00 p.m. in his room or the woman in midafternoon in her kitchen are convinced that they cannot resist the desolation, in all likelihood they will succumb. If both *consider* right *in the desolation*, as they sit in their respective rooms, that *they can resist*, and further consider the reason why they can resist—because though they do not clearly feel it, God is giving them all the grace (sufficient grace) they need to resist—they are in fact much more likely to resist. Such is the power of this third thought that Ignatius proposes in rule 7.

I conclude with this question: "What if the man at 10:00 p.m., the woman in midafternoon, or any of us in spiritual desolation, call to mind and consider that this experience has meaning, that it is a trial permitted by God and within his loving providence; that the reason for this trial is so that we may resist the desolation and by resisting grow in the ability to resist; and that we *can* resist because God's grace always supports us sufficiently to enable us to resist? What will happen to how they and we resist the desolation? The strength that consideration of these three thoughts provides is clear.

As we apply each successive rule, we are growing in the ability to resist and reject spiritual desolation. Captives are being set free.

16

Give Hope to Your Listeners
Consolation Will Return Soon
Rule 8

I introduce rule 8 with a passage from the spiritual journal of the Servant of God, Frenchwoman Elisabeth Leseur (1866–1914). When I use this passage and share a little of Elisabeth's fascinating story, my listeners are quickly be engaged—all the more if, like Elisabeth, they live the married vocation.

Elisabeth and her husband had a lifelong happy marriage. Felix, however, was a militant atheist. His attacks on her Christian faith caused Elisabeth to explore that faith more deeply, leading her to a deep life of union with the Lord and of faithful service to the Lord in her married life. Her one sorrow was that she could not share her life of faith with her husband. Elisabeth never pressured Felix but simply lived her family life with all the love she could.

After Elisabeth's death, Felix found her spiritual journal, the existence of which he had known nothing. As he read, he was struck to realize that there was a deep part of his wife that he had never known. (Here, when my listeners are married men and women, I can hear a pin drop; they ask themselves how deeply they know their own spouses.) Felix learned, too, from his wife's journal of her great longing that someday he would come to faith in Christ. As he read, Felix's heart was changed. He embraced faith in Christ, was eventually ordained a Dominican priest, and dedicated his life to sharing his wife's spiritual writings and message.

In one of her journal entries, Elisabeth writes,

> Cowardice, weakness, awkwardness in my demeanor with others—things that can harm the ideas I cherish; acute physical suffering and deep moral suffering. [Here I ask my listeners, "What is Elisabeth experiencing?" My listeners readily identify the nonspiritual desolation here, that is, the "acute physical suffering." I ask further, "Is Elisabeth also experiencing spiritual desolation?" We discuss this briefly. I note that the language suggests this possibility without, thus far, giving full clarity. I add that what follows will suggest even more strongly that Elisabeth is experiencing spiritual desolation as well. Such repeated questions, as we go through the rules, greatly help my listeners to apply the categories learned and grow in confidence that they can identify these experiences in their own lives.]
>
> [Before I read the next lines, I invite my listeners to note in them *how Elisabeth responds* to her spiritual desolation. In this way, I introduce the heart of rule 8, to which we will turn immediately after reading Elizabeth's words.] In the midst of this a will unshakably turned to God, a plenitude of confidence in him and love for him; daily duties performed at whatever cost by great effort, without fervor [here the language of spiritual desolation is more clearly present], but still performed [this is the portrait of a woman *who will not give up* in time of spiritual desolation—"a will unshakably turned to God, "daily duties performed at whatever cost by great effort"; when the burden of spiritual desolation urges Elisabeth to give way, to give up, to relax her efforts . . . she will not give up; she will stay the course. I say to my listeners, "If we can see, can sense, can feel, this unshakable resolve of Elisabeth *to stay the course* in time of spiritual desolation,

then we have grasped the heart of rule 8."]; then, little by little, calm returning to me, and divine strength penetrating me again; new and energetic resolutions, the hope that God will help me to do my duty, all my duty—that is the tale of these last weeks and of my soul during this time.[1]

Later in the journal, Elisabeth continues,

> More than two months in the dejection of almost continual physical suffering, and with terrible anxiety on Juliette's [Elisabeth's sister who was very ill] account; the miserable belief that my illness will last as long as I do, always impeding my life. Complete resignation, but without joy or any inner consolation. [Here I ask, "What is Elisabeth experiencing?" All readily answer that she is experiencing nonspiritual desolation (physical suffering, anxiety with regard to her sister's illness) and most likely spiritual desolation as well (no joy, no inner consolation).]
>
> [Again I invite my listeners to note how this wonderful woman of God responds to her spiritual desolation.] The resolve to use my misfortunes for the good of souls. To fill my life with prayer, work, and charity. To maintain serenity through everything. To love more than ever those who are the dear companions of my life.[2]

This is a really amazing response to spiritual desolation! Not only does Elisabeth stay the course when burdened by desolation but she also resolves "to use my misfortunes for the good of souls," desiring that in the Body of Christ, her burdens serve for the spiritual good of others. Elisabeth also resolves, in time of spiritual desolation, "to fill my life with prayer, work, and charity." She strives to "maintain serenity through everything." And not only this, but in the darkness of spiritual desolation, she also seeks "*to love more than ever* those who are the dear companions of my life," that is, those of her family and others who are part of her life. I tell my listeners that this is a superabundant application of rule 8 to which we will now turn—the person who, in time of spiritual desolation, will not give up but will faithfully stay the spiritual course.

We turn now to the text of rule 8. As we read, I observe that there are three interrelated parts to this rule:

> Eighth Rule. **The eighth: let one who is in desolation work to be in patience** [first part: patience is the key virtue in time of spiritual desolation; I cite the original Spanish, "*trabaje de estar en paciencia,*" and note that my translation, "work to be in patience," is clumsy in English but portrays exactly Ignatius's sense that, to remain patient, to stay the course in time of desolation, will require effort], **which is contrary to the vexations which come to him, and let him think that he will soon be consoled** [second part: a thought to be recalled in time of desolation that will greatly assist the effort to be patient, that is, to stay the course], **diligently using the means against such desolation, as is said in the sixth rule** [third part: the active steps to be adopted in time of spiritual desolation, that is, the four spiritual means given in rule 6].

We now examine each of these three parts.

"Work to Be in Patience"

I specify for my listeners that the word *patience* derives from the Latin *patior*, to bear, to endure, to suffer. This is the virtue of the person who undergoes a trial and who does not flee, but remains constant and faithfully carries the burden. Here, Ignatius gives us the key virtue, the key attitude needed in time of spiritual desolation: that we work to be in patience; that, like Elisabeth, we strive not to give up, not to give in to the desolation, but to remain faithful to our spiritual course, that is, to our life of prayer and service of the Lord in our various vocations.

At times I cite parallel examples from life more generally: the marathon runner who continues to run in the last miles when it would be so easy to give up; the person who cares for a family member with a prolonged illness, and who, out of love, will not desist from this service though tired or worn; the student who has taken several exams and still has more to take, who, though tired, continues to prepare for the remaining exams; the worker in a time of pressure to complete a project who perseveres until it is finished. All of these people "work to be in patience" and faithfully stay the course.

I then supply examples directly related to the spiritual life: the woman who prays with Scripture for a half hour every morning and who, today, in a time of spiritual desolation, would like simply to omit or at least shorten the time—and who does not, who completes the full time of prayer as planned; the man who is making a weekend retreat and, finding himself in desolation, would like to withdraw from the talks and times of prayer, or simply leave—and who does not, who continues to make the retreat as best he is able; the married woman who has undertaken new efforts to love in her family and who now, in a time of desolation, feels no energy for these efforts and is inclined simply to omit them and return to earlier, less loving patterns of action—and who does not, who faithfully, as best she can, strives to maintain her new efforts to love. The examples can be multiplied as needed.

This, Ignatius says, is the key attitude in time of spiritual desolation: to work to be in patience, *not to give up* but to stay faithful to our spiritual path.

"Let Him Think that He Will Soon Be Consoled"

I explain for my listeners that the effort to work to be in patience in time of spiritual desolation is not simply a matter of willpower, of sheer effort of will. Obviously some effort of will is involved, but Ignatius immediately supplies help for this effort. The first of these is a *thought*—"let one who is in desolation . . . *think"*—and precisely *"that he will soon be consoled."*

I note how helpful this thought is in time of spiritual desolation. Desolation—that is, the enemy speaking through the desolation—tries to have us believe that "it will always be this way." As we have already said, desolation (the enemy) claims power over the future and paints the present desolation—for the man at 10:00 p.m., the woman in midafternoon, or any of us in desolation—as a condition that will last the rest of today, tomorrow, next week, for months and even years without end. With a certain emphasis, I add, "The desolation says to us, *thirty more years* . . . " My listeners laugh, but they know of what Ignatius speaks: in desolation, we have all felt this sense that "This will just go on and on . . . " Obviously if we believe this lie, the desolation will be hard to resist.

Right in the desolation, therefore, Ignatius urges us to call to mind, to think that "we will soon be consoled." This thought contains three elements: we are to reflect that the present desolation will *not* last forever, that it will pass; that consolation will return, that is, that a time will come when we will again experience consolation; and, finally, that this consolation will return *soon*, much sooner than the desolation would have us believe. The contrast between this thought and the endless days, months, and years of burden presented to us by the desolation is evident. The courage to "work to be in patience" that this thought inspires is also evident.

I employ a comparison.[3] Here is a hospital room with two beds. In each is a patient. Each has different symptoms but roughly the same physical discomfort. The doctor enters the room. He stops at the bed of the first patient, asks some questions, and reviews the patient's charts. The doctor says to the patient, "I know that you are feeling some discomfort, and I wish I could tell you otherwise, but I need to tell you that you'll continue to feel this discomfort for several weeks yet."

The doctor then approaches the second patient. Again he asks questions and reviews the charts. He says to this patient, "I know that you are feeling some discomfort, but I can tell you that by tomorrow you'll be feeling as good as new." The doctor then leaves the room.

How do these patients react—these two who are experiencing roughly the same discomfort? The first falls back on his bed, stares out the window, and then picks up the remote control, flipping mindlessly through the channels. The long weeks of discomfort that lie ahead discourage him, and he feels little energy for anything constructive.

The second calls his wife immediately, and they plan for his return home. He also calls his boss, and they begin discussing the next project he will undertake at work. Already his thoughts turn creatively to this task. He moves about the room, packing his belongings. He finds himself desiring exercise and walks the corridor, speaking cheerfully to those he meets.

The doctor's words do not change the two patients' physical discomfort. The knowledge, however, that this discomfort will endure at length or pass soon changes everything. Our spiritual situation when in desolation, Ignatius tells us, is that of the second patient. If in time of desolation we can *think*, consider, call to mind this truth—that consolation will return *soon*—the spiritual discomfort of the present desolation will be much easier to endure.

I apply once more the example of desolation at 10:00 p.m. Two men sit alone in their rooms at 10:00 p.m. Both are in spiritual desolation. One believes the lie of the desolation that this heaviness will continue for days, weeks, and months. The other, remembering rule 8, consciously *thinks*, calls to mind, the truth that spiritual consolation will return *soon*. How do the two respond to their desolation this evening? The first may well succumb; the second is much more likely to resist energetically.

As time allows I may add other examples.[4] Some years ago I met a wonderful religious woman whom I will call Sister Mary.

She was seventy-five at the time, and has now gone to God. She told me that when she experienced desolation, she would say to herself, "Was it like this yesterday?" This was a perfect application of Ignatius's rule 8 and his counsel to consider that consolation will return soon. Sister Mary's practice was this: in time of desolation, she consciously adverted to the fact that the desolation lasts only for a time—"Was it like this yesterday? No, there was a time before this desolation began when I did not feel this burden. There will also be a time before much longer when I will no longer feel this desolation and will again experience peace in God." That thought helped break the desolation's hold on her and gave her energy to resist and reject it.

I explain to my listeners that at times, I have done the following. When I sense that I am in desolation, I take my journal and describe what I am feeling. Then, with rule 8 in mind, I add, "This desolation will pass. There will come a time when I will read what I am writing now and will no longer be in desolation." And such is always the case. When I write those words, it is an *act of hope*, of trust in God's love and in the truth of Ignatius's rule 8. When I reread them after the desolation has passed and consolation has returned, it is *an experience* of the truth of this rule. Each time I do this, I am strengthened in readiness to do it again in future desolation. For me, this practice more than any other helps me grow in applying rule 8.

"Diligently Using the Means"

If the *thought* mentioned will help the person in desolation work to be in patience, a choice to *act* in certain ways will further strengthen this effort—"Let one who is in desolation work to be in patience . . . *diligently using the means* against such desolation, as is said in the sixth rule."

I ask my listeners to name the means given in the sixth rule, and with a little effort they do so: prayer, meditation, much examination, and suitable penance. This is also a good opportunity to reinforce the teaching of rule 6! Ignatius here renews his call to those in desolation to employ actively the spiritual means that help them reject desolation.

This, then, is the complete teaching of rule 8. Like rules 5 through 7, rule 8 supplies tools for the person now in spiritual desolation. It calls for a "patience," a constancy, an unswerving fidelity in time of desolation, and it supplies two aids for such constancy: a thought and a set of spiritual actions. If we consider that thought and actively adopt those means, we will grow in solid patience when in spiritual desolation.

Alternations of Spiritual Consolation and Desolation: A Normal Experience

Before concluding rule 8, I address an important point raised by this rule. "One who is in desolation," Ignatius writes, is to "think that he will soon be consoled." Underlying this rule is Ignatius's understanding that alternations of spiritual consolation and spiritual desolation are normal in the spiritual life. Spiritual consolation does not last forever. It passes, and eventually we experience spiritual desolation. Neither does the desolation last forever; it, too, passes, and spiritual consolation returns. At times, as we have already said, we will experience neither spiritual consolation nor spiritual desolation but rather the "tranquil time" when we serve God in an affectively calm space.

The precise measure of these different spiritual experiences is always individual. It is shaped by God's loving providence in each life and by our readiness to cooperate with grace and resist the enemy—to be discerning. But that we experience such alternations is normal in the life of all who love and serve the Lord.

I offer an example from a spiritual classic.[5] Julian of Norwich (1342–1416), an English figure of holiness, provides a striking illustration of these alternations in her book of *Showings*.[6] She writes,

And after this he revealed a supreme spiritual delight in my soul. In this delight I was filled full of everlasting surety, powerfully secured without any painful fear. This sensation was so welcome and so spiritual that I was wholly at peace, at ease and at rest. . . . [Here—predictably for my listeners by now!—I ask, "What is Julian experiencing?" All readily answer, "Spiritual consolation."]

This lasted only for a time, and then I was changed, and abandoned to myself, oppressed and weary of my life and ruing myself, so that I hardly had the patience to go on living. I felt that there was no ease or comfort for me except faith, hope and love, and truly I felt very little of this. [I ask, "What is Julian now experiencing?" All readily answer, "Spiritual desolation."]

And then presently God gave me again comfort and rest for my soul, delight and security so blessedly and so powerfully that there was no fear, no sorrow, no pain, physical or spiritual, that one could suffer which might have disturbed me. [Once more, the question, and my listeners answer, "Spiritual consolation."]

And then again I felt the pain, and then afterwards the delight and the joy, now the one and now the other, again and again, I suppose about twenty times. . . . [This may be the clearest witness in spiritual writing to the alternations of spiritual consolation and spiritual desolation that Ignatius understands as normal in the spiritual life, "now the one and now the other . . . about twenty times."]

The sequel to the text reveals Julian's serenity amid these alternations, aware that God's loving providence is at work in them.[7] Her absence of self-recriminations, of self-centered anxiety, and her serenity invite a like serenity and trust in us as we experience them as well.

I also cite Thomas Green, SJ, who writes matter-of-factly, "Desolations will come; they are, in fact, as normal a part of human life as are rainy days."[8] *As normal a part of human life as are rainy days.* I like the calm tone of this sentence, and it, too, helps set my listeners at ease with their own experiences. I note that rainy days are an inconvenience, but if we never had them other serious problems would arise.

Here I restate and reemphasize some basic truths. "If any one of us," I tell my listeners, "experiences ups and downs in the spiritual life, times of spiritual energy (consolation) and times of spiritual heaviness (desolation), then know that *you are not the only one.* Sometimes we think that others seem to sail along peacefully in the spiritual life, while 'I always struggle with these ups and downs.' You are not the only one! All of us share this experience. You are *spiritually normal.*" As I say this, I often see smiles and burdens lifting.

I pursue the word *normal* a little further. "You go to the doctor for a full checkup," I say, "and the doctor orders a series of tests. A week later, the doctor calls and tells you that all the tests came out normal. You feel great! It's wonderful to know that everything is normal!" I continue, "In the spiritual life, when you experience alternations of consolation and desolation, you can say, 'It's wonderful to be normal!' What matters," I emphasize, "is to be discerning—to be aware, understand, and take action to accept the spiritual consolation and to reject the spiritual desolation."

Sometimes I add that I have taught these rules for thirty-five years and to groups of all kinds of cultural and educational backgrounds. "No one," I say, "has ever said to me, 'I don't know what you're talking about!'" My listeners laugh at this point, because all of them, too, know what I'm talking about when I share Ignatius's teaching on spiritual consolation and desolation. It *is* wonderful to be normal in the spiritual life. Rule 8 further cements the note of hope that fills the entire set of rules.

17

Answering the Question
Why Does God Permit Desolation
Rule 9

I begin the presentation of rule 9 by saying something like this: "Ignatius now addresses a very real and key question, 'Why does a God who loves us permit us to undergo times of spiritual desolation?' Why, for example, does God permit that man at 10:00 p.m. or the woman in midafternoon—or any of us—to undergo the darkness of spiritual desolation? Why does God permit people who love him and are sincerely trying to serve him to experience such dark times? Couldn't God spare them this darkness? They have given their lives to God and are doing their best to live their vocations faithfully. Why then this darkness?"

I apply this question to our group and ask, "Who of us here has not asked this question, and very likely, at times, in great pain of heart?" Because all of us have, at this point I have my listeners' rapt attention. I continue, "No treatment of discernment and in particular of spiritual desolation would be complete without addressing this question. This is what Ignatius does in rule 9." I specify that Ignatius's purpose is not merely speculative, that is, he does not address this question dispassionately for the sake of abstract clarity. Rule 9, like the preceding four rules, seeks to help people who are in spiritual desolation, struggling with it, and who need help to resist and reject it. A clearer grasp of why God permits desolation—the question rule 9 seeks to answer—will help them understand their experience and so resist desolation with greater insight and courage.

"It Is Better for You That I Go"

I present the dynamic of rule 9 through an example from the Gospel.[1] It is Holy Thursday night, and Jesus has told his disciples, "But now I am going to the one who sent me." He knows that this reference to his impending departure saddens his disciples, and so he continues, "Because I told you this, grief has filled your hearts." Then Jesus adds, "But I tell you the truth, it is better for you that I go. For if I do not go, the Advocate will not come to you. But if I go, I will send him to you" (Jn 16:5–7)[2]—that is, if I do not ask you to go through the temporary, painful separation of my passion and death, the work of redemption will not be completed, the Church will not be born, and the Spirit will not be poured out upon you, equipping you for the task that lies ahead. But if I go, all of this will occur.

I tell you, it is better for you that I go. I note how powerful these words are for the whole spiritual life and for discernment in particular. Why does God allow us to experience the darkness of spiritual desolation in which we feel "as if separated from our Creator and Lord" (rule 4)? Why does a God who loves us permit us to undergo the heaviness of spiritual desolation? The answer is precisely because God loves us, and that, at times, in his loving providence he knows that *it is better that I go,* that is, if I do not ask you to go through the temporary darkness of spiritual desolation, certain kinds of growth that I wish to give you will not be attained. But if I do ask you to undergo spiritual desolation, and if you strive to resist and reject it, this growth will be given.

As is evident, Jesus here attempts to guide his disciples' attention *away from* the pain of the separation and *on to* the reason for it. If they can grasp the reason for the painful separation—that is, if they perceive the fruit that God wishes to give them through it—then the separation will be easier to bear, and they will more likely gain that fruit. Such is the dynamic of rule 9: when we see the fruit that God desires to give through the spiritual desolation, we are strengthened to engage the struggle against it.

I observe for my listeners that spiritual desolation, as a tactic of the enemy, does not of itself bear any positive fruit. If the man at 10:00 p.m., the woman in midafternoon, or any of us surrender to it, the desolation will only cause the harm the enemy intends. But *if we resist it*, if we do our—most likely—imperfect but sincere best to reject it, then the experience of spiritual desolation will bear fruit, and we will be stronger for having passed through it.

I turn now to the text. Ignatius writes,

> Ninth Rule. **The ninth: there are three principal *causes* for which we find ourselves desolate.**

I explain that *cause* signifies here the reason for which God permits the desolation, that is, the fruit that God desires to give us if we are discerning—if we are aware of, understand, and take action to reject the desolation. There are, Ignatius tells us, three principle causes. I examine each now with my listeners. I begin each by reading the part of rule 9 in which Ignatius speaks of that cause.

Because of the length of rule 9—the longest of the rules thus far—and its division into three parts (three causes), I do not read the entire rule at once. Rather, I read the text regarding each cause at the start of my treatment of that cause. I believe that this helps my listeners better to absorb the text.

First Cause: Our Faults and the Gift of Conversion

We now read Ignatius's description of God's first reason for permitting spiritual desolation:

> **The first is because we are tepid, slothful, or negligent in our spiritual exercises, and so through our faults spiritual consolation withdraws from us.**

A first reason, Ignatius tells us, for which God may permit spiritual desolation is "because we are tepid, slothful, or negligent" in our spiritual exercises, that is, in the context of daily life, our prayer, and all that constitutes our spiritual life. In this case, the loss of spiritual consolation and the advent of spiritual desolation is due to "our faults." God permits this as a wake-up call: the burden of the spiritual desolation alerts us to our negligence and so invites us to conversion from that negligence. Underlying this first cause is a love that calls us to freedom from negligence and tepidity.

Here I recall the two fundamental directions in the spiritual life that Ignatius describes in rules 1 and 2: a person may be *essentially regressing* in the spiritual life, heading away from God and, in a confirmed way, "going from mortal sin to mortal sin" (rule 1); or a person may be *essentially progressing* in the spiritual life, heading away from sin and "rising from good to better" in God's service (rule 2). Rule 9 adds a further nuance: a person may be essentially progressing toward God and yet, in a determined moment, regress in one or another area in the spiritual life. The person continues essentially to progress toward God, but now one area is no longer integrated into that progress; in that area, the person is regressing—there the person is "tepid, slothful, or negligent." God may, as we have said, seek to heal that area of regression by permitting spiritual desolation as a wake-up call and an invitation to conversion.

As so often, an example helps clarify the teaching.[3] Six months ago, a woman began dedicating twenty minutes to prayer each morning. Before the activity of the day, she would spend these minutes meditating on the Gospel of the day's Mass. She grew to love this practice and experienced its fruits. Since she began this prayer, she found that her faith was more alive. Sunday Mass now meant more to her, and she felt God's presence more readily throughout the day. She grew more patient with her children and more loving in general. She knew that the change in her had become a blessing for the whole family.

Three weeks ago, all of her children caught a severe flu. There were visits to the doctor and largely sleepless nights. At the same time, her husband was working overtime on a pressing business project, and she had less help at home than usual. Christmas was close, and the season also added to the pace of life. In the midst of chaotic days, of constant demands on her time and energy, and a growing tiredness, the twenty minutes of prayer in the morning were swept away.

The children's illness passed, her husband completed his project, and the holiday season ended. Life returned to its normal pace. Today, several weeks later, she is driving to school to meet the children. As she drives, she realizes that she no longer feels the closeness with the Lord that she has loved in this past year. Her faith seems less alive, her confidence in God diminished, and her sense of God's love less present. She finds herself missing and desiring her former daily relationship with God. She then realizes that she has not resumed the twenty minutes of prayer dropped some weeks earlier in the time of pressure. Now that she sees this, she immediately resolves to begin again the next day.

In the light of the example, I repeat the teaching. Such is the first reason why God may allow spiritual desolation. When people who love God and are generally progressing toward him regress in a specific aspect of the spiritual life, God may allow desolation to alert them to this regression. The discomfort of desolation alerts the person to the area of regression and so to reintegrate it into a life generally progressing toward God.

I add a further example from Ignatius' *Spiritual Diary*. This example, like others explored thus far, illustrates the rule at hand and also reinforces the categories learned thus far. On April 2, 1544, Ignatius writes,

> Later, at another time, when much consoled, I thought that . . . it was better not to be consoled by God our Lord, if the lack of his visitation was due to my not

having disposed myself or helped myself throughout the day, or in giving place to some thoughts that distracted me from his words in the sacrifice [the Mass] and from his divine majesty [at this point in his life, Ignatius lives in such habitual communion with God that he can note those times in the day or in the celebration of Mass when he has allowed his heart to slip from that communion, "not having disposed myself" or "in giving place to some thoughts that distracted me"], and so *I thought it would be better not to be consoled in the time of my faults* [the highlighted words are pure rule 9, first reason], and that God our Lord orders this (*who loves me more than I love myself*) [these highlighted words are the real reason why I cite this example; these lovely words lay bare the deep truth of rule 9, first reason—Who of us would ever want spiritual desolation? but God, *who loves us more than we love ourselves*, will permit desolation "in the time of our faults" as a loving call to conversion and so to the full integration of our person in his love and service, our deepest, truest source of joy], for my greater spiritual benefit, so that it is better for me to walk straight, not only in the sacrifice, but throughout the day, in order to be visited.[4]

Second Cause: A Trial and the Gift of Learning

I title the second cause "a trial and the gift of learning," and explain it this way: God may permit spiritual desolation as a *trial* from which *learning* results. I comment that other words might be used for *learning*: *wisdom, growth, progress,* and the like.

At this point I raise a question, adding that I do not wish a verbal answer.[5] The question is a way to highlight a possible view of spiritual desolation. "How many of us," I ask, "if we were to say why God allows us to experience spiritual desolation, would consider the question fully answered in Ignatius's rule 9, first reason, that is, 'because we are tepid, slothful, or negligent in our spiritual exercises'?" In this view, if God permits us to experience spiritual desolation, this is *always* because we are in some way at fault: we are tepid, slothful, or negligent. The question helps my listeners realize that they may have this understanding of spiritual desolation. Some—perhaps many—do.

But I explain that Ignatius's view is evidently different. Our faults are *one* reason for which God may permit spiritual desolation, but only one. Two additional reasons follow, neither of them linked to any negligence on our part. When my listeners perceive this, they are further strengthened to resist desolation. Once again, Ignatius's teaching lifts burdens, and a note of hope enters the discussion of rule 9.

I then read the text of the second cause:

> **The second, *to try us* [here Ignatius refers to God's second reason for permitting spiritual desolation as a *trial*] and see [something is *learned*] how much we are and how much we extend ourselves in his service and praise without so much payment of consolations and increased graces.**[6]

As always, I turn to examples. Lucia has just completed a time of retreat and is now traveling home.[7] During her retreat she has felt close to a loving God. In the following account, she relates to her retreat director what she experienced as she traveled home:

> That experience I had as I was leaving after my retreat a month ago made quite an impression on me. It certainly took me by surprise! My mind was in such confusion that I couldn't comprehend what was happening to me. I didn't understand how I could feel so bad so fast after feeling so good for so long. On my way home I was second-guessing my entire retreat and felt that due to my failure it had been a complete waste of time. I figured that I must have some serious problem and that maybe I had

been dishonest by not bringing it up during the retreat. And since I didn't even know what the "problem" was, I concluded that I was probably incapable of making a "good" retreat because I was incapable of being honest and open. The thought came to me that I should not waste your time and mine with these retreats. When I thought of calling you about it, I ran into still more obstacles. I felt that I really had no right to bother you—after all, my retreat was over. If things weren't resolved during the retreat, that was my own fault.[8]

Lucia is evidently experiencing spiritual desolation with all the darkness, confusion, and heaviness of heart it involves. We have no indication that she has been negligent, slothful, or tepid in any way. On the contrary, she has just concluded a time of faithful and richly blessed prayer. Why then does God permit such desolation?

After this time of struggle, Lucia does call her retreat director and, in conversation with the director, finds the answer to her fears and a further confirmation of God's gift during her retreat. Now Lucia writes further to the director:

> So it was truly the grace of God that prompted me to make that phone call, and your words and prayers revealed the truth to me. I realize now *more than ever* how much God loves me, how much I need him; and I am *more determined than ever* to "keep my eyes fixed on Jesus," to follow him, to serve him, to do his will.[9]

I ask my listeners, "If you and I can say of any experience we have undergone that because we have undergone that experience we now realize more than ever how much God loves us, is there a reason why a God who loves us would permit us to undergo that experience?" My listeners nod their assent. Further, "If you and I can say of any experience we have undergone that because we have undergone that experience we now realize more than ever how much we need God, is there a reason why a God who loves us would permit us to undergo that experience?" Once more, nods of assent. Again, "If you and I can say of any experience we have undergone that because we have undergone that experience we are more determined than ever to keep our eyes fixed on Jesus, to follow him, to serve him, and to do his will, is there a reason why a God who loves us would permit us to undergo that experience?" Further nods of assent, and the point is made. Such learning "in the flesh" of key spiritual truths—perceiving more than ever before that she is deeply loved and that she needs God, with a new resolve to center her life on Jesus—reveals why God permits Lucia's trial of spiritual desolation.

I then quote an example from an early Franciscan text.[10] I invite my listeners to watch how St. Francis gives spiritual direction. This catches their attention!

In this text, we read of a Franciscan brother who was struggling with temptations that he felt helpless to resist. He knew that Francis was well aware of his inner conflict, and one day, when alone with Francis, he begged this holy man for help. He said,

> Pray for me, kind Father, for I am sure that I will be immediately freed from my temptations if you will be kind enough to pray for me. For I am afflicted above my strength and I know that this is no secret to you.

We then read Francis's answer. I note how consoling Francis's response must have been for this brother in his time of trouble:

> St. Francis said to him: "Believe me, son, for I think you are *for that reason more truly a servant of God* [we can "feel" the uplift of heart in this brother as he hears these words]; and know that *the more you are tempted, the more will you be loved by me.*" [Again, we can sense how profoundly consoling these words must have been

for the brother.] And he added: "I tell you in all truth, *no one must consider himself a servant of God* until *he has undergone temptations and tribulations*. [This is rule 9, second cause: growth in God's service through spiritual tribulations—spiritual desolations—and their accompanying temptations.] "Temptation overcome," he said, "is in a way a *ring* with which the Lord espouses the soul of his servant to himself." [A lovely metaphor, and one that often speaks warmly to my listeners' hearts.][11]

The tribulation that this brother thought an indication of his spiritual deficiency Francis knows to be rather the sign that this brother is a true servant of God. This, I observe, is the encouragement that Ignatius would give us in describing God's second cause for allowing the trial of spiritual desolation.

Finally, I comment that without spiritual desolation, we would remain spiritual children.[12] If I judge it helpful, I repeat this sentence: *without spiritual desolation, we would remain spiritual children*. I note that certain kinds of growth are given through the joy of spiritual consolation and that we all readily recognize this as we review our lives. Other kinds of growth, I continue, are normally given through the trial of spiritual desolation. The darkness of desolation almost compels us to take new spiritual steps—to reach out for help, to pray with new intensity, to approach the sacraments more frequently, and the like. I add that we can all see the truth of this when we consider our own lives. Yes, without times of spiritual desolation, we would likely remain spiritual children. God, who loves us so deeply, desires more for us and so prepares for us the path to growth.

Third Cause: Poverty and the Gift of a Humble Heart

We turn then to the third cause. I begin by reading the text with a brief commentary:

The third, to give us true recognition and understanding [a clear understanding in the mind] **so that we may interiorly feel** [a felt perception of the heart, an affective grasp] **that it is not ours to attain** [to cause spiritual consolation to arise] **or maintain** [to cause it to continue] **increased devotion, intense love, tears or any other spiritual consolation, but that all is the gift and grace of God our Lord** [this is the key: to know, from personal experience, that all spiritual consolation is the "gift and grace" of God. Thus far in his text on the third cause, Ignatius has told us that when we experience spiritual desolation, *we know* "in the flesh" that our experiences of spiritual consolation are not our doing but are the "gift and grace" of God. Now he turns to *the attitude* that this awareness is intended to awaken in us] ; **and so that we may not build a nest in something belonging to another, raising our mind in some pride or vainglory,** [this is the potential pitfall from which God would save us by permitting, at times, the experience of spiritual desolation; avoiding this pitfall, we remain humble and thereby richly open to grace] **attributing to ourselves the devotion or the other parts of the spiritual consolation.**

I remark that the text of the third cause is longer than that of the first and second combined, and longer than several of the rules in their entirety.[13] Rule 9, third cause, seems the one place in the rules in which Ignatius loosens his spare and essential style and describes his point in detail. These textual considerations, I tell my listeners, suggest that Ignatius ascribes a particular importance to this third cause. In fact, in his *Spiritual Exercises*, Ignatius presents humility—together with the evangelical poverty and bearing of wrongs for Christ that lead to it—as the rich spiritual space that leads "to all the other virtues" (*SpirEx* 146).

I apply the teaching. At times, we experience the joy of spiritual consolation perhaps for a day, a week, several weeks, or longer. During such times, almost insensibly we may "build a nest in something belonging to another," "attributing to ourselves the devotion or the other parts of the spiritual consolation." When God permits spiritual desolation to return, then we know "that it is not ours to attain or maintain increased devotion, intense love, tears or any other spiritual consolation, but that all is the gift and grace of God our Lord." Thus we are rooted in humility—this rich biblical space of openness and dependence on God (Mt 5:3; 11:29; Lk 1:48)—and so are open to all spiritual growth.

When a week ago I was in spiritual consolation, and now I am in spiritual desolation, *I know* that that spiritual consolation was God's gift. Thus I remain humble and receptive to God's grace.

Three Expressions of Love

I conclude rule 9 by noting that each of these three causes, in its own way, reveals God's love for us.[14] God permits spiritual desolation, Ignatius tells us, *to heal us* from areas of regression in our spiritual lives (first cause), to provide *opportunities for growth* (second cause), and to *save us from a possible pitfall* (third cause). Healing, growth, and protection from a pitfall: understood in the light of God's loving providence, spiritual desolation grows easier to resist. At this point, Ignatius has supplied a rich reply to the question that underlies rule 9: Why does a God who loves us, and whom we are seeking to love, permit us to experience the heaviness of spiritual desolation?

18

To Listeners in Consolation
Prepare for the Future
Rule 10

I begin rule 10 by reading the text:

> Tenth Rule. **The tenth:** let the one who is in consolation think how he will conduct himself in the desolation which will come after, taking new strength for that time.

Sometimes I comment that this is the shortest of the rules, which does not mean that I have the least to say about it! My first question for my listeners is, "For whom is rule 10?" By now, they expect these questions that underline elements in the text and can answer them with increasing ease. All reply, "For a person in spiritual consolation."

This question highlights for my listeners the shift as we move from rules 5 through 9 to rule 10. Rules 5 through 9 are for the person now experiencing spiritual desolation; rule 10, on the other hand, is for "one who is in consolation."

Having noted the shift, I immediately indicate that although in rule 10 Ignatius addresses the person in consolation, his goal remains the same as that of rules 5 through 9: to help the person reject spiritual desolation—in this case, not a present but a future desolation: "let the one *who is in consolation* think how he will conduct himself *in the desolation which will come after*, taking *new strength for that time.*" Rules 5 through 9 tell the person now in desolation how to resist and reject the desolation when actually in it; rule 10 tells this person, now in consolation, how to live this time of consolation in such a way as to gain strength to resist desolation when it returns, as eventually it will. Rule 10, therefore, adds a new refinement to resistance to spiritual desolation: we can begin to resist such desolation even before it begins!

I refer to the basic paradigm (be aware; understand; take action, accept/reject) and indicate that in rule 10, as in rules 5 through 9, Ignatius continues to focus on taking action to reject desolation. The paradigm gives visual support to this point. I underscore the word *reject*:

>BE AWARE
>UNDERSTAND
>TAKE ACTION
>   (ACCEPT/REJECT)

The Other Action: Accepting Spiritual Consolation

Rule 10, then, like the preceding five rules, offers help toward rejecting spiritual desolation. Because, however, this is the one rule in which Ignatius speaks of "one who is in consolation," before proceeding further I pause to make another important point. This rule for one in consolation provides an opportunity to focus on the other action to be taken in discernment, that is, to "accept" in time of consolation.

At times, people are unsure of whether or not they should accept spiritual consolation. Is it not better to seek "the God of consolations" rather than "the consolations of God"?[1] What of John of the Cross's strictures on spiritual gluttony?[2] Spiritual consolations come and go: Is it not best to serve God with a firm will rather than depend on such fluctuating experiences? Might God be more pleased that we serve him so? Such questions are raised with sincere goodwill, and they are important.

I address this question through an example in the life of St. Elizabeth Seton, wife, mother, widow, founder of a community of sisters, and initiator of parochial schools in the United States.[3] The experience I cite takes place when Elizabeth is fifteen. She longs for the love of her father, who remarried after the death of Elizabeth's mother and is less present than Elizabeth would have wished. On a warm, sunny day in May, Elizabeth sets out into the woods, finds a chestnut tree with moss under it, and stops there, "with a heart as innocent as human heart could be, filled even with enthusiastic love to God and admiration of his works."

Elizabeth continues, "God was my Father, my all. I prayed, sang hymns, cried, laughed, talking to myself of how far he could place me above all sorrow. Then I laid still to enjoy the heavenly peace that came over my soul; and I am sure, in the two hours so enjoyed, grew ten years in the spiritual life." With the sure intuition of the saints, Elizabeth knows that her call in this blessed time of spiritual consolation is simply to receive the gift. Having received it, she grows greatly, "in *the two hours so enjoyed, grew ten years in the spiritual life.*" I tell my listeners that we will seldom find a clearer example of Ignatius's "accept" in time of spiritual consolation.

I cite a further instance from St. Bonaventure's biography of St. Francis of Assisi. St. Bonaventure writes, "Francis would never let any call of the Spirit go unanswered; when he experienced it, he would make the most of it and enjoy the consolation afforded him in this way for as long as God permitted it. If he was on a journey, and felt the near approach of God's Spirit, he would stop and let his companions go on, while he drank in the joy of this new inspiration; he refused to offer God's grace an ineffectual welcome (cf. 2 Cor 6:1)."[4] Here, too, a saint perceives the call in time of spiritual consolation, "he would *make the most of it and enjoy the consolation afforded him in this way for as long as God permitted it.* . . . He refused to offer God's grace an ineffectual welcome." I note that like Elizabeth, Francis knows that the primary call in time of spiritual consolation is to receive the grace that God is giving, aware that this strength and light will bear fruit in blessed ways.

I stress for my listeners that we should never let anything—not even Ignatius's rule 10!—hinder us from this primary call in time of spiritual consolation: simply to accept God's gift, to delight in it, to allow this grace to heal, encourage, enlighten, and strengthen us. At this point, my listeners' questions, if they have them—and most often some do—are answered; they are set free to receive God's spiritual consolations with receptive hearts and with joy.

In Consolation, Think Ahead to Future Desolation

I return now to the example of Elizabeth and develop it further in the light of rule 10. Nothing, I repeat for my listeners, should ever weigh on our primary call in time of spiritual consolation simply to accept the gift. We can, however, live times of spiritual consolation in a way that joins to this *primary good* an *additional good*, also a source of much blessing. This additional good is the focus of Ignatius's rule 10.

I present this first through a caricature, telling my listeners that they will sense how harsh, discordant, and wrong this is. Suppose, I say, that during those two blessed hours of spiritual consolation beneath the chestnut tree, Elizabeth were to say to herself, "This is lovely and wonderful, and I delight in this heavenly joy. But . . . Ignatius says in rule 10 that in time of spiritual consolation we should think ahead to future spiritual desolation and take in strength for that time. So I need to interrupt receiving this joy and do that right now. I need right now to think about future desolation and how I will face it when it returns." Elizabeth, with the sure intuition of the saints, does not do this! She knows that her primary call, on which nothing ever should weigh, is to accept, to receive, to drink in and be fortified by the grace of the consolation given her in those two hours.

But, I continue, we could easily imagine Elizabeth that evening, perhaps out walking in the nature she loved, still warmed by the spiritual consolation of those two hours. As she walks, now Elizabeth can think ahead to times when desolation will return, and now, yes, prepare for those times. With her heart warmed by the love of her heavenly Father, she can think of how she will face those harder times and, with her God, "take new strength" for those times. Elizabeth thus joins to the primary good of spiritual consolation an additional good that will significantly aid her when desolation returns.

Such is Ignatius's counsel in rule 10. In the overall experience of spiritual consolation, there will be times when, still gladdened by that consolation, we can think ahead with the Lord to future desolation and take new strength for it. During an evening, a day, several days, or a week of consolation, while exercising, seated before the Blessed Sacrament, out walking, in the quiet of our room, waiting to pick up the children after school, or in any setting that permits quiet reflection, we can, in the joy of that consolation, think ahead to future desolation and take new strength for it.

I employ a biblical comparison. The dynamic of rule 10 is similar to that of Joseph and the seven years of plenty followed by the seven years of famine (Genesis 41). During the years of plenty, Joseph stores up grain *that he does not need*. But that stored-up grain will be crucial for survival in the years of famine that follow.

I ask, "What if, in time of spiritual consolation, we *do not* think ahead to the return of spiritual desolation and prepare? What will happen when the desolation does return?"[5] I answer that it will come with a disconcerting and perhaps prostrating shock of surprise. Our daily program of prayer, our spiritual initiatives, our efforts to live our vocations, and our service of the Lord may collapse in some—at times significant—measure. A collapse of this kind may require arduous and prolonged effort to overcome.

At times, I employ a comparison from years of sailing. You are moving well through the water with a fresh breeze. The sails are full, the boat is heeled over, and you are leaning out over the rail on the high side to keep the boat more level. Everything is functioning well, and the boat is forging ahead. Then, suddenly, the wind drops or you go under the wind shadow of a larger boat. In an instant, the boat slams down into the water, the sails flap wildly, water splashes into the boat, you struggle to regain your balance and not fall into the water. That is an image of what can happen spiritually if we are unprepared for desolation when it returns. From your own experiences, you will find the illustrations that work best for you in conveying this point to your listeners.

I often add a further instance.[6] Two people are riding a city bus on the way to work. Both are standing and support themselves by clasping the vertical metal rods placed for that purpose. At the moment, the bus is traversing a long, straight stretch of the street.

The first person is engaged with his smartphone, reading the newspaper, or simply gazing at the passing scenery. Because the street at this point is straight, a loose hold on the metal rod suffices. Up ahead on the bus's trajectory, however, is a sharp curve. When the bus enters the curve, this person's hold on the rod no longer suffices. He goes flying, and he hits the floor of the bus, tearing his suit jacket. His briefcase also hits the floor and spills open. It is not a matter of life and death but it does put a dent in his day, and some energy is required to recompose himself.

The second person is also engaged with his smartphone, reading the newspaper, or simply gazing at the passing scenery. For him, too, during the straight stretch of the street, a loose hold on the metal rod suffices. This person, however, looks up ahead from time to time to see what lies ahead on the bus's trajectory. He sees the sharp curve approach, widens his stance a little and tightens his grip on the metal rod. As the bus negotiates the curve, he sways a little . . . and that is all there is to it! I tell my listeners that this is where Ignatius would lead us in rule 10: if we have foreseen the return of desolation and prepared, negotiating (rejecting) the desolation will be greatly eased.

Ways of "Taking New Strength"

How do we take new strength in time of consolation to prepare for desolation? How do we do this concretely? I believe it important to supply my listeners with practical suggestions in this regard. At this point, therefore, I present a series of counsels on how to prepare for desolation when in consolation.[7] The following is how I discuss and exemplify each counsel. You will find your own ways of doing this.

- *Pray for Strength in Future Spiritual Desolation.* When we are in spiritual consolation, a morning, a day, a week . . . time is always available to think ahead to the return of desolation and to pray for help. One person does this during a long drive, another while out walking, another while exercising, yet another while sitting in church. "Jesus, that 10:00 p.m. time is a time when I can be vulnerable. Help me resist when I find myself there another time." "Mary, that early afternoon time alone in the kitchen is a time when I am exposed to desolation. Be with me the next time that happens. Be my spiritual mother then, and bring me close to Jesus and his love." Another person asks for this help while at Mass, praying a part of the Liturgy of the Hours, or saying the Rosary for this intention. I may ask my listeners, "Do we ever do this?"

- *Meditate on Truths That Will Sustain in Spiritual Desolation.* When we are in the peace of spiritual consolation, we consciously call to mind the truths of faith that will sustain us when desolation returns. A woman meditates on

Psalm 27:1, "The Lord is my light and my salvation; whom should I fear? The Lord is my life's refuge; of whom should I be afraid?"[8] Having done so, this verse will be fresh in her heart when desolation returns; it will be an arm against the desolation's urging to "lack of confidence." I tell my listeners, that all of us have favorite scriptural passages that tell us of God's faithful love. We can call these to mind, reflect on them, meditate on them when in consolation. Another woman, when in consolation, sings her "anti-desolation song." A man sits before the Lord and recalls the Lord's faithful love in dark times in the past, strengthened in the surety that the Lord will protect him in future desolation. I tell my listeners that I recall those words "I have been here before"; reflecting on them, my awareness that the Lord will guide me safely through future desolation grows. I note for my listeners that Ignatius offers these first two counsels to the person in spiritual desolation (rule 6); here we indicate that we can employ them when in spiritual consolation, *before* the desolation even begins—and when they will more likely be easier to employ because of the joy of the consolation.

- *Consider the Value of Spiritual Desolation for Growth.* When in the warmth of spiritual consolation, we might review rule 7 (why God allows the trial of spiritual desolation, that we *can* resist it) or rule 9 (three reasons why God permits us to undergo desolation and the fruits he desires to give us through it: healing, growth, protection from a potential pitfall). We might reflect on the truth that "without spiritual desolation, we would remain spiritual children."

- *Reflect on Past Personal Growth through Spiritual Desolation.* This takes the preceding counsel and renders it personal. The invitation is to recall and reflect on the growth we have experienced through undergoing spiritual desolation in the past, how at times the desolation almost compelled us to take what proved to be the most helpful spiritual steps of our lives. I share my own reflection on that difficult moment as I walked along the street with the question in my heart, "Why is this happening? I'm just trying to do the best I can," and the strengthening words, "I have been here before, and you guided me through the struggle not only safely but with growth as well." I share how the pain of that experience led me to take courses, participate in programs, and do systematic reading that opened up a new phase in my life—that I probably would never have written on discernment and would not now be presenting this teaching were it not for the stimulus of that difficult time. This remembrance and reflection helps prepare me to stand firm when desolation returns.

- *Resolve to Make No Changes in Time of Spiritual Desolation.* Here we prepare to apply rule 5 when desolation returns. I suggest to my listeners that when they are in consolation they review past times when they *did* make harmful changes to their spiritual proposals in times of spiritual desolation. When made, those changes were harmful; now, reflecting on them in spiritual consolation, they become helpful—they root us more deeply in our purpose to apply rule 5 in the future. In a certain sense, those harmful changes of the past are now redeemed.

- *Review These Ignatian Rules.* I take a little time on this because I consider this key to the sustained application of the rules. I observe, "You and I right now are in a rarified situation. We have nothing to do right now but consider these rules. When we are back in the press of life and its busyness, how much of this will we remember? How much will we remember a week from now? A month? A year? Five years?" I make my point, "If we wish these rules to be effective in our lives, we need two things: we need to learn them—that is what we are doing now—and we need a way to keep them fresh in our consciousness." I ask my listeners, "How might we do this?" I invite suggestions. This is always an interesting time for my listeners (and for me!) as various persons offer suggestions. Their suggestions are helpful and offer me an opportunity to comment and amplify as I deem useful. One may suggest keeping the text of the rules at hand. I tell my listeners of people I have known who have kept them on their nightstands, taped them to the door of their rooms or to the dashboard of their cars, or kept them on the desks where they work. Another may suggest posting them on the smartphone. I speak of persons who program their phones to send them regular reminders of the rules. Yet another may describe writing a short, personal summary of the rules and carrying this constantly. I speak of persons who have done this and carry the rules in their pocketbooks or wallets. Another speaks of teaching the rules, and I observe that teaching them is among the best ways to learn them. The suggestions continue . . . and we enjoy discussing them. As we do this, my listeners begin to consider how they will keep the rules fresh in their awareness. When all the suggestions have been made (or time permits no more), I say the following: "I invite all here, before we finish our time together, to take five to ten minutes and consider how you will keep the rules fresh in your consciousness. I can promise you this: if you do, a time will come when you will look back with gratitude at those minutes and what has come from them."[9]

- *Plan for Specific Situations of Spiritual Desolation.* We may know that in certain situations we are especially vulnerable to spiritual desolation. When in spiritual consolation, we can think ahead to these times and prepare.[10] This counsel can be particularly helpful in overcoming repeating patterns of spiritual desolation. I give examples. A man knows that a meeting at work on Thursday afternoons can leave him discouraged and so prone to desolation. The bells of a church near his office building ring at noon every day. He decides that the bells, when they ring on Thursday, will remind him to pray for strength in that meeting and to avoid any consequent discouragement and desolation. In my own life, I tell my listeners, the time after a retreat or seminar, when I am tired and the people are no longer present, can be an occasion for spiritual desolation.[11] I find myself in an airport or on a plane, alone and tired. In that space, the trap of spiritual desolation can enter the normal nonspiritual desolation (tiredness, aloneness) that follows the expenditure of energy and involvement with people in the retreat. The desolation may persist after I return home in the time when I attempt to rest and recover my energy. When I am spiritually aware, therefore, already in the airport and on the plane I pray for help to resist spiritual desolation. Again, as throughout, you will find your own illustrations.

19

Living the Discerning Life
Humble in Consolation, Trusting in Desolation
Rule 11

I begin rule 11 by reading the text of the rule:

> Eleventh Rule. The eleventh: let one who is consoled seek to humble himself and lower himself as much as he can, thinking of how little he is capable in the time of desolation without such grace or consolation. [Now the second part of the rule.] On the contrary, let one who is in desolation think that he can do much with God's sufficient grace to resist all his enemies, taking strength in his Creator and Lord.

I then ask a question already familiar to my listeners: "For whom is rule 11?" They answer readily, "For both the person in spiritual consolation and the person in spiritual desolation." I explain that after a set of rules for the person in spiritual desolation (rules 5 through 9) and one for the person in spiritual consolation (rule 10), now Ignatius gives us a rule that includes both. What he does, I tell them, is to paint the portrait of the mature person of discernment.

I note for my listeners that this is the final rule of these fourteen in which Ignatius speaks of spiritual consolation and spiritual desolation, and that there will be a slight shift as we move into the final three rules (12 through 14). I say that it almost seems as though before leaving consolation and desolation, Ignatius wishes to tie together all that he has said about them. In this "portrait of the mature person of discernment," Ignatius addresses first spiritual consolation and then spiritual desolation.

Humble in Spiritual Consolation

I review with my listeners the what, why, and how of this first half of rule 11: *What* are persons in spiritual consolation to do, *why* should they do it, and *how* should they do it?

What They Should Do

One who is consoled, Ignatius counsels, is to "seek to *humble himself* and lower himself as much as he can." This person is to avoid any sense of self-satisfaction—"Look at me. I have arrived. I'm doing well in the spiritual life."—and of pride and overconfidence. One, therefore, in the joy and warmth of spiritual consolation should seek to be humble, and should do so with a certain energy—"as much as he can."

Why They Should Do It

One does not "humble himself" just because humility is, generally speaking, a good thing, but because careless overconfidence sets us up for a fall. Ignatius would help us avoid precisely such falls and their painful aftermath.

I find an example employed by Jules Toner, SJ, useful in this regard.[1] Toner applies to rule 11, first part, the dialogue between Jesus and Peter in Mark 14:27–31. It is Holy Thursday night, and Jesus and the disciples have gone to the Mount of Olives. Once there, Jesus tells them, "You will all fall away."[2] Peter replies, "Even though they all fall away, I will not." Jesus answers Peter, "This very night, before the cock crows twice, you will deny me three times." Peter vehemently insists, "If I must die with you, I will not deny you." We know the sequel.

In the warmth and security of Jesus's presence (spiritual consolation), Peter presumes on his strength, confident that he can overcome any temptation in the ensuing trial. I tell my listeners that what I say next is a hypothetical case, just to make a point. "What if," I ask, "when Jesus told the disciples that they would all fall away that night, Peter had said to himself, 'You know, I've been pretty sure of myself a few times before, and things haven't always gone that well.' And what if Peter had then turned to Jesus and said, 'Jesus, you know that the last thing I would ever want is to fall away from you. But I know that I'm weak and that I could become afraid in the trial. Jesus, help me, stay with me, give me the courage I need to stand by you faithfully in this trial.'" Then I ask, "If Peter had done this, would he have had to go through the pain of the betrayals and the bitter tears that followed? Might he have found strength in Jesus to withstand the trial? Yes, Jesus later heals his heart with great sensitivity at the lakeshore (Jn 21:15–17), but might Peter have never fallen at all?"

I comment that this is the pitfall that Ignatius wishes to help us avoid in the first part of rule 11: a thoughtless overconfidence, an excessive trust in our own strength in time of spiritual consolation when all seems easy and possible. Such overconfidence may lead us to attempt spiritual steps beyond our strength and ability to sustain—it sets us up for a fall. When the fall comes (in the example, a thoroughly frightened Peter denies Jesus three times), much pain may follow. In this painful deflating of our spiritual overconfidence, our preceding steps of growth may collapse, and we may easily fall prey to spiritual desolation. The danger is real!

How They Should Do It

I note once more for my listeners that Ignatius is always practical. He does not simply counsel us to remain humble in spiritual consolation but also provides a means toward growing in such humility: "*thinking* of *how little he is capable* in the *time of desolation* without such grace or consolation." I observe that, as always, Ignatius calls us to the reflective spiritual life:

thinking—not simply carried along blindly in the spiritual life but conscious, aware, noticing, and reflecting, in this case so as to avoid the pitfall of overconfidence. Of what precisely is the person in spiritual consolation to think in order to remain humble? This person is to think "of *how little he is capable* in the *time of desolation* without such grace or consolation."

Over the years I have found the following effective at this point. I ask my listeners, "How many of us here would be happy, right now, to have the video playing on the screen before us of how we handled our last desolation?" I don't ask for a verbal answer! I tell my listeners that I would not wish this. I comment, "There would probably be a few refrigerators, smartphones, and similar things in that video." At this, all smile, and all also get Ignatius's point: If, in time of spiritual consolation, we recall past—perhaps not very far past—spiritual desolation and how we struggled in that time to pray, maintain our proposals, avoid flight into diversion, and the like, we gain a true perception of our spiritual abilities. We grasp how much we need God's help and are therefore more likely to remain humble in the present time of consolation. In this way we avoid the pitfall mentioned.

Trusting in Spiritual Desolation

We look then at the second part of rule 11: "On the contrary, let one who is in desolation think that he can do much with God's sufficient grace to resist all his enemies, taking strength in his Creator and Lord." Again I highlight Ignatius's call to reflection, to *think*. This person burdened by spiritual desolation is to think the following encouraging thought: "he *can do much* with *God's sufficient grace* to *resist all his enemies*, taking strength in his Creator and Lord." I underline the hope in Ignatius's "all"; though the desolation would have us believe the contrary, there is *no spiritual enemy* that we cannot resist because God's grace is always *sufficient*—God will always give us all the grace we need to resist the desolation and emerge from it not only without harm but even with growth. Thus this person "takes strength in his Creator and Lord" to resist and reject spiritual desolation.

Now I draw the conclusion, that is, the portrait of the mature person of discernment depicted in rule 11. This person is neither carelessly and naively "high" in time of spiritual consolation nor blindly and despairingly "low" in time of spiritual desolation. Rather, this person is *humble* in time of spiritual consolation and *trusting* in time of spiritual desolation. In this way, the person progresses solidly toward God.

Rule 11 in Practice: An Example

In keeping with the pedagogy employed throughout, I now turn to an example. My listeners find the following example engaging. It illustrates rule 11 well and also reinforces many points made earlier.

I explain that the following is an account of an eight-day, silent, individually directed Ignatian retreat. Jane, who makes the retreat, is a faithful and dedicated person. As is customary in such retreats, Jane prays with Scripture for an hour four times each day and meets daily with her retreat director to share her experience and receive guidance. The account follows.[3]

> *Day 1*: Jane begins the retreat in peace, with a quiet expectation of meeting Christ. She reflects, as directed, on chapter 55 of Isaiah and is attracted to verse 1: "All you who are thirsty, come to the water!"; and verse 12: "Yes, in joy you shall depart, in peace you shall be brought back." She is confident that the Lord will nourish and refresh her for her ministry. [Here I ask my listeners, "What does Jane appear to be experiencing on day 1?" They answer readily, "Spiritual consolation." I confirm the answer and note the signs of such consolation: her

hopeful attitude as she begins ("quiet expectation"), her attraction to the verses suggested, and her confidence that the Lord's grace will work in this retreat. Jane appears to be experiencing a gentle spiritual consolation on day 1. As so often before, such questions reinforce the teaching. I have learned over the years how pedagogically effective these questions are. My listeners enjoy them and gain confidence that they can identify spiritual consolation and desolation.]

Day 2: In praying over the assigned Scripture verse, "Come to me . . . I will refresh you" (Mt 11:28), Jane experiences an inner cleansing and refreshment as if she were drawn into a fountain of fire and water. She is filled with wonder and joy. The blissful feeling remains with her throughout the day, and she experiences the nearness of Jesus as she ponders other assigned Scripture readings and listens to what the Lord is saying to her. [I ask my listeners, "What does Jane appear to be experiencing on day 2?" All readily reply, "Spiritual consolation." I confirm the answer and add that this is very beautiful and very strong spiritual consolation.]

Day 3: She arises early the next morning quietly hoping for similar experiences of the Lord. She prays over the assigned section of the Canticle of Canticles and experiences a sweet joy at the thought of the Lord's love for her. [I ask, "What is Jane experiencing on day 3?" Again, all reply, "Spiritual consolation."]

She then decides to prolong her praying periods from an hour to an hour and a half each so as to become more immersed in Christ. She does not inform her director about this plan. She spends seven hours that day in prayer. Her excitement grows. That night she cannot fall asleep. [At this point, I ask my listeners, "What do you think of Jane's choices on day 3?" Here the conversation grows interesting! Various responses arise: she is pushing herself too hard, she won't be able to sustain this, and the like. I ask, "Why doesn't Jane tell her director about this change from four to seven hours of prayer?" The answer comes, "Because she knows that her director will most likely ask her to keep a less intense daily rhythm of prayer, and in the joy of her spiritual consolation she does not want this limitation." Now I propose several questions directly related to rule 11, first part. I ask, "On day 3, is Jane trying, in her time of spiritual consolation, to humble and lower herself as much as she can, thinking of how little she is capable in time of spiritual desolation when she does not have such warmth and consolation?" All reply, "No." Then, "On day 3, is Jane 'myself-in-consolation' or 'myself-reflecting-on-myself-in-consolation'?" All reply, "myself-in-consolation"—she is simply carried, unreflectively, by the great joy of her consolation. Again, "Can we see that for Jane, on day 3, the first half of rule 11 has gone by the board?" All nod agreement. I immediately add, "Let's not be hard on Jane. We've all been there. We've all lived times of spiritual energy when we've not wanted anyone to moderate the initiatives in prayer or active service we desire to take." Finally, I ask, "How long can Jane keep this up—seven hours of prayer and an excitement that does not allow her to sleep?" All perceive that Jane cannot sustain this intense pace.]

Day 4: Jane gets up with a bad headache, feeling exhausted and under strain. She cannot pray well. All joy has evaporated. She is tired and sad and moody. [I ask, "What is Jane now experiencing?" All answer, "Desolation." For teaching purposes, I pursue the question further: "Yes, she is obviously in desolation. Is this nonspiritual or spiritual desolation?" Usually, without my assistance my listeners give the answer, "Nonspiritual desolation." I reply, "Yes. Jane has simply pushed her physical and emotional energies too hard. Of course, therefore, she is 'tired and sad and moody.'"]

Finally in the evening she tells the director about her action of the previous day and its results. [I remark, "Here our hearts lift. Now that Jane has spoken openly with her director—the "finally" suggests that this is not totally easy for her—we know that something good will follow." I add that Jane here applies rule 13, a rule we will soon explore.] The director advises cutting down on prayer time and resting more. [I note that this is a good director who gets everything right. My listeners usually smile at this point!]

Day 5: She follows the advice, prays less, but still has no enthusiasm and is filled with gloom. [Again I ask, "What is Jane experiencing on day 5?" All answer, "Desolation." I pursue the question further: "Is this nonspiritual or spiritual desolation?" Now the answers are more hesitant and divided. I observe, "Yes, it is harder now to know whether this is still simply nonspiritual desolation or whether the enemy has now brought spiritual desolation into the nonspiritually vulnerable space—Jane's physical and emotionally tiredness." I comment, "When this is the case, and it's hard to be sure, it may mean that we are seeing the transition from nonspiritual to spiritual desolation."

These questions now permit me to ask another important question: "What should we do when we are aware (first step in discernment) but unable to understand (second step in discernment)?" I reply, "We should never force a clarity that we do not have. Rather, we should simply continue to be aware and notice the experience. As it continues to unfold, this experience will very likely grow clearer. And as for Jane, conversation with a wise and competent spiritual person—here, her retreat director—will help her understand her experience." Anticipating (and so preparing for) rule 13, I affirm that for Ignatius the discerning life is never lived alone but always presumes competent accompaniment.]

Day 6: At her morning prayer she becomes very much disturbed. She begins to doubt the Lord's presence to her even in the opening days of the retreat. Probably, she thinks, she should attribute everything to her overactive imagination. Who is she to be given a taste of the sweetness of the Lord? She begins to grow discouraged at the thought that she is not meant for a deep prayer life. Her desire for God is just an illusion. The rest of the day is one of disquietude, confusion, and a sense of discouragement. [I ask, "What is Jane now experiencing?" All immediately reply, "Spiritual desolation." I confirm the answer. If time allows, I may highlight various classic qualities of spiritual desolation that appear on day 6: lack of confidence ("She begins to doubt"—it was all "her overactive imagination"); the claim to interpret Jane's spiritual past ("She begins to doubt the Lord's presence to her even in the opening days of the retreat") and to predict her spiritual future ("She begins to grow discouraged at the thought that she is not meant for a deep prayer life"), obviously all in a dark key. You can indicate for your listeners other qualities of spiritual desolation here if you desire and time permits.]

[Now I ask a set of questions related to rule 11, second part. These questions are parallel to those I proposed earlier (day 3 of Jane's retreat) regarding rule 11, first part. My listeners readily perceive the parallelism, and it serves to reinforce the content of the two parts of rule 11 in combination. I ask, "On day 6, is Jane trying, in her time of spiritual desolation, to think that she can do much with God's sufficient grace to resist all her enemies?" All reply, "No." Then, "Is Jane, on day 6, 'myself-in-desolation' or 'myself-reflecting-on-myself-in-desolation'?" All reply, "myself-in-desolation"—she is simply carried, unreflectively, by the discouragement of her desolation. Again, "Can we see that for Jane, on day 6, the second half of rule 11 has gone by the board?" All nod in agreement. I immediately add, "Let's not be hard on Jane. We've all been there in our own times of spiritual desolation." I conclude, "It is discouragement like Jane's that Ignatius would help us avoid in the second half of rule 11."]

Day 7: The director urges her to trust her earlier experiences. [When Jane doubts the authenticity of her spiritual consolation in the earlier days of the retreat, the director is able to reassure her that this was true spiritual consolation, a gift of God. In terms of the paradigm of discernment (be aware, understand, take action), when Jane is not able on her own to reach the second step (to *understand* her earlier experience clearly), with the director's help she is able to reach that understanding and so find more peace. I take the opportunity to highlight the importance of accompaniment in the discerning life, again preparing for rule 13]. Her director also urges her to hope in the Lord that he will bring good even from this desolation. [The director applies rule 9: there is a reason why a God who loves Jane permits this time of spiritual desolation.] She directs her to pray over John 14, especially the opening verses, "Do not let your hearts be troubled."

She prays quietly over the passages, rests more, and takes walks in the garden [a well-chosen scriptural passage and healthy nonspiritual choices].

Day 8: On the closing day she returns to chapter 55 of Isaiah: "Come to the water. . . . In joy you shall depart" (vv. 1, 12). A calm settles on her mind and spirit. She knows that she is loved by God. She also knows at her deepest level that the experience of the second day was genuine. [On day 7, Jane needed the director's help to understand the authenticity of the earlier spiritual consolation; now she is able to see it herself.] She has become more [I invite my listeners to note the repeated "more" in this account of day 8; this "more" expresses the fruit God has given her through permitting her time of spiritual desolation] aware of her weaknesses, especially her undisciplined imagination and her rapidly fluctuating emotions. [These led her to overextend herself through enthusiasm and so harm herself.] She prays for light and strength to manage these and become more balanced emotionally. She ends the retreat in quiet gratitude. She looks forward now in hope to her ministry—a more wise and serene woman. [I ask my listeners, "What is Jane experiencing as she concludes her retreat?" All answer, "Spiritual consolation." I confirm the answer: on this day, Jane does appear to experience a gentle spiritual consolation.]

I now return to a "rule 9" question. I ask, "Couldn't a God who loves Jane have spared her the spiritual desolation of days 4 through 6? Here is a woman who loves God and who, with very goodwill, has set aside eight days to pray. Why does God allow such painful and discouraging days?" Jane's retreat provides an excellent opportunity to reinforce the teaching of rule 9, that God's providential love is at work even in permitting spiritual desolation. Again, I highlight the "more." Jane grows both through the richness and beauty of her times of spiritual consolation (days 1 through 3) *and also*, in significant measure, through her trial of spiritual desolation (days 4 through 6). Through that trial she gains a self-knowledge that will bless her greatly in days to come: "She ends the retreat in quiet gratitude. She looks forward now in hope to her ministry—a more wise and serene woman." In his letter to Sister Teresa Rejadell, we saw Ignatius refer to both spiritual consolation and spiritual desolation as "lessons." Here we perceive clearly what that vocabulary expresses: Jane learns, grows, profits ("lesson") *both* from her times of spiritual consolation and spiritual desolation.

20

Teaching Your Listeners How to Resist Temptation

Rule 12

I introduce rule 12 by noting the shift in the rules at this point. Thus far, Ignatius has essentially dealt with spiritual desolation and how to reject it. After rule 11, Ignatius does not mention spiritual desolation again. He turns now to the other garden-variety tactic of the enemy: temptation. I indicate the difference between the two: *spiritual desolation* is a heaviness of heart (discouragement, sadness, anxiety) on the spiritual level; *temptation* is a deceptive suggestion of the enemy ("Why don't you let your prayer go till later? You can probably get it in then." "You can let yourself see that. It doesn't always have to get too far out of hand."). Spiritual desolation always involves heaviness of heart; temptation, initially at least, may present itself as attractive.

I note that "garden-variety" does not mean that we may take these two tactics lightly. If we do not resist spiritual desolation and if we succumb to temptation, these will work great spiritual harm—which is the enemy's intention. "Garden-variety" simply means that these are the two basic tactics of the enemy that all of us experience. The magnitude of Ignatius's contribution is evident: if we know and practice his rules, we will find increasing freedom from these two tactics.

If time allows, I recall rules 4 and 7 in which Ignatius explicitly links spiritual desolation and temptation: "disquiet from various agitations and *temptations*" (rule 4: description of spiritual desolation), and "so that he may resist the various agitations and *temptations* of the enemy" (rule 7: why God allows the trial of spiritual desolation). Following Ignatius, I tell my listeners that, generally, temptations (deceptive suggestions of the enemy) will be present in time of spiritual desolation. I say something like this: "We can expect that the enemy's temptations will be floating in and out of our times of spiritual desolation." Having focused earlier on spiritual desolation, Ignatius now turns more explicitly to temptation.

Finally, I add that though the shift in the rules and the distinction between spiritual desolation and temptation are real and to be noted, we do not need to overemphasize this. The shift is slight. Further, as just mentioned, spiritual desolation and temptation will often be found together. And it is the same enemy, with the same goal, who works in both.

I now observe that in the last three rules, Ignatius highlights three qualities of the enemy in his temptations. If we can see these clearly, we will be better equipped to resist them. My listeners now grasp Ignatius's objective in the rules we are about to explore.

The Metaphors of the Final Three Rules

At this point, we must deal with the metaphor of rule 12: "the enemy acts like a woman"! This issue is part of a larger issue, that is, the function of the metaphors in rules 12, 13, and 14.

I note to my listeners that the text of the final three rules tends to be longer than that of the preceding rules. The reason is that in each, Ignatius—as a good pedagogue—presents a metaphor, a parable, a briefly outlined situation, and then draws from it the teaching he wishes us to grasp. These metaphors are the woman fighting with a man (rule 12), the false lover seeking to use another for his selfish purposes (rule 13), and the leader of a group of thieves desiring to sack and pillage a castle (rule 14). I observe for my listeners that, evidently, each situation has something "unnatural" about it, something "anti-human," something contrary to the way God intends things to be. Such *must be* the case because these are metaphors of *the enemy's action*, the one who is, according to the expanded title Ignatius adopts in these three rules, "the enemy of human nature."

Turning now to the metaphor of rule 12—that of the woman fighting the man—I comment that if this metaphor grates on us, if it feels wrong and we find ourselves resisting it, then *we are hearing it well*. This is a metaphor of *the enemy of human nature*; it portrays an anti-human situation: God never intended that woman and man should fight each other but rather that they live in mutual love and self-giving, each for the sake of the other.[1]

In practice, I have never found the metaphor of rule 12 problematic. By this time—it is a blessing that this metaphor is found in rule 12 and not rule 1!—my listeners are convinced of Ignatius's wisdom and are open to his words. The explanation just given generally resolves any difficulties regarding the metaphor. Nonetheless, because these woman-man issues are so culturally charged today, I find it helpful to shift the metaphor. Following another author, I cite the example of parents and a spoiled child.[2] Again, the unnatural quality is present—children are not intended by God to be spoiled—but the metaphor is gentler and easier to apply. The same point can be made without the cultural issues that accompany the original metaphor.

The Text of Rule 12

Now I read the text of rule 12 with some commentary:

> Twelfth Rule. **The twelfth: the enemy acts like a woman in being weak when faced with strength and strong when faced with weakness** [*"weak when faced with strength and strong when faced with weakness"*: this is the quality of the enemy in his temptations that Ignatius wants

us to see]. For, as it is proper to a woman, when she is fighting with some man, to lose heart and to flee when the man confronts her firmly, and, on the contrary, if the man begins to flee, losing heart, the anger, vengeance and ferocity of the woman grow greatly and know no bounds, [this is the metaphor; now the application] **in the same way, it is proper to the enemy to weaken and lose heart, fleeing and ceasing his temptations** [first I highlight the vocabulary of *temptation*, noting Ignatius's use of this word. Then I refer to Ignatius's language at this point of the rule and ask, "Have we ever thought of the enemy as *weakening*, as *losing heart*, as *fleeing*, and just giving up—*ceasing*—his efforts to tempt?" This is wonderful vocabulary! I explain that it is heartening to think of the enemy in these terms, and Ignatius wants us to see this: the enemy's weakness is revealed when we respond to his temptations in the way Ignatius will immediately describe. I add that the enemy is not weak compared to us—he is of a higher (angelic) order of being than we—but to the power of Christ's grace in us] **when the person who is exercising himself in spiritual things confronts the temptations of the enemy firmly, doing what is diametrically opposed to them** ["Why don't you let your prayer go till later?" "No! I planned to pray now, and I will pray now just as I planned." The person does what is diametrically opposed to the enemy's temptation—and the temptation is over. The enemy weakens and flees. . . .]; **and, on the contrary, if the person who is exercising himself begins to be afraid and lose heart in suffering the temptations** ["Why don't you let your prayer go till later?" "Yes, maybe I could. I don't really feel like it now. I'm kind of tired. Perhaps later would be better. I should be able to get it in after supper . . ." I ask, "Will this person ever pray this day?" After a pause to allow my listeners to reflect, I answer, "Very likely, no."], **there is no beast so fierce on the face of the earth as the enemy of human nature** [*the enemy of human nature*: here is the expanded title] **in following out his damnable intention with such growing malice** [a weak response when the temptation first presents itself allows it to grow in power].

Presenting the Key Point

Now I turn to the key point of rule 12, express it, and exemplify it. Ignatius wants us to see, above all, that when the enemy brings his temptations, he is *weak* when *faced with strength* and *strong* when faced with *weakness*.

I return to the metaphor of the spoiled child, and express it like this: "We've all seen those situations in airports or shopping malls in which a young, spoiled child acts out. We know how at times these situations can get totally out of hand. It is as if, Ignatius says, the spoiled child just gets started acting out, stops, cocks his head, looks at his parents, and sees that they are helpless, wringing their hands, supplicating—*on he comes*, and the situation can get totally out of hand. But here is the same spoiled child who just gets started acting out, stops, cocks his head, looks at his parents—and in their eyes sees storm clouds gathering and swift justice about to descend [my listeners are now smiling]—it's over! The only possibility the spoiled child has of acting out is the weakness of his parents in responding when he begins. In the example, I presume that these are loving parents who seek only the good of their child."

Another metaphor has proven very effective. I say it this way: "Here is a high mountain, covered with snow [with arm raised and finger extended, I indicate this high place; all are very attentive at this point]. And here, at the peak, a snowball is just getting started. You can put out a finger and stop it [the gesture of my arm raised and the index finger reaching out to stop the snowball as it just begins is telling—my listeners remember it]. But let the same snowball continue halfway down the mountainside, gaining mass and speed—it will run you over!" [Every eye and every ear in the room is now on me.]

"If this is so," I continue, "then what is the key moment in resisting the enemy's temptations? When is it easiest to resist these temptations? When is it easiest, for example, for the man at 10:00 p.m. to resist the temptation to pick up the smartphone in a 'low and earthly' way?" The group answers readily, "At the very beginning. Before the first touch of the screen." I confirm the answer: "Yes, and we know that after the tenth, fiftieth, and one hundredth touch, the temptation grows harder and harder to resist—and so with other temptations. Temptation is easiest to resist," I conclude, "*in the very beginning*, before the 'snowball' even begins.

"This is why," I add, "rule 12 can save us so much suffering and burden in the spiritual life. This is also why in my book I entitled this chapter 'Standing Firm in the Beginning.'[3] *Stand firm in the very beginning of temptation*: this is Ignatius's insistent invitation in rule 12."

Rule 12 in Practice

With the basic point of rule 12 now clear, I turn to examples to apply and reinforce this teaching. I explore two of these with my listeners.

The Example of Steve

The first example is the experience of Steve. This occurs in a retreat that Steve makes on the verge of ordination to the diaconate.[4]

> Steve has completed seven years of seminary training and is on the verge of ordination to the diaconate, as a preparation for priesthood. He has reached, therefore, the

moment of final preparation for the clerical state of life. [Steve is just weeks away from his definitive commitment to the clerical vocation. In the vocation to marriage, for example, this would be the equivalent of the weeks immediately preceding one's wedding—obviously an important time in the person's life.] His preparation for ordination includes an eight-day Ignatian retreat [in silence, personal prayer with Scripture, and daily meetings with the retreat director], to be made a few weeks before the ceremony. Steve welcomes the opportunity to pray more deeply as he approaches this key moment in his life and willingly prepares for these days of silence and recollection. Steve is an occasional smoker and, before the retreat, decides to abstain from smoking during the eight days of retreat. [I have learned over the years that I must explain this carefully! Steve is an occasional smoker: he might smoke a cigarette once a week or even every two weeks. Steve's decision, therefore, not to smoke during the eight days of the retreat is reasonable; it is a simple and easily achievable ascetical choice for the purpose of being more open to the Lord in these days of prayer. I also comment that, in this scenario, I am not addressing medical issues regarding smoking—only the spiritual significance of Steve's decision and what follows from it.]

The retreat begins and Steve dedicates himself to the daily rhythm of liturgical prayer with the other seminarians, personal prayer with Scripture, and his individual meeting with the director. He finds the silence helpful and enjoys the setting of natural beauty that surrounds the retreat house. He experiences times of peace-filled closeness to God in prayer and an overall sense of well-being in the retreat. [I ask my listeners, "What does Steve appear to experience on these days of the retreat?" All answer readily, "Spiritual consolation."]

After supper on the fourth day, Steve finds that he has lost his former sense of peace. He goes for a walk, but a vague interior disquiet persists. [Here I ask my listeners, "What is Steve experiencing at this point? What can we say about this?" All recognize that Steve is experiencing some desolation. As a learning exercise, I press the question further: "Is this spiritual or nonspiritual desolation?" After some conversation, we conclude that we do not know enough to answer clearly and need to continue to watch the experience as it unfolds. It is useful for my listeners to see that we may not always find clarity immediately when we examine spiritual experience, and that in such cases we do not become anxious but simply continue to be attentive.]

Steve decides to smoke a single cigarette and does so. [I ask, "Spiritually speaking, good decision or bad decision?" All reply, "Bad decision." I ask, "Which rule is involved here?" All answer, "Rule 5." I confirm the answer: "Yes, in a time of at least nonspiritual desolation and perhaps spiritual desolation, Steve changes a spiritual proposal that he had in place before the desolation began—his proposal not to smoke during the retreat." Then I ask, "Spiritually speaking, is the fact that Steve smokes one cigarette during his retreat a matter of life and death?" All answer in the negative. I confirm this answer as well, "Probably not."] He then goes to his room for his final hour of prayer that evening, unhappy that he has not maintained his resolve to avoid smoking during the retreat. As he begins his prayer, he continues to feel restless and ill at ease.

The prayer is distracted and dry, and Steve, finding it difficult, ends the prayer period after forty-five minutes. [Steve had planned to spend an hour in prayer and now, because the prayer is difficult, shortens it to forty-five minutes. I ask, "Good decision, bad decision?" All answer, "Bad decision." I ask, "Which rule?" All answer, "Rule 5." I ask further, "Spiritually speaking, is the fact that Steve shortens his prayer this evening by fifteen minutes a matter of life and death?" All answer in the negative, and I confirm the answer, "Probably not."]

Steve awakens late the next morning and barely arrives in time for morning prayer with the other seminarians. He continues with the times of prayer as planned but finds them empty and burdensome. God seems far away and Steve becomes increasingly frustrated as he strives to pray. [I ask, "What is Steve clearly experiencing now?" All answer, "Spiritual desolation."]

A thought comes to him: "You are about to be ordained a deacon, and you wish to become a priest. Look at you! You can't even keep a simple resolution not to smoke for eight days. You can't complete an hour of prayer as planned. You are unable to pray with any fruit at all, after all these years of training. If you can't even do these simple things, how are you ever going to handle the responsibilities of priesthood for the rest of your life?" [I ask, "Can you see that this sequence has now gotten deadly? Here is Steve, on the verge of his definitive commitment to the clerical state, experiencing thoughts that directly undermine his assurance of this calling." I then ask, "Can you see that *the snowball has now gotten halfway down the mountainside*?" Further, "Can you see that, in terms of waking hours, this is a sequence of only a few hours, the late evening and the next morning? The 'snowball' need not require much time to grow in mass and speed." Then I ask, "What if, the evening before, Steve had not smoked the cigarette? Would the rest of the sequence ever have happened?" I ask further, "And what if Steve *had* smoked the cigarette, but had not shortened his next hour of prayer by fifteen minutes? Would the rest of the sequence ever have happened?" Then I comment, "Can you see that the choices we make in response to seemingly small temptations, when they first come, have much to say about whether the temptations will grow or not?" At this point, the teaching of rule 12 and its power to help us have been made clear.]

In the early afternoon, Steve meets as usual with the retreat director and shares openly with the director all that he has experienced since the day before. [Here our hearts lift, and we sense that Steve's open sharing about this experience with his director will help him find the clarity he needs. I note for my listeners that in speaking openly with his director, Steve is applying rule 13, as we will see shortly.] The sharing relieves his frustration and doubts, and the director helps Steve discern the spiritual movements at work in him. [Be aware, *understand*, take action. When Steve is unable to reach this understanding on his own, he does reach it with the help of his director—again, the point of rule 13 to which we will turn soon.] Steve recovers his peace, continues his retreat with his habitual goodwill, and, a few weeks later, is ordained a deacon. His ordination is the beginning of a rewarding year of diaconate and leads, later, to a fruitful priesthood.

Two Responses to the Tempter

Next, I compare Eve's and Jesus's response to the tempter. In Genesis 3, the tempter approaches Eve and asks, "Did God really say, 'You shall not eat from any of the trees in the garden?'"[5] Eve enters into dialogue with the tempter and answers, "We may eat of the fruit of the trees in the garden; it is only about the fruit of the tree in the middle of the garden that God said, 'You shall not eat it or even touch it, or else you will die. . . .'" The tempter replies, "You certainly will not die. . . ." The process continues—the snowball gains mass and speed—and Eve succumbs, with the unhappy consequences that we know.

In Matthew 4, the tempter approaches Jesus, "If you are the Son of God, command that these stones become loaves of bread." Jesus's reply is immediate, definitive, and it shatters the temptation *in the very moment of its beginning*: "It is written, 'One does not live by bread alone, but by every word that comes forth from the mouth of God.'" Jesus's response to the following temptations is equally immediate and definitive—*and the tempter is undone*. I explain for my listeners that this is where Ignatius would lead us in rule 12.

St. Francis of Assisi

In an early biography of St. Francis of Assisi, we read,

> The saint, therefore, made it a point to keep himself in joy of heart and to preserve the unction of the Spirit and the "oil of gladness" [Ps 45:7]. He avoided with the greatest care the miserable illness of dejection, so that if he felt it creeping over his mind even a little ["*even a little*," that is, when it first begins; this is pure rule 12—we witness here how Francis responds *at the very beginning* of the burden], he would have recourse very quickly to prayer. [The two adverbs *very quickly* perfectly illustrate the response to the enemy's burdens that Ignatius intends: when the discouragement is just beginning, Francis is quickly aware of it and turns *immediately* to prayer.] For he would say, "If the servant of God, as may happen, is disturbed in any way, he should rise immediately [I highlight the adverb *immediately* with a question, "When should he rise?" All reply, "Immediately."] to pray and he should remain in the presence of the heavenly Father until he "restores unto him the joy of salvation" [Ps 51:12].[6]

The Man at 10:00 p.m. and the Woman in Midafternoon

Now I return to the example employed repeatedly in earlier rules: the man who had the disappointing experience that morning at work, who did not go to Mass as usual on his lunch hour, did not pray as usual when he returned from work, and now at 10:00 p.m. he sits at his desk in spiritual desolation, poised between the Bible and the smartphone, feeling the pull to "low and earthly things"; and the woman whose difficult conversation with her college-age daughter left her discouraged and now sits alone in her kitchen in midafternoon, in spiritual desolation, poised between the Bible with the psalms she usually prays at this time and the remote control.

I ask my listeners, "What if, when the disappointing experience occurs at work that morning, the man stops to become aware of what he is feeling, realizes that desolation is just beginning and could grow heavier, turns immediately to prayer, resolves to maintain his usual rhythm of prayer, goes to Mass on his lunch hour, and pray as usual when he returns from work? Then the difficult situation at 10:00 p.m. *will most likely never even occur*. The snowball has been stopped at the top of the mountain. The same can be said of the woman when her discouragement *first begins*; if she, too, responds immediately or shortly after the discouragement begins, she may never even experience that desolate time in midafternoon." When I apply rule 12 in this way to the experience of this man and woman—really, applying it to the experience of us all—I can feel the surge of hope that fills the room.

St. Benedict

I take a final example from St. Benedict's classic Rule.[7] In this Rule, the saint supplies seventy-two "Instruments of Good Works."[8] With my listeners, I examine the fiftieth of these. I cite the beginning of Benedict's text: "As soon as wrongful thoughts come into your heart," and then pause. *As soon as*: I comment that this is pure rule 12—an exploration of how we are to respond in the very beginning of the enemy's temptations.

Then, as an exercise, I invite my listeners to suggest the completion of this sentence: "Before I read the remainder of this text, how might we complete it?" My listeners offer various replies: "As soon as wrongful thoughts come into your heart," "Turn to prayer," "Bring them to the Lord," "Examine the situation," and similar suggestions. I affirm them all, and then read Benedict's full text: "As soon as wrongful thoughts come into your heart, *dash them against Christ* [The figure is striking. We can imagine a piece of pottery, ugly and misshapen because it represents the temptations of the enemy, hurled against a solid mass of stone and so utterly shattered that it can never be restored. This, Benedict says, is what we are to do *as soon as* these wrongful thoughts present themselves], and disclose them to your spiritual father [again, an anticipation of Ignatius's rule 13].[9]

21

A Key Counsel
In Time of Trouble, Do Not Keep Silent!
Rule 13

I begin the presentation of rule 13 in the following way: "When we looked at rule 5, I begged you never to forget this rule, saying that it would get you safely through almost any darkness you might face in the spiritual life. Now I'll complete that statement. I beg of you never to forget rules 5 and 13. These two rules together will get you safely through any darkness you may ever face in the spiritual life. *Do not make changes in the darkness*, and *speak to a wise and competent spiritual person*. If you do these two things, you will come safely through any spiritual darkness you may ever face." As may be imagined, I immediately have the attention of every listener.

I then turn to the text of rule 13 and read it with some commentary:

> Thirteenth Rule. **The thirteenth: likewise he** [the enemy] **conducts himself as a false lover** [the enemy's pleasures are apparent (rule 1) and his reasons false (rule 2); his "love" also is a false love] **in wishing to remain secret and not be revealed.** [This is what Ignatius wants to highlight in rule 13—the enemy's wish, when he brings his burdens to our hearts, *to remain secret and not be revealed.*] [Now the metaphor.] **For a dissolute man who, speaking with evil intention, makes dishonorable advances to a daughter of a good father or a wife of a good husband,**

wishes his words and persuasions to be secret, and the contrary displeases him very much, when the daughter reveals to her father or the wife to her husband his false words and depraved intention, because he easily perceives that he will not be able to succeed with the undertaking begun. [The metaphor is evident. When the dissolute man approaches the upright woman for his selfish ends, his whole urging to her is, "Don't talk about this. You can't talk about this," because he knows that *in the moment itself* that the daughter speaks to her father or the wife to her husband, the game is up. It can only go on as long as she keeps silent; hence his urging to her to keep his "words and persuasions" secret, hidden, unrevealed.]

[Now the application of the metaphor.] **In the same way, when the enemy of human nature** [again, the expanded title of the enemy] **brings his wiles and persuasions to the just soul, he wishes and desires that they be received and kept in secret** [now, in the application of the metaphor, this is the tactic of the enemy that Ignatius highlights]; **but when one reveals them** [this is to be our response to the enemy's tactic: *to reveal them to a wise and competent spiritual person*] **to** [Ignatius will now delineate two profiles of such wise and competent spiritual persons] **one's good confessor or to another spiritual person, who knows his deceits and malicious designs, it weighs on him very much, because he perceives that he will not be able to succeed with the malicious undertaking he has begun, since his manifest deceits have been revealed.** [As in the metaphor, the enemy knows that the "game" is up.]

Highlighting the Elements of Rule 13

With my listeners I review the various elements of the rule. I examine these following the text itself.

A Key Counsel 219

The Enemy's Tactic: Keep These Burdens Secret

This is what the enemy wants: when we feel his discouraging, energy-sapping, heavy burdens in our hearts, *we keep these secret*, that we speak of these with no one. The enemy desires that these burdens "be *received* [when they first arise] and *kept* [in the subsequent days, weeks, months, even years] in secret." In this way, the burden will continue to weigh, to reduce our freedom to love and serve the Lord.

What We Are to Keep Hidden

What does the enemy "wish and desire" that we keep hidden? Ignatius describes this as the enemy's "wiles and persuasions": his troubling temptations, doubts, fears, the burdens that cause us to lose our peace in the spiritual life.

"Here," I tell my listeners, "perhaps more than at any other point in this teaching, I need to speak with great reverence. I know that this may touch deep places in our hearts. These burdens may include things that have happened in the past, even many years ago, about which we've never said anything. They may involve things happening in our lives now about which we've never spoken to anyone. At times, we feel God's love come close, and we say to ourselves, 'I would feel so free to receive God's love and to love God in return . . . were it not for . . . And there it is: the burden, the thing that holds me back, the weight in my heart that makes me afraid.' And the enemy's urging is, 'You can't speak about this. About other things, yes, but not about this.'" As may be imagined, the room is deeply attentive as I express this. Rule 13 is speaking to my listeners' hearts. We must present this with great reverence!

The Nonspiritual and the Spiritual

"This," I tell my listeners, "is another point in which the distinction between the nonspiritual and the spiritual is of great importance for the accurate application of a rule. If a person bears deep psychological wounds, perhaps resulting from trauma of one kind or another, it would be a terrible misapplication of rule 13 to say to this person, in the name of this rule, 'Well, Ignatius says that we must not keep silent. And so, though it tears your heart apart, you need to find someone and say everything about this now.'

"This person," I continue further, "does need to find freedom from this burden. This is a nonspiritual (psychological) captive who needs to find nonspiritual (psychological) freedom. This person *does* need to speak with someone. But deep psychological wounds should be shared with a professionally trained and competent psychologist or counselor, able to understand and wisely assist the person toward freedom. This psychologist or counselor, however, will never insist that in a first meeting the person put everything into words. He or she will allow a relationship of trust to build over time, so that the person, most likely gradually, will find increasing ease in speaking and so move toward freedom."

I continue, "Having said this, it remains true that we may carry spiritual burdens in our hearts that we *can*, perhaps with some courage, speak about with a wise and competent spiritual person and so find freedom from them. This is Ignatius's warm and insistent invitation in rule 13."

With Whom Should We Speak?

We should not speak with just anyone! With economy of words, Ignatius presents two profiles of the person with whom we should speak. I unpack for my listeners the dense content of Ignatius's description of both.

The first is "one's good confessor." Each of these three words is significant. This is a priest, a *confessor*, one who hears sacramental confessions. This is not just any priest, any confessor, but a *good* confessor. "Good," in this context, as Ignatius immediately clarifies, means more than devout, as commendable as this is. "Good" here signifies *knowledgeable*—one "who *knows* his [the enemy's] deceits and malicious designs." This is a priest who, when people share their spiritual burdens, will be competent to understand their sharing and wise in helping them because he *knows* the enemy's tactics. Finally, this is *one's* good confessor, that is, the person has had sufficient contact with this priest in the sacrament of Confession to know personally that this is a good (knowledgeable) confessor. It is a compelling portrait of a priest!

The second profile is broader: "or another spiritual person, who knows his [the enemy's] deceits and malicious designs." This profile may include persons of all vocations—lay, religious, and clerical. What qualifies this person to be the recipient of another's sharing is that this person is *spiritual*. Again, as Ignatius immediately specifies, "spiritual" here means more than devout, as commendable as this is. This person is spiritual because this person "*knows* his [the enemy's] deceits and malicious designs." Like the confessor, this man or woman is knowledgeable, conversant with the enemy's tactics, and so competent to receive the sharing of one burdened by them. This spiritual person will understand what is being said and know wisely how to assist the troubled person to freedom. Again, this is a compelling portrait!

I emphasize for my listeners that when our hearts are burdened by the enemy, care must be taken to speak to a person who fits one or the other of these profiles. To share with a person who, though devout, is not knowledgeable, may well lead to unintended but real harm.

I comment that one of the happiest things in my work as a retreat director, spiritual director, and confessor has been those times when I receive another's sharing of spiritual burdens: *you see before your eyes* captives set free.

St. Thérèse of Lisieux: An Example of Rule 13 in Practice

I now explore in some detail an experience of St. Thérèse that aptly illustrates rule 13.[1] This event occurs the evening before

Thérèse professes perpetual vows as a Carmelite. I explain for my listeners the background to this account. From an early age, Thérèse has been sure of her vocation to Carmel. She desires to enter at age fifteen, and moves heaven and earth to attain this goal. Thérèse gains her father's permission and, after some struggle, that of her uncle. When the priest entrusted with the direction of the monastery withholds permission, Thérèse speaks to the bishop. When the bishop, too, is not ready to permit her entrance at so young an age, Thérèse—breaking all protocol—begs the permission of Pope Leo XIII when she encounters him during a pilgrimage to Rome. The pope refers Thérèse to her superiors and tells her that she will enter if God wills it.

The vicar general of the diocese, however, who witnessed this scene, grew convinced of the authenticity of Thérèse's vocation, even at so young an age, and assisted her entrance into Carmel at fifteen. Thérèse has entered, has lived the years of postulancy and novitiate, ever certain of her vocation, and now has reached the threshold of her vows. To prepare, Thérèse makes a retreat that will end only with the ceremony of her vows. This is the final day of retreat, and it is now evening.

The community has gathered to pray the Divine Office for a final time this day. After the Office, the sisters remain in silent prayer for some minutes and then go to their rooms to rest. The silence will continue until the ceremony the next morning. Such is the setting for Thérèse's account. She writes,

> The *beautiful day* of my wedding [her perpetual vows, her espousal to Christ as a religious sister] finally arrived. It was without a single cloud; however, the preceding evening a storm arose in my soul, the like of which I'd never seen before.
>
> Not a single doubt concerning my vocation had ever entered my mind until then [it would be difficult to find, in our spiritual tradition, a vocation that was embraced

earlier in life and with similar certainty: from age nine, no doubt about her Carmelite vocation has ever entered Thérèse's mind], and it evidently was necessary that I experience this trial. [In this we can hear Ignatius's rule 9, the second reason why God allows spiritual desolation: as a *trial* from which growth results. Thérèse demonstrates a remarkable clarity in her perception of this experience—the lucidity of the saints.]

In the evening, while making the Way of the Cross after Matins [the final prayer of the Divine Office for which the sisters have gathered], my vocation appeared to me as a *dream*, a chimera. I found life in Carmel to be very beautiful, but the devil inspired me with the assurance [*assurance*—this is a strong word!] that it wasn't for me and that I was misleading my Superiors by advancing on this way to which I wasn't called. The darkness was so great that I could understand one thing only: I didn't have a vocation. Ah! how can I possibly describe the *anguish* in my soul? [We can perhaps glimpse a little of this anguish. Here is a young woman who has overcome all obstacles to her vocation, has never doubted it, has prepared in the monastery for the past years, is on the verge of perpetual vows, with all prepared for the ceremony the next morning—and now, in the silence of this evening, understands that she never was called to Carmel, that she was misleading her superiors . . . Anguish is certainly the right word.]

It appeared to me (and this is an absurdity that shows it was a temptation [Thérèse names the experience clearly for what it is] from the devil [she names its origin with equal clarity]) that if I were to tell my Novice Mistress about these fears, she would prevent me from pronouncing my Vows. [I ask my listeners to note the *imagined scenario* that runs through Thérèse's mind: Thérèse sees herself approach the novice mistress, ask her to speak, sees the novice mistress agree, sees them find a quiet room, sees herself share this new certitude that she is not called to Carmel, sees the novice mistress gently nod agreement and tell her that, if this is the case, we'll cancel the ceremony for tomorrow, let your family know, and set things in motion so that you can return home. The *imagined scenario* says: if you talk about this with your novice mistress, it will be unbearably painful; it will be the death of all you've ever hoped for vocationally.] And still I wanted to do God's will and return to the world rather than remain in Carmel and do my own will. [Thérèse never wavers in her desire to do God's will; it is only her understanding of God's will that, in this darkness, has become confused.]

I made the Novice Mistress come out of the choir [The choir is the place of common prayer for the community. I say to the group that most likely women, more than men, will understand the courage this requires of Thérèse. Here is the youngest member of the community, whom all know to be on verge of vows, in full sight of all and in obvious distress asking the novice mistress to speak. The sisters will not find it difficult to guess that vocational struggles may be involved. But if Thérèse is to speak with her novice mistress this evening, this is her last opportunity. Within minutes, the novice mistress will retire to her room until the next morning. Thérèse is shown here to be a woman of courage, a woman of spiritual steel.] and, filled with confusion [this is not easy for her], I told her the state of my soul. Fortunately, she saw things much clearer than I did, and she completely reassured me. [The novice mistress is Thérèse's wise and competent spiritual person. She is an experienced religious, has probably seen many times such struggles in the imminence of vows, knows Thérèse well, and has no difficulty in reassuring

A Key Counsel

Thérèse of the authenticity of her vocation. The sequel has abundantly vindicated the novice mistress!] The act of humility I had just performed put the devil to flight since he had perhaps thought that I would not dare admit my temptation. [*since he had perhaps thought that I would not dare admit my temptation*: this is precisely the tactic of the enemy that Ignatius highlights in rule 13— you can't speak about this, you have to keep this hidden, unrevealed.]

My doubts left me completely as soon as I finished speaking.[2] [I say to my listeners, "You could take this sentence, print it in elegant letters, frame it, and put it on the wall of your room. These are words of spiritual beauty: "My doubts left me *completely* as soon as I finished speaking." These words are pure rule 13. I invite my listeners to note a further aspect of these words. When do Thérèse's doubts leave her? *As soon as she finishes speaking.* Simply expressing her doubts openly to the proper competent spiritual person completely undoes them, and Thérèse is set free. Finally, I ask my listeners to note the difference between the *imagined scenario* (I tell the novice mistress of my new certitude that I have no vocation to Carmel, she agrees, she sets things in motion for me to return home, it is unbearably painful and the death of my vocational hopes) and the *real scenario* (I tell the novice mistress of this my certitude that I have no vocation to Carmel, she fully reassures me, my doubts leave me completely, and the road to vows once more lies open for me). *The difference between the two* lays bare the enemy's tactic. I tell my listeners that there will always be an imagined scenario, and it will always be painful. The real scenario, that is, when we speak openly with a wise and competent spiritual person, will be very different.]

Nevertheless, to make my act of humility even more perfect, I still wished to confide my strange temptation to our Mother Prioress, who simply laughed at me. [I ask my listeners, "Do you remember Ignatius's counsel to persons in desolation who are tempted to shorten their prayer? What does Ignatius advise them to do?" The group answers, "Add a little more time to the prayer." I continue, "That is what Thérèse does here. The enemy is already defeated, but Thérèse takes a further step as well to utterly destroy the enemy's temptation: she also speaks of it with her prioress. The prioress, who knows Thérèse well, simply laughs, "Thérèse, we know you. We know there is no doubt about your vocation."]

In the morning of September 8, I felt as though I were flooded with a river of peace, and it was in this peace "which surpasses all understanding" [Phil 4:7] that I pronounced my Holy Vows. [I ask my listeners, "What is Thérèse experiencing as she professes her vows?" All answer, "Spiritual consolation."]

Now I ask my listeners two questions. "What if," I ask, "that evening, Thérèse had *not* spoken with her novice mistress? Would she have professed her vows the next morning in 'a river of peace'?" All reply, "Most likely not." I pursue the question further. "What might she have carried in her heart for years? We all know that every genuine vocation can be tested, at times severely, and there it would be: 'You knew that you weren't called, and you didn't say anything.' The door to all that anguish and doubt," I continue, "*is shut*, because Thérèse no sooner feels the enemy's burdens than she immediately approaches her wise and competent spiritual person, shares openly, *and it is over*."

I then say, "Let's ask a second question. What if, that evening, Thérèse *had* spoken, not to her novice mistress but perhaps to another novice, no further along in religious life than she? Would she have professed her vows in 'a river of peace'? What might she have carried for years to come?" Again, my listeners grasp the point clearly: speak to the right wise and competent spiritual person.

Thomas Merton: Rule 13 Applied— After Some Hesitation!

If time allows, I add a second example, this time from Thomas Merton's *The Seven Storey Mountain*.[3] This serves as a helpful foil to Thérèse's experience. Thérèse applies Ignatius's counsel quickly and fully: she speaks immediately with her wise and competent spiritual person. Merton also applies rule 13 but only after some delay and with greater struggle than Thérèse. His experience may, at times, be more like our own!

Merton has entered the Catholic Church and is teaching at St. Bonaventure University in southwestern New York State. While there, he visits the Trappist monastery in Gethsemane, Kentucky, and for the first time wonders if God might be calling him to priesthood in the monastic life. Months pass, and the question returns from time to time. This evening, at St. Bonaventure's, it surfaces with great urgency. Merton writes, "By now, the question had resolved itself into one practical issue: Why don't I consult somebody about the whole question?" Obviously, we are in rule 13 terrain!

Merton struggles with a significant spiritual issue. As he does, a competent spiritual person is available, Franciscan Father Philotheus, whom Merton describes as "a wise and good philosopher." Merton knows that Father Philotheus will be willing to speak with him and that the conversation will be helpful. But Merton hesitates, as he explains, "There was one absurd, crazy thing that held me up. . . . It amounted to a vague subconscious fear that I would once and for all be told that I definitely had no vocation. It was the fear of an ultimate refusal." Like Thérèse,

Merton experiences an *imagined scenario*: if you speak, it will be the death of your vocational hopes; it will be unbearably painful.

Merton makes a first attempt to speak with Father Philotheus. He goes out to the courtyard and sees that the light is on is Father Philotheus's room. Instead of approaching the room, however, Merton bolts out into the darkness and heads for a shrine on the university grounds dedicated to St. Thérèse. Merton paces in front of her statue and prays for the courage to speak to Father Philotheus. Finally, he returns, approaches the priest's room, nears the door—and again runs out into the evening darkness and the shrine.

After anguished prayer and further hesitation, Merton makes a third attempt. When he returns to the building, he sees that the light is now out in Father Philotheus's room. One hope remains, the priests' common room, a room Merton has never dared to approach before. Now he knocks on the door, opens it, and finds only one priest there—Father Philotheus. Merton asks to speak with him, and the priest agrees. Merton writes, "That was the end of all my anxiety.... As soon as I proposed all my hesitations and questions to him, Father Philotheus said that he could see no reason why I shouldn't want to enter a monastery and become a priest." Merton reflects, "It may seem irrational [it won't to us, in light of rule 13], but at that moment it was as if scales fell off my own eyes, and looking back on all my worries and questions, I could see clearly how empty and future they had been.... Already I was full of peace and assurance—the consciousness that everything was right, and that a straight road had opened out, clear and smooth, ahead of me."

Again, the difference between the *imagined scenario* (I speak with Father Philotheus, he confirms that I should not pursue priesthood, it is the death of my vocational hopes, it is unbearably painful) and the *real scenario* (I speak with Father Philotheus, he answers my worries and questions, the path to priesthood lies open before me, I find great peace and clarity) is evident. One

A Key Counsel

thing is different, however, in the two accounts: whereas Thérèse speaks immediately with her competent spiritual person, Merton hesitates, and we witness a "back-and-forth" as he attempts to speak, fails, tries again, fails once more, and finally, on his third attempt, finds the courage to speak.

I comment for my listeners, "At times, we may be like Merton. We know that we need to speak about a burden in our spiritual lives. We also know that there is a competent spiritual person with whom we could speak. But a month goes by . . . then a second month, and perhaps more time still—until, by God's grace, we find the courage to approach this person and speak." My listeners all recognize this dynamic. When we do speak, as Ignatius says, "it weighs on him [the enemy] very much, because he perceives that he will not be able to succeed with the malicious undertaking he has begun, since his manifest deceits have been revealed."

At this point, I recall the experience of Steve (rule 12) who makes the retreat, smokes the cigarette, shortens his prayer, enters spiritual desolation, and begins to doubt his vocation to the priesthood. I say to my listeners, "Steve got every other rule wrong, but *he got rule 13 right*: he spoke openly with his director about his desolate experience. And rule 13 saw him safely through his darkness." I add, "If we can use this term of spiritual things, this is a 'success' story." Because he follows Ignatius's counsel in rule 13, Steve remains unharmed by the enemy's attempts to weaken his vocational certitude. I affirm once more the power of rule 13 to bring us safely through times of spiritual darkness.

Identifying the Enemy's Tactic in Practice

Over the years, I have found it helpful to express the enemy's tactic in the ways my listeners may experience it in their own lives.[4] If you do this with your listeners, you must speak with great reverence: what you say may touch deep places in your listeners' hearts. And this must be a message of hope! Ignatius's message in rule 13 is *the call to freedom* from the enemy's urging to secrecy.

I exemplify the various ways that we may experience the enemy's incitement to silence. I present these by saying, "We might seldom articulate the enemy's urgings this clearly, but if we were to put the enemy's tactic into words, it might sound something like this:

"I Could Speak with Him or Her, But He/She Is Too Busy."

Always let that person make this decision. You need not hesitate for this reason to approach him or her. Spiritual guides will take responsibility for their own time and will let you know whether or not they are too busy to meet.

"I Wish I Could Speak with Him/Her, But I Am Too Busy."

If this is an especially pressured week or two, I can grant that this may be so. But if three, four, or six months have passed, and you are still too busy, then you need to begin to think in terms of rule 13: there is an enemy who does not wish you to speak.

"If I Talk about This, He/She Will Laugh at Me."

This may be the most painful imagined scenario of all. Do not let this stop you. If the person you approach is truly the good confessor or spiritual person Ignatius describes, this person will not laugh but rather reverence the deep place in your heart that seeks healing.

"If I Talk about This, He/She Will Never Understand Me."

Again, if this person is truly the good confessor or spiritual person whom Ignatius intends, this person will understand. When you have identified such a person, do not let this imagined scenario prevent you from speaking.

"If I Talk about This, He/She Will Be Kind about It But Will Never Respect Me in the Same Way Again."

The same as the preceding. Genuinely competent guides will love and reverence your courage in speaking about this burden. Their respect for you will increase.

"If I Talk about This, He/She Will Gently Reply, 'If That Is Part of Your Life and That Is Who You Are, Then We Can No Longer Work Together.'"

The same as the preceding.

"What's the Point of Talking about This? There Is Nothing Anyone Can Say That Will Change Things."

This imagined scenario says that "no words of any spiritual person can help in my situation." This is obviously not true, as experience repeatedly shows. But even if the spiritual person were to say little, the simple act *of putting the burden into words* in that setting will already effectively begin healing. Never let this thought stop you from speaking.

"We Always Have Need of a Guide"

Having expressed the above, we can now make a fundamental point to our listeners about the discerning life: we are not intended to live this alone, in isolation. As rule 13 clearly shows, Ignatius always presumes accompaniment in the discerning life.[5]

I cite God's words from the very origins, "It is not good for the man to be alone" (Gn 2:18).[6] The creation of woman and the mutual belonging of man and woman follow. This principle—that it is not good for us to be alone—applies broadly to human experience. It applies to the spiritual life and it underlies Ignatius's rule 13: it is not good for us to be alone on the spiritual journey, and certainly it is not good for us to be alone in living the discerning life.

Benedict XVI writes,

> To advance toward the Lord [this is what all of us want, not to remain static in the spiritual life but to advance, progress, grow, in love and service of the Lord; we would not be here today were this not our desire], we always have need of a guide [this could not be said more clearly], of a dialogue [some setting in which we are not spiritually alone, in which we can speak]. We cannot do it with just our own reflections. [I say to my listeners, "If I may reverently say this, those of us who *have* tried to do it just with our own reflections, know the truth of this, know how we felt 'stuck' in the spiritual life, like the hamster in the cage, running, expending energy, but always with the same doubts, the same uncertainties."] And finding this guide is part of the ecclesial nature of our faith. [This is why Jesus founded a church: we are not meant to be alone in the spiritual life but to assist each other along the way.]"[7]

I have my listeners' full attention as I make these comments: they are reflecting on their own experience and asking themselves how they might benefit from such accompaniment in the future.

Finding Accompaniment in the Discerning Life

If time permits and the group desires—often my listeners will raise this question—I review various forms of accompaniment in the discerning life.

- *Spiritual Direction.* This generally entails a monthly meeting for an hour with a competent spiritual director. Where this is possible, this is a classic and fruitful way to be accompanied in the discerning life. If regular meetings are not possible, the occasional meetings that are possible may prove very helpful.

- *Confession.* If we can find a confessor (Ignatius's "good confessor") who is helpful and to whom we can go regularly, his brief words of spiritual accompaniment may assist us greatly. This means is accessible to many; if we find it, we have found a spiritual treasure.
- *Retreats.* If we make an annual retreat of a day, a weekend, or more days, as our commitments allow, we will have, at least annually, a chance to speak with a director. A conversation or two in such retreats may open other possibilities of accompaniment and bless the entire year.
- *Spiritual Friends.* Here, no one attempts to be a spiritual director but simply a friend in the Lord with whom it is possible to speak about spiritual things. A meeting for coffee, a phone conversation, a video conversation, a gathering of friends for brunch: in many settings, such sharing with a friend or group of friends may provide great encouragement in living the rules.
- *The Parish.* Liturgical prayer together, activities, groups of spiritual formation: in many ways, the parish may offer avenues of accompaniment on the spiritual journey.
- *Married Couples.* Where possible, husbands and wives—in a way unique to this vocation—may accompany each other in the discerning life. Neither attempts to be the spiritual director of the other; they simply accompany each other, provide a place for sharing and mutual encouragement on the journey.
- *Mixtures of These Forms of Accompaniment.* If more than one and even several of these means are adopted simultaneously, each will strengthen the other.

I invite my listeners to consider how they will find accompaniment in living the Ignatian wisdom we are exploring. Finally, I note for my listeners that this accompaniment will most likely be decisive in regards to *sustaining* the discerning life. If we desire that the Ignatian wisdom we have learned here not fade, that it remain a part of our lives, grow, and become increasingly helpful, the absence or presence of some form of accompaniment will most likely determine this outcome.

22

Hope Where Your Listeners Have the Least Hope
Rule 14

I begin rule 14 with a quick glance at rules 12 and 13 that prepares for the newness of rule 14: "If in rule 12, Ignatius wants us to see the enemy's weakness if we are willing to stand firm in the beginning of his temptations; and if in rule 13, Ignatius wants us to see the enemy's desire that we keep his temptations and burdens secret; in rule 14, Ignatius wants us to see the *enemy's astute sense of our weakest point*, the fact that he will *attack us right there*, and *how we can undo his tactic.*"

Then I say, "Ignatius, in a sense, saves the best for last. It may be that one or another of us, as we've gone through these rules, has said to himself or herself, 'Well, Fr. Gallagher, all of this is good, and I can see how it's going to help in some ways. But . . . there is still this one area, this one matter, this one struggle that is not going to change and in which I'm going to continue to fail.' Said with different words, 'In general, I can resist the enemy, but not in this one area.' *Right there*—Ignatius wants to bring hope. He does not wish his rules to end without addressing this deep place in our hearts and awakening hope where we feel the least hope."

As I say this, I sense that these words speak to my listeners, and to some in particular, in a deep way. Rule 14 has already taken on life for them.

Then I make a further key point, and one that frees my listeners to receive rule 14 with open hearts. I tell them, "Just as there is no shame in experiencing spiritual desolation, *there is no shame in having a weakest point.* We all do. It may arise from our individual temperaments, from the years of our lives, from experiences we've undergone, or all of this together. This is simply what it means to live in a fallen, redeemed, and loved world." I pursue this further: "There is no shame in having a weakest point. What *does matter* is to be aware, understand, and take action—to know that weakest point and to work to strengthen it. Then the weakest point becomes the cutting edge of growth. If this weakest point is where we are most vulnerable and exposed to attack, it is also, therefore, the point where growth will most help us."

If we say this to our listeners, then any sense of shame or burden as we explore rule 14 is removed. Here, as throughout, it is essential that we reverence the hearts of our listeners. When our listeners feel safe, they will receive the teaching. And these words are not simply a well-intentioned attempt to comfort; these words comfort *because they are true.* Our listeners sense this as we speak.

The Text of the Rule and Commentary

Now I read and comment on the text of rule 14:

> Fourteenth Rule. **The fourteenth: likewise he** [the enemy] **conducts himself as a leader, intent upon conquering and robbing what he desires.** [The word *robbing* tells us that this is not a noble leader fighting for a just cause. This leader—as we would expect in a metaphor of the enemy—is ignoble, the head of a band of brigands and thieves, whose single purpose is to pillage, sack, and rob for material gain, with utter disregard for the pain and death he inflicts.] **For, just as a captain and leader of an army in the field, pitching his camp and exploring the fortifications and defenses of a stronghold, attacks it at the weakest point** [this is the metaphor; now the application],

in the same way the enemy of human nature, roving about, looks in turn at all our theological, cardinal and moral virtues [this is Ignatius's way of saying, in classical theological language (our theological, cardinal, and moral virtues)[1], that the enemy explores the whole of our spiritual lives—our prayer, our ministry, our life in the church, our vocation, our relationships with others, what gives us hope and strength, what discourages us and makes us afraid, everything]; **and where he finds us weakest and most in need for our eternal salvation, there** [*por allí*, "right there"] **he attacks us and attempts to take us.**

The Metaphor in More Detail

I return now to the metaphor and examine it in more detail. My listeners follow with close attention. A slide with an image of the kind of town Ignatius intends adds life to the narration.

I recall for my listeners how in Ignatius's Europe, towns were built in elevated places and surrounded with walls for reasons of defense. "Here," I say, "is one such town in Ignatius's Spain. On this day, the townspeople look out over their walls and see in the distance a band of motley and rag-tag, but deadly, brigands approaching. As they watch, the brigands set up camp on the plain below. And as they continue to watch, they see the leader of these brigands, accompanied by his lieutenants, ride up the hill and closer to the walls, still safely out of distance of shot, and slowly ride the circuit of the walls. They see him study the approach of the land, the strength and repair of the walls, the towers, and the gate. And as they watch, they see the moment when he *finds the weakest point in their defenses*. A less experienced eye might not perceive the weakness of this point—perhaps, for example, behind a facade of strength, the masonry at that point is weak and crumbling—but the astute eye of this leader misses nothing. Shortly after, the attack begins precisely at that point."

I continue, "Of what value to the townspeople are walls ten feet thick of stone, if in one place the walls are in disrepair and exposed to assault? The defenses *are only as strong as the weakest point*."

I ask, "Now if that is the tactic of the enemy, what is to be our response?" I return to the metaphor and make explicit the response that Ignatius intends. "Here," I say, "is a day of peace, when the townspeople are not under attack. They gather together, and the leader says to them, 'You know, from time to time bands of plunderers attack us. Let us examine the state of our defenses.' And so the leader, accompanied by his assistants, rides out of the gate, and at a short distance from the walls, slowly examines the entirety of the defenses. He studies the approach of the land, the strength and repair of the walls, the towers, and the gate. And the moment comes when *he finds the weakest point*—that place where, behind the outer appearance, the masonry is weak and crumbling. The townspeople now set to work. They strip away the crumbling stone and replace it with strong and solid masonry."

I continue, "Then a day comes when the band of brigands approaches. The townspeople see them set up camp on the plain below. As they watch, the leader, accompanied by his lieutenants, rides up the hill and closer to the walls, still safely out of distance of shot, and slowly makes the circuit of the walls. They see him study the approach of the land, the strength and repair of the walls, the towers, and the gate. But this time, things are different. *The weak point is no longer weak*. Now the enemy has only two choices: to attack at that point in the face of strong defenses, or to attack at another point that also will be stronger than the former weak point. The enemy's task is now much harder and his victory less certain."

I tell my listeners, "This is where Ignatius leads us in rule 14. This is what we must do spiritually: know, see clearly, our weakest point, and work to strengthen it."

Identifying the Weak Point

I then propose a series of questions to help my listeners begin, at least, to name the weak point.[2] This, too, must be done with reverence, knowing that it may touch deep places in my listeners, and always with a view to hope: such self-knowledge is the first step toward freedom—toward strengthening the weak point. It is beautiful to see people who, perhaps at length, have had no hope, begin to hope that freedom is possible.

I tell my listeners that all of the following questions are variations on a single question:

- *Is there some situation that frequently discourages me? That frequently strips me of spiritual energy?* I note the word *frequently*: things are going well spiritually, and then this happens again.

- *Are there circumstances in which I often become afraid?* Afraid in my relationship with God. This happens often enough that I can see a pattern.

- *In which I often become worn out?* Tired, worn down spiritually.

- *In which I feel spiritually helpless?* With the sense that "I can't avoid this," "I'm going to fail," "I'm helpless."

- *Is there one recurring way in which I find myself spiritually weakened?* "Recurring"—one way that I can identify as standing out, repeating more often than others, and more debilitating.

- *Does one thing seem to diminish most of my energy to love and serve others?* Life is going on, my spiritual practices are in place . . . and then this happens, and all my spiritual energy fails. I sit in my room, feeling like I can't do this anymore.

- *Is there something that habitually disheartens me in prayer?* That makes it hard for me to approach God with joy, with openness.

- *Is there something that causes me to doubt God's love for me?* We need to be aware that this question can touch places of pain in our listeners' hearts: "That vulnerable place is touched, and it's hard to feel that God loves me."

- *Is there a repeating pattern of these experiences?* The repeating pattern of attack in this place that hurts and weakens me is the sign that I am in rule 14 terrain.

I conclude the review of these questions with a strong reaffirmation of the hope rule 14 offers: once we identify this vulnerable point and work to strengthen it, something very happy begins to occur. On a deep level, we are set free—right where we felt ourselves most captive.

Know Thyself

Self-knowledge, therefore, is central to rule 14. I remind my listeners of the ancient adage: Know thyself. To forestall any uneasiness, I examine briefly what these two words mean. To know ourselves is, before anything else, to know *that we are loved.* Most deeply, we are beloved sons and daughters of our heavenly Father, brothers and sisters of the Jesus who loved us to the death. This is our fundamental identity. Self-knowledge, understood thus, is a joyful thing!

Having recalled this profound truth, we may then approach self-knowledge in the sense of where this deep, joyful identity is most vulnerable to attack—the focus of rule 14. We desire to know this vulnerable point so that, perceiving it, we may fortify it and grow increasingly free to live our identity as God's beloved sons and daughters.

If time allows and as seems appropriate for the specific group, I review the spiritual means that help us strengthen the vulnerable point: a life of faithful daily prayer and the sacraments, some form of spiritual accompaniment, the examen prayer, spiritual reading with regard to this point, and the like.[3] I also mention that if nonspiritual issues (psychological pain and the like) underlie the spiritually vulnerable point, suitable nonspiritual means (for example, counseling) may assist the effort to strengthen the spiritually weak point. As classic theology teaches, grace presupposes and builds on nature—all that strengthens our humanity creates a richer base for grace to work.

Rule 14 in Practice: An Example

The story of Venerable Matt Talbot engages my listeners and helps illustrate rule 14 in practice. I find, too, that because his most vulnerable point was alcohol, my listeners—most of whom do not have this problem or, if they have had it in the past, have now overcome it—can hear his story without feeling personally questioned. Matt's story of conversion is fascinating and beautiful. It exemplifies rule 14 well and engenders hope that liberation is possible even from long-standing and deep-seated vulnerabilities.[4]

On June 7, 1925, a man walking through the streets of Dublin on his way to Sunday Mass collapsed and died. At the hospital, he was identified as Matt Talbot, a sixty-nine-year-old worker in a timber yard. The instruments of penance found on his body first alerted viewers to his remarkable spiritual journey. Many attended his funeral on June 11, and six years later his cause of canonization was introduced. In 1975, Pope Paul VI declared him venerable, an official witness to his heroic virtue.

When Matt was twelve, he abandoned the little education he had received, equivalent to the first and a part of the second grade. He began work as a messenger boy for a firm of wine merchants and by the following year was a complete alcoholic. For the next fifteen years, he lived an alcoholic's life, spending his wages at the pubs and then begging, pawning, doing whatever he could to obtain the alcohol his body craved.

The moment of grace arrived when Matt was twenty-eight. One day, when he had no money, he stood outside the pub as his "friends" entered, hoping that someone would invite him in for a drink. None did, either because they did not care or because they pitied what he had become. He went home to his mother and told her that he was going to take the pledge, a promise to abstain from alcohol. She told him not to take it unless he meant it. Matt took the pledge for three months, then six, then for life. From that day, he never touched a drop of alcohol.

But it was a bitter struggle. Matt knew that he was too weak to be on the streets where the pubs awaited. He also knew that he needed a place where he would find strength. He began attending Mass in the early morning before work; when work was finished, he returned again to church. He stayed in church for several Masses on Sundays. And this man, desperate for God's help, attempted to pray, while every cell in his body cried out for alcohol. Again and again, Matt made this prayer: "Lord, in your mercy, give me the gift of prayer." Slowly prayer grew less painful. Gradually it became easier and then began to draw him. Finally, it transformed him.

Matt sought the help of a priest who guided him in his efforts. This laborer in a timber yard, who had had so little education, began reading spiritual books. Slowly, painstakingly, he read the Bible, the Confessions of St. Augustine, the writings of St. Francis de Sales, and others. On lunch break one day, a fellow worker saw Matt reading the *Apologia pro Vita Sua* of John Henry Newman. When his companion asked if Matt found the reading difficult, Matt simply replied that the Lord helped him.

Matt knew that he could not hope to deny his body alcohol if he allowed it all else it desired. So he began a life of strict penance.

He simplified his food. He observed the fasts of the Church and more. He slept on a wooden plank with a block of wood for a pillow. And he adopted the instruments of bodily penance found on him at his death.

His fellow workers knew Matt simply as a quiet man and good worker, ready to help others. His full story was discovered only after his death, and it remains an inspiration for thousands. This was a man *who knew his weakest point*. He built his whole spiritual life on strengthening that weakest point, and *it made him a saint*. This is the hope and the gift of rule 14.

I conclude for my listeners that our individual points of vulnerability may be, like Matt's, evident and dramatic. More often they may be hidden, known just to a few or only to us who experience their effects in our lives. To identify them and strengthen them releases great energy and fosters great growth on the spiritual journey.

23

Concluding the Teaching

When I present the rules, I always try to leave time at the end for questions. I enjoy this part of the presentation. The "work" is done at this point, and my listeners have a solid grasp of the material. Invariably, their questions are good; they complete and consolidate the teaching received.

Generally, I do not invite questions earlier. Most often, questions arise spontaneously during the teaching, and I answer them as they are raised. This interaction with my listeners is welcome to me and to them, and the questions are usually helpful for the group. If the questions are not helpful, I reply in a way that reverences the one asking and is useful for the listeners as a whole.

But generally I do not ask for questions earlier, and for two reasons. One is that time is limited: fourteen rules—or as many as time allows—are a lot to cover! The other is that if I invite questions too soon—this is different from answering questions when my listeners themselves raise them—time will be lost. Many of these questions will be answered by the subsequent unfolding of the material. When a listener raises a question that I know will be addressed later in the teaching, I tell him or her that we will be addressing this soon. I add that the question is excellent and shows that the listener is thinking right with Ignatius, who also knows that this question must be addressed. I may ask that if the question does not seem adequately answered later on, the person raise it again. This way that person knows that I am not trying to dodge the question!

Concluding the Teaching

Now that the presentation is complete, however, a time for questions is opportune. Generally my listeners—and I with them—welcome this. The length of time we spend depends on the number of questions and the time available.

When all the questions have been raised or time requires that we conclude, I offer a few final remarks. My goal is to confirm in my listeners the hope that they can truly live the discerning life.

I ask, "When Ignatius's eyes were opened, how much were they opened?" Because we have quoted this phrase so often, all immediately reply, "A little." Then I add, "That 'little' was all God needed to transform his life." That "little" opening of our eyes, that imperfect but sincere effort we make to live with new spiritual awareness—that is all God needs to transform our lives as well.[1]

At this point, I may quote G. K. Chesterton who cites the saying, "If a thing is worth doing, it is worth doing well," and reverses it: "If a thing is worth doing, it is worth doing badly."[2] I tell my listeners that Chesterton is right. If the best we can do is live the discerning life imperfectly, with lapses of awareness, struggles to understand, and failures to take the appropriate action—and this, I add, will be true for all of us, including the presenter!—*this daily effort is worth doing.* God's grace will unite with it, and we will rejoice to see the spiritual newness that enters our lives.

I conclude by quoting John 16:33. I note that these are the final words of Jesus to his disciples before he goes to his passion. John 17 gives us his priestly prayer to the Father, and in John 18, the passion begins.

Jesus knows that his disciples' hearts are heavy. They do not fully understand all that he has said at the Last Supper, but they do know that, in some form, trials and separation from him lie ahead. And so Jesus says to them, "In the world you have tribulation"—and we do. He continues, *"But be of good cheer, I have overcome the world."*[3]

I tell my listeners that this is the spirit in which we live the discerning life: with hope and, on a deep level, with confidence. Christ has overcome, and in him, the door to freedom lies open for us as well. My final word is this: may that hope bless us daily on the spiritual journey.

PART THREE

The Context of the Teaching

24

The Proximate Preparation for the Teaching

If you are reading this, then at some point the wisdom of the rules has touched your heart. This wisdom awakened enthusiasm, and you found it a blessing in your life. You also grew convinced that "this is important!" and needs to be shared with others. From this was born the desire to teach the rules. You set about learning them in more depth and shaped a way to present them to others. You have begun to teach them, or you wish to begin teaching them. If you have begun, you love the response in your listeners—the new clarity and hope the rules impart. You delight in seeing others share your own enthusiasm and the sense that "this can make a great difference in my life."

The study, prayer, and preparation that led you to undertake this teaching is the remote preparation for this teaching. Such remote preparation is of great importance: without it, the teaching will lack substance and accuracy. For me, this remote preparation was serious and in depth; I have never stopped trying to learn more about the rules. Years ago, I spoke with one of my Jesuit professors in Rome, an internationally renowned Ignatian scholar. At one point in the conversation, he grew thoughtful and said, "You think that you know everything there is to know about Ignatius's Spiritual Exercises, and then you find that there is always more." This is certainly true of the rules—blessedly, there is always more to learn.

Presuming this remote preparation, I wish now to address the proximate preparation for the teaching: the preparation that immediately precedes each new presentation of the rules. I find that this is a key component of my teaching, and I believe that this is true for all who teach the rules.

Prayer

We need to pray that God make our teaching fruitful. This is humble and confident prayer, asking that the preparation and the teaching be enveloped in God's grace—the grace that alone can make the teaching beneficial for our listeners.

For some years now, before each presentation I also ask others to pray. These are people who have offered to pray that God bless my listeners, me as the teacher, and the teaching. I repeatedly experience the difference these prayers make: spiritually speaking, you add two and two (my preparation, the organization of the event, and the like) and you get one hundred—the teaching bears fruit in ways that only this prayer can explain. I would not wish to teach without the support of these prayers! I am deeply grateful to those who offer them.

Review of the Material

As the years pass, I find the review of the material the most demanding and most important part of teaching the rules. The quality of my teaching, after prayer, depends most of all upon this detailed review. It allows me to teach the rules each time, no matter how often I have done this, with freshness, enthusiasm, and from the heart. Because of this review, there is never a sense in my listeners that "he's done this so many times that it's become rote."

The review is also the main source of new insights into the rules. Because of it, I continue to learn more about the rules. I understand Ignatius's words more deeply as time passes; for example, I see the components of his lengthy description of God's third reason for allowing spiritual desolation (rule 9). I see connections between rules as, for example, the link between rules 5 (the changes we *should not* make in desolation) and 6 (the changes we *should* make in desolation). I find new metaphors to express the teaching, like the two boys learning to ride a bicycle (rule 7), the two patients in the hospital room (rule 8), and the snowball at the top of the mountain (rule 12). Because of this repeated review, the teaching constantly grows richer. Much of what I now say when I teach the rules comes from insights gained through this review.

This review also helps me adapt the teaching to the specific audience and especially to choose examples suited to that particular group. If I have students, for example, I teach rule 2 (the person growing toward God) with the example of a student who has drifted from God, feels the need for a change, begins to attend Mass on Sunday, speaks with the chaplain, makes a retreat, changes certain harmful practices, begins to pray . . . and the students know that I am speaking *to them*. If I have lay adults, the example is a man or woman who undergoes a similar growth in the setting of marriage, family, work, and parish life. Again, my listeners are engaged and feel that I am speaking directly to them.

This review requires effort! There are no shortcuts. A wonderful high school teacher, revered by her many students, told me that she has read *Huckleberry Finn* twenty-six times, each time that she has taught the book. The review is easier when accompanied by prayer.

Because of this review, your listeners will feel that you are presenting the rules "for the first time" and with love. The teaching will be fresh and new each time. Josef Pieper writes, "A teacher sees the reality just as the beginner can see it, with all the innocence of a first encounter, and yet at the same time with the mature powers of comprehension and penetration that the cultivated mind possesses."[1] This is a beautiful image of a teacher: *all the innocence of a first encounter* and *with mature powers of comprehension and penetration*.

Through this preparation, you not only renew your intellectual grasp of the rules but also ready *your heart* to teach. A spark, an uplift of heart, a sense that "now I'm ready to teach" arises within. Now you are indeed prepared to teach. Now the teaching will have an impact on your listeners.

Consolation and Desolation in the Teacher

I must add a word on consolation and desolation in the context of this preparation and in the teaching itself. First, desolation. This preparation may be a time when the enemy brings desolation: "Why did I get myself into this?" "I don't want to do all this work again." "It's not going to go well." "I don't feel able to teach this well," and similar discouraging thoughts. I have experienced this many times!

Such discouraging thoughts and feelings are to be expected. The enemy does not want this teaching. Of course not! Through it, his lies are unmasked and captives are set free to love and serve the Lord. As teachers, we must be serenely aware that we may be attacked by desolation. If, as we prepare, we turn to the Lord with humble and confident prayer, we will find the help we need. God's grace is always there to help, and I have learned this through experience. In fact, over the years this "pre-event desolation" has become familiar, and I now see it—at least when I am spiritually aware and discerning—even as a good sign. It tells me that God's grace will work in the teaching and that good will come of it.

Such desolation may arise, as just said, when preparing for the teaching. It may also arise during the teaching or after. Generally, the desolation will not be dramatic, just a sense of discouragement, of heaviness, of lack of desire. We may feel tired, alone, worried that some do not like the presentation. We are wise to use healthy human (rest, exercise, time with friends, and the like) and spiritual (prayer, discernment, spiritual accompaniment, and

The Proximate Preparation for the Teaching 253

similar means) remedies for such desolation. We must not permit such desolation to hinder our teaching!

Above all, however, we will experience the joy and consolation of our service to our listeners. I teach the rules because I know the value of this teaching and wish to share this treasure with others. I also teach them because I love this ministry and find joy in the hope and renewed energy they give my listeners. It is this joy, the fruit of prayer, study, preparation, the teaching itself, and primarily of grace, that we will experience in our teaching above all. We have undertaken a worthy and important task, and its fruits, in us and through us for others, are abundant.

25

Tools for the Teaching

I will discuss here three tools that I find helpful for my teaching: handouts, paradigms, and PowerPoint (or some other version of digital images). Such tools continue to evolve with the progress of technology, and new forms will likely be available by the time you read this. Nevertheless, whatever form—whiteboard, hard-copy handouts, electronic handouts, digital images, computer-based aids of various kinds, or other—these tools may take with time, they remain valuable for our teaching. In combination, I find them highly effective. I will review them here as I use them in their present state.

Handouts

I use two handouts. One supplies the text of the fourteen rules, and it is our basic working text. Close examination of the text requires, obviously, that people have the text in hand. I have translated the rules as closely to the original Spanish as English allows in order to facilitate direct access to Ignatius's own words. Thus, for example, when Ignatius asks that one in desolation *"trabaje de estar en paciencia"* (rule 8), I have translated these words as "work to be in patience." The English is clumsy but gives the Spanish original exactly, and that was my goal in translating. This almost transliterated translation serves well the approach I follow in the teaching.

The second handout is longer and includes the examples I employ to teach each rule. Many of the examples are taken from my books on these rules;[1] others I add as I encounter them in the many ways life speaks to us. I find it helpful that people have these in hand, can write notes on these pages, and can relax and listen because they already have the texts. They can also take them home for future reference.

I create different forms of this second handout according to different kinds of listeners and the examples that will speak to each. Much of the handout is the same for all groups, but some elements change according to the specific group. I continue to update and adapt this handout as I find additional or better examples to illustrate the rules. My proximate preparation for teaching the rules consists largely in reviewing this handout and reflecting on the examples once again.

Paradigms

I employ three paradigms. I present them either on a whiteboard or as PowerPoint slides, or if helpful, in both ways. Each appears when opportune in the unfolding of the teaching; once it does appear, I keep it constantly before my listeners. In this way, through continued visual exposure, they assimilate it well. I will present all three here; they may also be seen in the accompanying figures.

The first is the key paradigm. It renders visual the understanding of discernment that Ignatius outlines in his title statement, "Rules for *becoming aware* and *understanding* to some extent the different movements which are caused in the soul, the *good, to receive* them, and the *bad to reject* them" (*SpirEx* 313):

> BE AWARE
> UNDERSTAND
> TAKE ACTION
> (ACCEPT/REJECT)

This brief paradigm has proven highly effective in teaching the rules. It is simple and clear. Having learned it, my listeners know exactly what Ignatius intends by discernment of spirits—this threefold spiritual action, each step preparing the next. I return to this paradigm repeatedly as we explore the various examples. For this reason, I keep it constantly before my listeners.

The second helps especially in teaching rules 1 and 2. It illustrates the "persons who are going from mortal sin to mortal sin" (rule 1) and the "persons who are going on intensely purifying their sins and rising from good to better in the service of God our Lord" (rule 2):

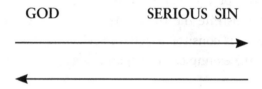

The first line represents the persons of rule 1; the second, those of rule 2. This simple paradigm greatly facilitates the teaching of these two rules. When, for example, I speak of the young Augustine before his conversion (example of the person of rule 1), I need simply indicate the first line. At a glance, my listeners grasp his spiritual situation and the spiritual profile Ignatius intends in rule 1. Likewise, when I wish to describe Augustine's spiritual situation after his conversion, I point to the second line. This new situation is again clear. The second line also portrays the spiritual situation of most, generally all, of my listeners.

This same paradigm assists later as well, notably in teaching rule 9. A slight addition to the second line as seen here illustrates well the first reason why God allows spiritual desolation: lesser areas of regression ("we are tepid, slothful, or negligent in our spiritual exercises") within a life generally progressing toward God:

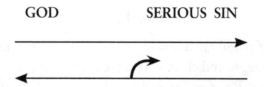

I post the third paradigm when presenting rule 6 or, at the latest, rule 8. The paradigm is the following:

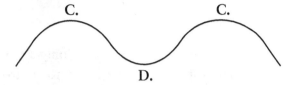

The C and D represent, obviously, consolation and desolation. This paradigm depicts their alternations in our spiritual experience: times of spiritual consolation, which eventually pass, followed by times of spiritual desolation, which also eventually pass, followed by the return of spiritual consolation, and so on. I note for my listeners that our experience is less symmetrical than this paradigm shows, that this is simply a teaching tool intended to represent the alternations of consolation and desolation that Ignatius expects in a healthy spiritual life. I observe further that this paradigm does not include the third spiritual space, the tranquil time that we discussed earlier (rule 5).

This paradigm is effective in discussing many of the rules, especially rules 8 (in desolation, remember that consolation is coming soon), 10 (in consolation, prepare for the following desolation), and 11 (humble in consolation, trusting in desolation). Thus, for example, when teaching rule 10, I note that rules 5 through 9 supply tools to the person *now in desolation*, and I point to the low space on the line with its accompanying D. I then indicate the preceding higher space marked by C. and explain that we can do something at this point, *when in consolation*, that will strengthen us to resist and reject the following desolation. The paradigm visually supports the teaching—the combination of spoken explanation and visual representation renders the teaching clear.

These three paradigms help my listeners grasp many key points in the rules. Together with the handout, they greatly facilitate the teaching. Teachers may find other paradigms that serve their teaching.

PowerPoint

In my first years of teaching the rules, I used only a whiteboard and handouts. Then I presented the rules to a group that evangelized through media. They found me hopelessly out of date! One of them offered to create a PowerPoint presentation for me to assist the teaching. I gratefully accepted, and since then PowerPoint has become a key piece in my teaching. I mention PowerPoint because that is what I currently use. As mentioned, other programs (Prezi, Keynote, and similar) may be employed for the same purpose. Most likely still others will be available by the time you read this book.

Whatever the program adopted, the visual aid it permits has become an important tool for teaching the rules. Listeners are increasingly accustomed to images; younger people almost expect them. I find that such visual tools serve to engage my listeners and reinforce the teaching. Are such visual aids essential to teaching the rules? I would not say so. I taught the rules for years without them. Are these visual aids, when the teacher is able to employ them, useful for the teaching? The answer is certainly yes.

I am still learning the art of using these visual tools effectively. If overused, if employed as a crutch or to replace personal preparation, if the slides are too burdened with text . . . PowerPoint (or its equivalent) can hinder rather than help the teaching. Used wisely, it serves the teaching well.

My PowerPoint presentation is available through the link that accompanies this book.[2] Here I offer just a few examples of how I use the slides.

Some represent the above-mentioned paradigms:

Tools for the Teaching

Be Aware
Understand
Take Action
(accept/reject)

Rules 1 and 2

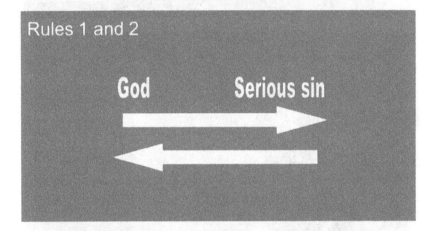

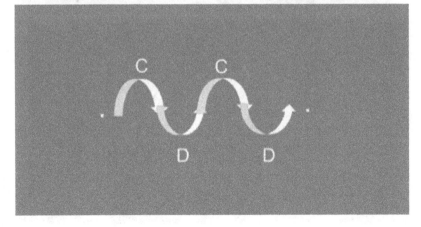

Others summarize a rule. Thus, for example,

> **Rule 5**
>
> "In time of desolation, never make a change."

> **Rule Ten**
>
> When in Consolation, Take in Strength for Desolation

> **Rule 12**
>
> Stand firm in the beginning

Still others represent a spiritual figure whom I cite. Thus my listeners see the person as we read his or her words. The following are St. Ignatius, St. Francis, and St. Elizabeth Seton:

Still other slides highlight key phrases in a rule (rule 13, the enemy "wishes to remain secret and not be revealed") or present lists of various kinds (rule 2, the four tactics of the enemy in a person progressing toward God). Thus, the tactics of the enemy in rule 2:

> enemy bite,
>
> sadden,
>
> place obstacles,
>
> disquiet with false reasons

Such lists help my listeners follow as I explore each element in succession.

I want the slides to contribute to the positive tone of the teaching emphasized earlier. Within the limits of my skill and copyrighted material, I want them to be clear, attractive, and hope-filled.

I find the combination of these three tools—handouts, paradigms, and PowerPoint (or equivalent)—valuable in teaching the rules. You will find your own tools for your presentations and your own ways of using them.

Groups for Discussion?

Is it helpful to provide time for personal reflection, small-group discussion, and large-group sharing with an opportunity to ask questions as well? Obviously, yes. The teaching touches our listeners' experience, often deeply, and they generally welcome time for personal assimilation and sharing.

The key question in this regard is time. Some formats readily allow time for such reflection, discussion, and sharing. Thus, for example, a group that meets once a week in a parish to explore the rules may easily provide time for this dynamic. A retreat or retreat-like setting may also accommodate such space. Other settings render this sharing more difficult. If, for example, I have only one day (perhaps four talks) to present the rules, I judge it more important to present the basics (title, rules 1 through 4) than to provide time for group work. In such cases, however, I try to give time for questions, at least before concluding the day. You will make your own best decisions in this regard.

26

What about the Second Set of Rules?

When I teach the fourteen rules, at times the question of the second set of rules is raised: "Doesn't Ignatius also have a second set of rules? You haven't mentioned them. What about them?" It is a fair question!

When I present the fourteen rules, unless I am asked questions of this kind, I never mention the second set of rules (*SpirEx* 328–336). Even when asked, my answer is adequate but brief. Behind this is a pedagogical choice of importance. I have addressed this issue in detail elsewhere;[1] here I will simply reply to the question just raised, one that you need to know how to answer.

Ignatius tells us in the title to the fourteen rules that "these rules are more proper for the first week" (*SpirEx* 313). *First Week* signifies a stage in the Spiritual Exercises (*SpirEx* 4), a time of purification from sin (*SpirEx* 45ff) that also awakens a deeper appreciation for the Savior and a growing openness to follow him in our lives (*SpirEx* 53, 60–61, 71).

A person may live this First-Week dynamic in daily life, outside of the formal retreat. When we seek growing freedom from sin, deeper gratitude for the love and mercy of the Savior, and a heart more ready to follow him in our lives, we are living the First-Week dynamic. Often this will be the situation of our listeners, good people who love the Lord and wish to "rise from good to better" (rule 2) in his service. This is a rich spiritual space.

In this *First-Week situation*, the enemy typically attempts to discourage through spiritual desolation and its accompanying temptations—all that Ignatius has described in the fourteen rules. When, therefore, people find themselves in this

First-Week spiritual situation, the fourteen rules apply and will greatly bless them.

Further along the journey, as progress continues, a different situation may arise. At this point, people have grown in generosity with God and have matured in the spiritual life. They are spiritually stronger and less likely to succumb to desolation and obvious temptations. In Ignatius's terms, these are no longer First-Week but *Second-Week* persons (*SpirEx* 9–10, 328).[2] The *First-Week situation* has given way to the *Second-Week situation*.

In the Second-Week situation, the enemy shifts his attack. Without fully relinquishing spiritual desolation, he "commonly" tempts in a different way, that is, "under the appearance of good" (*SpirEx* 10). The enemy awakens joy in the pursuit of something good—truly good—but not the good that God desires for this person.[3] In this new situation, with the enemy tempting in a new way, the person needs new guidance. Ignatius supplies this in *the second set of rules*, those, he says, that "help more for the second week" (*SpirEx* 328).

Obviously much more could be said about this and, as mentioned, I have done so elsewhere. For our purpose now, it is enough to note that the Second-Week situation is very different than the first.

An important pedagogical directive follows. When, Ignatius says, a person experiences the spiritual desolation and accompanying temptations described in the first set of rules (First-Week situation), the spiritual guide *"should not explain to him* the rules about different spirits for the *second week"* (*SpirEx* 9). Ignatius immediately explains, "because as much as those for *the first week will help him*, those for *the second week will harm him*, as being matter too subtle and elevated for him to understand (*SpirEx* 9)."

When the enemy brings spiritual desolation and its accompanying temptations to a person (First-Week situation), the First-Week rules—the fourteen that are the subject of this book—will greatly assist that person. *In this First-Week situation*, however, to speak of the Second-Week rules will *actually harm* the person. Not only does the person not need them, but the Second-Week rules will confuse—this is the "harm" of which Ignatius speaks—the clarity of the First-Week rules. The person will be left hesitant, unsure of how to proceed, and prone to harmful choices.

This was why I wrote separate books on the First-Week and Second-Week rules. Each book is helpful when a person experiences the spiritual situation presumed by that set of rules. At the same time, because they are separate, neither will confuse the application of the other.

When, therefore, we teach the fourteen rules to people who are learning them for the first time or who have as yet limited familiarity with them, it is best not to mention the second set of rules. I take this as a general norm with such groups of listeners.

To return to our initial question, when I have listeners, many or most of whom are learning the rules for the first time, and I am asked about the second set of rules, I answer something like this: "Yes, there is a second set of rules that I have not mentioned in this presentation. Those rules presume a different spiritual situation than that of the fourteen rules we have explored. I have discussed this second set of rules in the book entitled *Spiritual Consolation: An Ignatian Guide to a Greater Discernment of Spirits*, to which I refer you for more detail. I will also be happy to answer any questions you may have one-on-one after this session." This answer validates the question, indicates the importance of the second set of rules, and offers ways to pursue learning more about them. It carefully avoids, however, entering into the content of this second set of rules and so avoids the confusion this would cause for my listeners.

When teaching the rules to groups with more formation—for example, seasoned spiritual directors or those in training—the situation changes. We should be ready to learn both sets of rules, and we must know them in order to serve competently as spiritual directors. Even so, I believe it wise to teach the first set of rules and allow time for its practice and assimilation before teaching the second set. In the one-on-one of spiritual direction, directors will apply either set as needed.

27

Resources for Learning the Rules

Ignatian literature is vast. Here I will indicate only a few resources, print and digital, that I believe can help those who teach the rules. The more extensive your background, the richer will be the teaching. Such reading has proven invaluable for me in my own teaching. As I mention sources, I hope I may be forgiven for including my own books!

Books

I recommend reading the life of St. Ignatius. Knowledge of Ignatius's life illuminates a text that derives in significant part from Ignatius's experience. The most basic source is Ignatius's *Autobiography*.

O'Callaghan, Joseph, trans. *The Autobiography of St. Ignatius Loyola with Related Documents* (New York: Harper & Row, 1974).

Idígoras, José Ignacio Tellechea. *Ignatius of Loyola: The Pilgrim Saint*. Chicago: Loyola University Press, 1994.
    An excellent resource for engaging Ignatius's autobiography.

Dalmases, Candido de. *Ignatius of Loyola: Founder of the Jesuits*. St. Louis: Institute of Jesuit Sources, 1985.
    Drier, but based on solid scholarship.

Gallagher, Timothy. *The Discernment of Spirits: An Ignatian Guide for Everyday Living*. New York: Crossroad, 2005.
    Of the two books I have written on the fourteen rules, this is more basic and offers a systematic exposition of the rules through examination of Ignatius's words and many examples.

———. *The Examen Prayer: Ignatian Wisdom for our Lives Today.* New York: Crossroad, 2006.

This resource examines the examen prayer as the practical means for living daily discernment.

———. *Setting Captives Free: Personal Reflections on Ignatian Discernment of Spirits.* New York: Crossroad, 2018.

My second book on the fourteen rules explores further issues in the rules and offers many further examples.

Jules Toner, SJ, *A Commentary on Saint Ignatius' Rules for the Discernment of Spirits: A Guide to the Principles and Practice.* St. Louis: Institute for Jesuit Sources, 1982

A valuable resource for those who wish to pursue the rules more analytically.

———. *Spirit of Light or Darkness: A Casebook for Studying Discernment of Spirits.* St. Louis: Institute for Jesuit Sources, 1995.

The accompanying workbook to the resource immediately above.

For Those Who Read Spanish

Fiorito, Miguel Angel, SJ. *Discernimiento y Lucha Espiritual* (Buenos Aires: Ediciónes Diego de Torres, 1985).

Gil, Daniel, SJ. *Discernimiento según San Ignacio: Exposición y comentario práctico de las dos series de reglas de discernimiento de espíritus contenidas en el libro de los Ejercicios Espirituales de San Ignacio de Loyola (EE 313–336)* (Rome: Centrum Ignatianum Spiritualitatis, 1983)

You may pursue this reading as far as desired. Further reading might include other writings of Ignatius, for example, his Spiritual Diary and Letters; further writing on discernment; and the whole vast array of Ignatian sources.[1] The more we learn as teachers, the more we will have to give.

I have deliberately limited this list of books. One need not be an Ignatian scholar to teach the rules with fruit. A basic ability to present material to others, helpful talks and classes if these are available, the prayerful and reflective reading of well-chosen books—perhaps read more than once—a sincere effort to live discernment personally, guidance as needed, and use of the written and digital tools available will prepare one to begin the teaching. The rest is learning from experience and the ongoing search for deeper understanding of the rules. The effort is worth it! Many will be grateful to you for the light and hope your teaching will give them.

Digital Resources

Podcasts

I have presented the fourteen rules in a series of podcasts entitled *The Discernment of Spirits*. These are available on:

discerninghearts.com	Google Play
The Discerning Hearts app	YouTube
iTunes	FORMED

DVDs

This same material is also available in visual form as the DVD of a ten-part series I taught on EWTN, *Living the Discerning Life*. The DVDs are available on:

EWTN website: http://www.ewtnreligiouscatalogue.com/shop.axd/ProductDetails?edp_no=23867

My website:
https://www.frtimothygallagher.org/product-page/living-the-discerning-life-the-spiritual-teaching-of-st-ignatius-of-loyola

All of my print, electronic, and digital resources are available through my website: frtimothygallagher.org

Notes

1. In this book I discuss only the teaching of the first set of rules (*SpirEx* 313–327). This same pedagogical approach, however, also serves to teach the second set of rules (*SpirEx* 328–336), and I have done this in *Spiritual Consolation: An Ignatian Guide for the Greater Discernment of Spirits* (New York: Crossroad, 2007).
2. The rules in question are the fourteen rules of the first set—the "first week" rules, as Ignatius titles them (*SpirEx* 313–327). For the second set of rules, see the preceding note.
3. NABRE. Emphasis added.

1 How This Pedagogy Developed

1. For the life of Venerable Bruno, see Timothy Gallagher, OMV, *Begin Again: The Life and Spiritual Legacy of Bruno Lanteri* (New York: Crossroad, 2013).
2. Timothy Gallagher, OMV, *The Great Art of Our Sanctification: A Study of the* Direttorio degli Esercizi di S. Ignazio *of Pio Brunone Lanteri* (licentiate thesis, Pontifical Gregorian University, Rome, 1980); *Gli esercizi di S. Ignazio nella spiritualità e carisma di fondatore di Pio Bruno Lanteri* (Rome: Typis Pontificiae Universitatis Gregorianae, 1983).
3. Daniel Gil, SJ, *Discernimiento según San Ignacio: Exposición y comentario practico de las dos series de reglas de discernimiento de espíritus contenidas en el libro de los Ejercicios Espirituales de San Ignacio de Loyola (EE 313–336)* (Rome: Centrum Ignatianum Spiritualitatis, 1983).
4. Jules Toner, SJ, *A Commentary on Saint Ignatius' Rules for the Discernment of Spirits: A Guide to the Principles and Practice* (St. Louis, IL: The Institute of Jesuit Sources, 1982).
5. Miguel Ángel Fiorito, SJ, *Discernimiento y lucha espiritual: Comentario de las reglas de discernir de la Primera Semana del libro de los Ejercicios Espirituales de San Ignacio de Loyola*

(Buenos Aires: Ediciones Diego de Torres, 1985); *Buscar y hallar la voluntad de Dios: Comentario práctico a los Ejercicios Espirituales de San Ignacio de Loyola*, 2 vols. (Buenos Aires: Ediciones Diego de Torres, 1989); and his many articles in *Boletín de espiritualidad*.

6 All quotations of Ignatius's text of the rules are taken from the author's translation in *The Discernment of Spirits: An Ignatian Guide for Everyday Life* (New York: Crossroad, 2005), 7–10.

7 I presented only the rules for the first week (*SpirEx* 313–327) and not those of the second week (*SpirEx* 328–336).

8 Gallagher, *Discernment of Spirits*, 27–31.

9 Gallagher, *Discernment of Spirits*, 47–48.

10 Gallagher, *Discernment of Spirits*, 110–12.

11 Gallagher, *Discernment of Spirits*, 121–22.

12 Timothy Gallagher, OMV, *The Discernment of Spirits: An Ignatian Guide to Everyday Living* (New York: Crossroad, 2005); *The Discernment of Spirits: An Ignatian Guide to Everyday Living—Reader's Guide* (New York: Crossroad, 2013); *Setting Captives Free: Personal Reflections on Ignatian Discernment of Spirits* (New York: Crossroad, 2018). I employed the same pedagogy in *Spiritual Consolation: An Ignatian Guide to a Greater Discernment of Spirits* (New York: Crossroad, 2007), a study of the second set of rules (*SpirEx* 328–336).

13 Polish, Latvian, Spanish, Portuguese, Korean, and Vietnamese.

14 Timothy Gallagher, OMV, *The Discernment of Spirits*; *Setting Captives Free*; *The Discernment of Spirits: A Reader's Guide*. Also for second set of rules, *Spiritual Consolation*.

15 EWTN, *Living the Discerning Life*, and Catholic Television, *Discernment of Spirits*; discerninghearts.com, iTunes, Google Play, YouTube, and FORMED.

2 The Fruit of This Pedagogy

1 NABRE.

2 Among the many editions, *The Hidden Treasure* (Charlotte, NC: TAN, 2012).

3 The Heart of the Pedagogy

1. To explain the rules, Daniel Gil wrote a book of 389 pages and Jules Toner a book of 332 pages. See Daniel Gil, SJ, *Discernimiento según San Ignacio: Exposición y comentario práctico de las dos series de reglas de discernimiento de espíritus contenidas en el libro de los Ejercicios Espirituales de San Ignacio de Loyola (EE 313–336)* (Rome: Centrum Ignatianum Spiritualitatis, 1983); and Jules Toner, SJ, *A Commentary on Saint Ignatius' Rules for the Discernment of Spirits: A Guide to the Principles and Practice* (St. Louis, IL: The Institute of Jesuit Sources, 1982). Both books comment on the two sets of rules.
2. Jules Toner's book is a fine example of this approach. For that very reason, however, it is largely inaccessible to the broader audience of those who seek to apply the rules in their lives.
3. Timothy Gallagher, OMV, *Setting Captives Free: Personal Reflections on Ignatian Discernment of Spirits* (New York: Crossroad, 2018), xxviii.
4. Timothy Gallagher, OMV, *The Discernment of Spirits: An Ignatian Guide to Everyday Living* (New York: Crossroad, 2005), 7. Author's translation.
5. Letter of June 18, 1536, in William Young, SJ, *Letters of Saint Ignatius of Loyola* (Chicago: Loyola University Press, 1959), 19. Emphasis added. Cited in Gallagher, *Discernment of Spirits*, 40.
6. Manuel Ruiz Jurado, SJ, ed., *San Ignacio de Loyola: Obras* (Madrid: Biblioteca de Autores Cristianos, 2013), 42: *Autobiography*, para. 22. Emphasis added. Author's translation.
7. Gallagher, *Setting Captives Free*, 23–24.
8. Gallagher, *Setting Captives Free*, 30–31.

4 Getting to Know the Text

1. Taken from Timothy Gallagher, OMV, *The Discernment of Spirits: An Ignatian Guide to Everyday Living* (New York: Crossroad, 2005), 7–10.

2 Eldar Mullan, SJ, *The Spiritual Exercises of St. Ignatius of Loyola: Translated from the Autograph* (New York: P. J. Kenedy & Sons, 1914), xii. Also available online at http://www.ccel.org/ccel/ignatius/exercises.toc.html.

3 Of the many editions in Spanish, I recommend Candido de Dalmases, SJ, *Ejercicios espirituales: Introducción, texto, notas y vocabulario* (Santander: Editorial Sal Terrae, 1985).

4 Jules Toner's *Commentary* does follow this approach, though more loosely and with "detailed scholarship, and sometimes difficult textual analysis, or . . . critical discussion of conflicting interpretations" included in the commentary. Jules Toner, SJ, *A Commentary on Saint Ignatius' Rules for the Discernment of Spirits: A Guide to the Principles and Practice* (St. Louis, IL: The Institute of Jesuit Sources, 1982), xvi. This is an excellent book for those willing to read and study it patiently.

5 New York: Crossroad, 2018.

6 Daniel Gil, SJ, *Discernimiento según San Ignacio: Exposición y comentario práctico de las dos series de reglas de discernimiento de espíritus contenidas en el libro de los Ejercicios Espirituales de San Ignacio de Loyola (EE 313–336)* (Rome: Centrum Ignatianum Spiritualitatis, 1983); and Miguel Ángel Fiorito, SJ, *Discernimiento y lucha espiritual: Comentario de las reglas de discernir de la Primera Semana del libro de los Ejercicios Espirituales de San Ignacio de Loyola* (Buenos Aires: Ediciones Diego de Torres, 1985).

5 Choosing Examples

1 See Timothy Gallagher, OMV, *The Discernment of Spirits: An Ignatian Guide to Everyday Living* (New York: Crossroad, 2005), for all these examples.

2 "Throughout the ages, there have been so-called 'private' revelations, some of which have been recognized by the authority of the Church. They do not belong, however, to the deposit of faith. It is not their role to improve or complete Christ's definitive Revelation, but to help live more fully by it in a certain period of history." *Catechism of the Catholic Church*, no. 67: http://ccc.usccb.org/flipbooks/catechism/index.html#22. Examples of recognized private revelations include the apparitions of Mary in Lourdes in 1858 and in Fatima in 1917.

3 NABRE.
4 Ignatius, *Autobiography*, para. 6–8; Augustine, *Confessions*, 8.11.
5 *Autobiography*, no. 8.
6 *Confessions*, 8.11.
7 Gallagher, *Discernment of Spirit*, 11–15, 27–31.

6 Living the Rules Personally

1 See Timothy Gallagher, OMV, *The Examen Prayer: Ignatian Wisdom for Our Lives Today* (New York: Crossroad, 2006), and Gallagher, discerninghearts.com, "A Daily Prayer of Discernment," eight podcasts.
2 Gallagher, *Examen Prayer*, 132–35.
3 Gallagher, *Examen Prayer*, 115.
4 Commonly called the Nineteenth Annotation retreat, from para. 19 of the *Spiritual Exercises*, in which Ignatius describes this form of the Exercises.

7 General Principles

1 I am speaking here of the application of the rules in daily life, outside the context of the Spiritual Exercises.
2 Primarily my book *The Discernment of Spirits: An Ignatian Guide for Everyday Living* (New York: Crossroad, 2005) and the related podcasts: see chapter 27 for the references. In these resources, the listeners find the full presentation of all fourteen rules.
3 See the letter of Ignatius to Teresa Rejadell, 18 June 1536, para. 7, in William Young, SJ, *Letters of Saint Ignatius of Loyola* (Chicago: Loyola University Press, 1959), 22.
4 See Gallagher, *Setting Captives Free*, xxvii–xxix. Fiorito proposes two interpretations of "to some extent": the text of the rules is incomplete without the experience of discernment of spirits, and this first set of rules is incomplete without the second. *Discernimiento y lucha*, 19–22. He opts for the first. Gil proposes the second interpretation. *Discernimiento*, 33.

5 Timothy Gallagher, OMV, *Setting Captives Free: Personal Reflections on Ignatian Discernment of Spirits* (New York: Crossroad, 2018), xxix.

6 In the second set of rules (*SpirEx* 328–336), Ignatius speaks of "the evil spirit" (*SpirEx* 333, 336), "the evil angel" (*SpirEx* 331, 332, 335), and the "enemy" (329, 333, 334). In *SpirEx* 6–10, where Ignatius explains the different use of each set of rules, he employs both the word *enemy* (once) and the phrase *enemy of human nature* (twice), without employing the phrase *evil spirit*. See Gallagher, *Setting Captives Free*, 10–11.

7 Gallagher, *Discernment of Spirits*, 33–34. The classic triad is the world, the flesh, and the devil.

8 C. S. Lewis writes, "There are two equal and opposite errors into which our race can fall about the devils. One is to disbelieve in their existence. The other is to believe, and to feel an excessive and unhealthy interest in them." *The Screwtape Letters and Screwtape Proposes a Toast* (New York: HarperOne, 2012), xlvii.

8 Start with the Basics—the Title Statement

1 Timothy Gallagher, OMV, *Setting Captives Free: Personal Reflections on Ignatian Discernment of Spirits* (New York: Crossroad, 2018), xx.

2 *Autobiography*, paras. 1–8. See Gallagher, *Discernment of Spirits*, 11–15, and *Setting Captives Free*, xx–xxvii.

3 For this and the following quotations, see *Autobiography*, para. 8.

4 For further discussion of this line, see Timothy Gallagher, OMV, *The Discernment of Spirits: An Ignatian Guide to Everyday Living* (New York: Crossroad, 2005), 26; and *Spiritual Consolation: An Ignatian Guide for a Greater Discernment of Spirits* (New York: Crossroad, 2007), 14–29.

5 *Confessions*, 10. 27. Author's translation.

6 See Gallagher, *Setting Captives Free*, xxix–xxxiii, for a full list of these factors.

7 Blaise Pascal, *Pensées*, nos. 139–183, www.ntslibrary.com/PDF%20Books/Blaise%20Pascal%20Pensees.pdf. See Gallagher, *Discernment of Spirits*, 19–20; *Setting Captives Free*, xxxi–xxxii.
8 Gallagher, *Discernment of Spirits*, 18–20.

9 The Spirits in Persons Far from God: Clarity for Your Listeners—Rule 1

1 *Confessions*, 8.11.
2 *Confessions*, 2.1, author's translation. See Timothy Gallagher, OMV, *The Discernment of Spirits: An Ignatian Guide to Everyday Living* (New York: Crossroad, 2005), 28.
3 R. S. Pine-Coffin, trans., *Saint Augustine Confessions* (Harmondsworth, UK: Penguin Books, 1961), 175. The subsequent quotations are from this same source.
4 NABRE.
5 For a discussion of *mortal sin* understood as "capital sin," see Timothy Gallagher, OMV, *Setting Captives Free: Personal Reflections on Ignatian Discernment of Spirits* (New York: Crossroad, 2018), 4–8.
6 This will no longer hold true in the second set of rules (*SpirEx*, 328–336). In the experience presumed there, the enemy imitates the action of the good spirit. For a discussion of the second set of rules, see Gallagher, *Spiritual Consolation: An Ignatian Guide to a Greater Discernment of Spirits* (New York: Crossroad, 2007).
7 Francis Thompson, "The Hound of Heaven," in *The Oxford Book of English Mystical Verse*, ed. D. H. S. Nicholson and A. H. E. Lee (Oxford: Clarendon Press, 1917), https://www.bartleby.com/236/239.html.

10 The Spirits in Persons Growing Toward God: Addressing Your Listeners' Experience—Rule 2

1 Timothy Gallagher, OMV, *Setting Captives Free: Personal Reflections on Ignatian Discernment of Spirits* (New York: Crossroad, 2018), 19–21.

2 William Young, S.J., *Letters of Saint Ignatius of Loyola* (Chicago: Loyola University Press, 1959), 19. See Gallagher, *Discernment of Spirits*, 40.
3 *Autobiography*, para. 22. Author's translation.
4 Young, *Letters of Saint Ignatius of Loyola*, 22.
5 Young, *Letters of Saint Ignatius of Loyola*, 19. Emphasis added.
6 Gallagher, *Setting Captives Free*, 25–27.
7 RSVCE.
8 The following are the concluding words of this lovely message: "The Lord replied, my precious, precious child, I love you and I would never leave you! During your times of trial and suffering when you see only one set of footprints, it was then that I carried you." See www.wowzone.com/fprints.htm.
9 For this and the preceding example, see Gallagher, *Setting Captives Free*, 37–38.

11 Helping Your Listeners Recognize Spiritual Consolation—Rule 3

1 Jacques Maritain, ed., *Raïssa's Journal* (Albany, NY: Magi, 1974), 35. Emphasis in the original.
2 This distinction matters: "A married man, for example, finds himself attracted to another woman and knows that the attraction is reciprocal. When they converse, he finds his heart energized and uplifted. A priest finds himself drawn to a woman of the parish and also experiences an uplift of heart when speaking with her. Both, evidently, experience consolation: the uplift of heart that a man and woman feel when mutually attracted. If the married man or the priest, however, were to identify this consolation as the spiritual consolation of which Ignatius speaks in rule 3, and were to understand it as an indication of where God is leading, disastrous consequences would obviously ensue. Neither is experiencing *spiritual consolation*; both, rather, are experiencing *nonspiritual consolation*, the natural uplift of heart that a man and woman feel when placed together and mutually attracted. This nonspiritual consolation is not an indication of where God is leading: it is simply a

natural response to a natural situation. Such cases and many others like them, indicate why the distinction between spiritual and nonspiritual consolation must always be observed in discernment." Timothy Gallagher, OMV, *Setting Captives Free: Personal Reflections on Ignatian Discernment of Spirits* (New York: Crossroad, 2018), 51. I do not explain and exemplify this issue when presenting spiritual and nonspiritual consolation because the learners are still absorbing these two terms. If the listeners raise the question, "Why are we making this distinction between two types of consolation?" then I address this question more explicitly.

3 John Clarke, OCD, trans., *St. Thérèse of Lisieux: Her Last Conversations* (Washington, DC: ICS Publications, 1977), 60. In the original quote, Pauline's words are italicized and Thérèse's words set in roman type. I have removed the italics. See Timothy Gallagher, OMV, *The Discernment of Spirits: An Ignatian Guide to Everyday Living* (New York: Crossroad, 2005), 49–50.

4 NABRE.

5 NABRE.

6 Gallagher, *Setting Captives Free*, 54–66.

7 Quoted with author's permission.

8 Daniel Gil, SJ, *Discernimiento según San Ignacio: Exposición y comentario práctico de las dos series de reglas de discernimiento de espíritus contenidas en el libro de los Ejercicios Espirituales de San Ignacio de Loyola (EE 313-336)* (Rome: Centrum Ignatianum Spiritualitatis, 1983), 127.

9 NABRE.

10 "This is an increase in the level ordinarily experienced and perceived by the person, who perceives this in his examens as something of note." Gil, *Discernimiento*, 129.

11 Evelyn Waugh, *Monsignor Ronald Knox* (Boston: Little, Brown, 1959), 169–70. Emphasis added.

12 Helping Your Listeners Recognize Spiritual Desolation—Rule 4

1. Jules Toner, SJ, *Spirit of Light or Darkness: A Casebook for Studying Discernment of Spirits* (St. Louis, MO: Institute of Jesuit Sources, 1995), 63. See Timothy Gallagher, OMV, *The Discernment of Spirits: An Ignatian Guide to Everyday Living* (New York: Crossroad, 2005), 58–59.
2. Toner, *Spirit of Light or Darkness*, 66. See Gallagher, *Discernment of Spirits*, 59.
3. A secularized culture does not recognize the reality of specifically spiritual desolation and so subsumes it into nonspiritual desolation, the only kind it does recognize.
4. Timothy Gallagher, OMV, *Setting Captives Free: Personal Reflections on Ignatian Discernment of Spirits* (New York: Crossroad, 2018), 68–71.
5. On the difference between this darkness of soul and St. John of the Cross's dark nights, see Gallagher, *Setting Captives Free*, 71–75.
6. Gallagher, *Discernment of Spirits*, 63.
7. For the examen prayer, see Gallagher, *The Examen Prayer: Ignatian Wisdom for Our Lives Today* (New York: Crossroad, 2006). The examen prayer is a contemporary presentation of the classic examination of conscience that incorporates into it the discernment of spirits.
8. Gallagher, *Discernment of Spirits*, 65–66.
9. In William Young, SJ, *Letters of Saint Ignatius of Loyola* (Chicago: Loyola University Press, 1959), 21–22.
10. In the second set of rules (*SpirEx*, 328–336), this may change. I do not, however, mention this to the listeners: Ignatius advises against explaining the second set of rules to those who need the first set (*SpirEx*, 9). Because some listeners may know the second set, for precision I add the phrase, "In this set of rules." Regarding the relationship of the first and second set of rules, see Timothy Gallagher, OMV, *Spiritual Consolation: An Ignatian Guide for a Greater Discernment of Spirits* (New York: Crossroad, 2007), 17–29.

13 The Advice That Your Listeners Never Forget—Rule 5

1. Timothy Gallagher, OMV, *Setting Captives Free: Personal Reflections on Ignatian Discernment of Spirits* (New York: Crossroad, 2018), 107–8.
2. J. R. R. Tolkien, *The Fellowship of the Ring*, part 1 of *The Lord of the Rings* (New York: Ballantine Books, 1986), 488.
3. Timothy Gallagher, OMV, *The Discernment of Spirits: An Ignatian Guide to Everyday Living* (New York: Crossroad, 2005), 80–83. See these pages for a more complete commentary on this text of Ignatius.
4. Author's translation. See Gallagher, *Discernment of Spirits*, 196n7.
5. Gallagher, *Setting Captives Free*, 107.

14 Liberating Your Listeners: Never Be Passive in Desolation!—Rule 6

1. Once again, the original context of these rules is the Ignatian retreat in which a person applies these four means as part of the experience. In that context, Ignatius calls on the retreatant in spiritual desolation to "insist more" upon these four means, that is, to apply them more diligently in response to the heaviness of the desolation. A similar dynamic holds when, as in our treatment here, rule 6 is applied in daily life: the person employs spiritual means in daily life but is to "insist more" upon them—specifically the four Ignatius names in rule 6—in the time of greater need, that is, in the time of spiritual desolation.
2. See Jules Toner, SJ, *A Commentary on Saint Ignatius' Rules for the Discernment of Spirits: A Guide to the Principles and Practice* (St. Louis, IL: The Institute of Jesuit Sources, 1982), 165; and Timothy Gallagher, OMV, *The Discernment of Spirits: An Ignatian Guide to Everyday Living* (New York: Crossroad, 2005), 87–88.

3 Timothy Gallagher, OMV, *Setting Captives Free: Personal Reflections on Ignatian Discernment of Spirits* (New York: Crossroad, 2018), 122.
4 Gallagher, *Setting Captives Free*, 127.
5 RSVCE.
6 Gallagher, *Setting Captives Free*, 132–35.
7 "It is important to repeat that Ignatius is speaking of *spiritual* desolation here, as described in the fourth rule. He is not addressing situations of nonspiritual desolation as, for example, intense psychological stress or the various psychological disorders. Such afflictions exceed the limits of discernment of spirits and require other solutions, including professional help." Gallagher, *Discernment of Spirits*, 197–98n4. To attempt to examine such deep pools of psychological pain without professional help is unwise.
8 Gallagher, *Discernment of Spirits*, 89–90.
9 Jules Toner, SJ, *Commentary*, 151. See Gallagher, *Discernment of Spirits*, 91.
10 Gallagher, *Setting Captives Free*, 135–36.

15 Understanding Desolation: A Trial, Its Reason, and Its Fruit—Rule 7

1 Paul Lachance, trans., *Angela of Foligno: Complete Works* (New York: Paulist Press, 1993), 171. See Timothy Gallagher, OMV, *The Discernment of Spirits: An Ignatian Guide to Everyday Living* (New York: Crossroad, 2005), 95–97.
2 Timothy Gallagher, OMV, *Setting Captives Free: Personal Reflections on Ignatian Discernment of Spirits* (New York: Crossroad, 2018), 142–43.
3 Gallagher, *Setting Captives Free*, 143–44.
4 Gallagher, *Setting Captives Free*, 145–46.
5 If the enemy brings spiritual desolation into a notable emotional or physical depletion of this kind, then both nonspiritual (physical rest and emotional strengthening with appropriate means) and spiritual (Ignatius's rules for discernment and related tools from our spiritual tradition) remedies must be applied.

16 Giving Hope to Your Listeners: Consolation Will Return Soon—Rule 8

1. Elisabeth Leseur, *My Spirit Rejoices: The Diary of a Christian Soul in an Age of Unbelief* (Manchester, NH: Sophia Institute Press, 1996), 68. Timothy Gallagher, OMV, *The Discernment of Spirits: An Ignatian Guide to Everyday Living* (New York: Crossroad, 2005), 104–5.
2. Leseur, *My Spirit Rejoices*, 77.
3. Timothy Gallagher, OMV, *Setting Captives Free: Personal Reflections on Ignatian Discernment of Spirits* (New York: Crossroad, 2018), 155–56.
4. Gallagher, *Setting Captives Free*, 156–57.
5. Gallagher, *Discernment of Spirits*, 110–11.
6. Edmund Colledge and James Walsh, trans., *Julian of Norwich: Showings* (New York: Paulist Press, 1978), 204–5.
7. Colledge and Walsh, *Julian of Norwich*, 205.
8. Thomas H. Green, SJ, *Weeds Among the Wheat* (Notre Dame, IN: Ave Maria Press, 1986), 125. Gallagher, *Setting Captives Free*, 160–61.

17 Answering the Question: Why Does God Permit Desolation?—Rule 9

1. I take this application of John 16:7 from Toner, *Commentary*, 183. Timothy Gallagher, OMV, *The Discernment of Spirits: An Ignatian Guide to Everyday Living* (New York: Crossroad, 2005), 114; Timothy Gallagher, OMV, *Setting Captives Free: Personal Reflections on Ignatian Discernment of Spirits* (New York: Crossroad, 2018), 165–66.
2. NABRE.
3. Gallagher, *Setting Captives Free*, 167–68.
4. Simon Decloux, SJ, *The Spiritual Diary of St. Ignatius Loyola: Text and Commentary* (Rome: Centrum Ignatianum Spiritualitatis, 1990), 173. I have integrated into this translation the rendering of the Spanish original in S. Thió de Pol, trans., *La intimidad del peregrine: Diario espiritual de San Ignacio de Loyola* (Bilbao: Mensajero-Sal Terrae, 1990), 193. Gallagher, *Discernment of Spirits*, 117–18.

5 Gallagher, *Setting Captives Free*, 170–71.
6 For a closer look at what is seen, see Gallagher, *Setting Captives Free*, 170–71.
7 Gallagher, *Discernment of Spirits*, 42–43, 120–21. In this book, I cited Lucia's experience also to illustrate the enemy's tactic of disquieting with false reasons (rule 2).
8 Quoted from Jules Toner, SJ, *Spirit of Light or Darkness? A Casebook for Studying Discernment of Spirits* (St. Louis: Institute of Jesuit Sources, 1995), 38–39.
9 Toner, *Spirit of Light or Darkness?*, 39. Author's emphasis.
10 Thomas of Celano, *Second Life*, no. 118, in Marion Habig, ed., *St. Francis of Assisi, Writings and Early Biographies: English Omnibus of the Sources for the Life of St. Francis* (Chicago: Franciscan Herald Press, 1973), 460. Gallagher, *Discernment of Spirits*, 121–22.
11 Thomas of Celano, *Second Life*, no. 118, in Habig, *St. Francis of Assisi, Writings and Early Biographies*, 460. Emphasis added.
12 I have adapted the words of Jules Toner, SJ, in *A Commentary on Saint Ignatius' Rules for the Discernment of Spirits: A Guide to the Principles and Practice* (St. Louis, IL: The Institute of Jesuit Sources, 1982), 188, where he expresses this idea.
13 Gallagher, *Setting Captives Free*, 174–76.
14 Gallagher, *Setting Captives Free*, 176–77.

18 To Listeners in Consolation: Prepare for the Future—Rule 10

1 Timothy Gallagher, OMV, *Setting Captives Free: Personal Reflections on Ignatian Discernment of Spirits* (New York: Crossroad, 2018), 182–83.
2 *The Dark Night*, 1.6. See Kieran Kavanaugh, OCD, and Otilio Rodriguez, OCD, trans., *The Collected Works of Saint John of the Cross* (Washington, DC: ICS Publications, 1991), 371–73.
3 Timothy Gallagher, OMV, *The Discernment of Spirits: An Ignatian Guide to Everyday Living* (New York: Crossroad, 2005), 128; and *Setting Captive Free*, 185.

4 Marion Habig, ed., *St. Francis of Assisi, Writings and Early Biographies* (Quincy, IL: Franciscan Press, 1991), Major Life, 10, para. 2, p. 706.
5 Gallagher, *Discernment of Spirits*, 130–31.
6 Gallagher, *Discernment of Spirits*, 131–32.
7 Gallagher, *Discernment of Spirits*, 133–36. The first five of these points I have taken from Jules Toner, SJ, *A Commentary on Saint Ignatius' Rules for the Discernment of Spirits: A Guide to the Principles and Practice* (St. Louis, IL: The Institute of Jesuit Sources, 1982), 195–96. I have expanded upon his treatment of these five and have added the final two.
8 NABRE.
9 If it seems appropriate for the group, at this point I share my desire to see the rules represented in drawing, painting, music, poetry, video, digital form, and the like, as ways of diffusing their content. At times, some listeners have responded and created wonderful expressions of the rules in these forms.
10 This counsel is similar to rule 14: strengthening the weak point.
11 Gallagher, *Setting Captives Free*, 191.

19 Living the Discerning Life: Humble in Consolation, Trusting in Desolation—Rule 11

1 Jules Toner, SJ, *A Commentary on Saint Ignatius' Rules for the Discernment of Spirits: A Guide to the Principles and Practice* (St. Louis, IL: The Institute of Jesuit Sources, 1982), 197. See Gallagher, *Discernment of Spirits*, 140.
2 RSVCE. The subsequent verses are from this same source.
3 Jules Toner, SJ, *Spirit of Light or Darkness: A Casebook for Studying Discernment of Spirits* (St. Louis: Institute of Jesuit Sources, 1995), 65–66. See Timothy Gallagher, OMV, *The Discernment of Spirits: An Ignatian Guide to Everyday Living* (New York: Crossroad, 2005), 143–48.

20 Teaching Your Listeners to Resist Temptation—Rule 12

1. See Timothy Gallagher, OMV, *The Discernment of Spirits: An Ignatian Guide to Everyday Living* (New York: Crossroad, 2005), 150–52, for a more detailed treatment of this issue. The teacher might reference the Theology of the Body of St. John Paul II and his repeated emphasis on the gift of self as central to the love of man and woman.
2. David Fleming, SJ, *Draw Me into Your Friendship: A Literal Translation and a Contemporary Reading of the Spiritual Exercises* (St. Louis: Institute of Jesuit Sources, 1996), 257. See Gallagher, *Discernment of Spirits*, 152.
3. Gallagher, *Discernment of Spirits*, 149.
4. Gallagher, *Discernment of Spirits*, 155–56. This experience is shared with the permission of the person I am calling "Steve."
5. This and the following verses are from NABRE.
6. Thomas of Celano, *Second Life*, 125, in Marion Habig, ed., *St. Francis of Assisi, Writings and Early Biographies: English Omnibus of the Sources for the Life of St. Francis* (Chicago: Franciscan Herald Press, 1973), 465–66.
7. Timothy Gallagher, OMV, *Setting Captives Free: Personal Reflections on Ignatian Discernment of Spirits* (New York: Crossroad, 2018), 213.
8. *The Holy Rule of Our Most Holy Father Saint Benedict* (St. Meinrad, IN: Grail Publications, 1956), 13–16.
9. Translation from "Chapter 4: The Tools for Good Works," Monastery of Christ in the Desert, accessed June 15, 2018, https://christdesert.org/prayer/rule-of-st-benedict/chapter-4-the-tools-for-good-works.

21 A Key Counsel: In Time of Trouble, Do Not Keep Silent!—Rule 13

1. Timothy Gallagher, OMV, *The Discernment of Spirits: An Ignatian Guide to Everyday Living* (New York: Crossroad, 2005), 164–68. The text is from John Clarke, *Story of a Soul: The Autobiography of St. Thérèse of Lisieux* (Washington, DC: ICS Publications, 1996), 166.

2 Emphasis added.
3 Gallagher, *Discernment of Spirits*, 168–71. The quotations are from Thomas Merton, *The Seven Storey Mountain* (London: Sheldon Press, 1975), 333, 363–66.
4 Timothy Gallagher, OMV, *Setting Captives Free: Personal Reflections on Ignatian Discernment of Spirits* (New York: Crossroad, 2018), 225–27.
5 Gallagher, *Setting Captives Free*, 227–28.
6 NABRE.
7 General Audience, 16 September 2009, http://w2.vatican.va/content/benedict-xvi/it/audiences/2009/documents/hf_ben-xvi_aud_20090916.html. Author's translation, with some wording from other English translations.

22 Hope Where Your Listeners Have the Least Hope—Rule 14

1 Theological virtues: faith, hope, and charity; cardinal virtues: prudence, justice, temperance, and fortitude; moral virtues: patience, humility, chastity, obedience, and many others.
2 Timothy Gallagher, OMV, *The Discernment of Spirits: An Ignatian Guide to Everyday Living* (New York: Crossroad, 2005), 182; *Setting Captives Free: Personal Reflections on Ignatian Discernment of Spirits* (New York: Crossroad, 2018), 245–46.
3 See Gallagher, *Setting Captives Free*, 247–51, where I have examined these in more detail.
4 For the life of Matt Talbot, see, among others, Joseph Glynn, *The Life of Matt Talbot* (Dublin: Catholic Truth Society, 1942); Albert Dolan, O.Carm., *We Knew Matt Talbot: Visits with His Relatives and Friends* (Englewood, NJ: Carmelite Press, 1948); Eddie Doherty, *Matt Talbot* (Milwaukee, WI: Bruce Publishing Company, 1953); Mary Purcell, *Matt Talbot and His Times* (Chicago: Franciscan Herald Press, 1977); Susan Wallace, FSP, *Matt Talbot: His Struggle, His Victory Over Alcoholism* (Boston: Pauline Book & Media, 1992). See Gallagher, *Setting Captives Free*, 251–53 and these references.

23 Concluding the Teaching

1. For this and the subsequent paragraphs, see Timothy Gallagher, OMV, *Setting Captives Free: Personal Reflections on Ignatian Discernment of Spirits* (New York: Crossroad, 2018), 261–62.
2. G. K. Chesterton, *The Paradoxes of Mr. Pond* (New York: Dodd, Mead, 1937), 63.
3. RSVCE. Emphasis added.

24 The Proximate Preparation for the Teaching

1. Josef Pieper, *Guide to Thomas Aquinas* (New York: Pantheon, 1962), 95.

25 Tools for the Teaching

1. *The Discernment of Spirits: An Ignatian Guide for Everyday Life* (New York: Crossroad, 2005); *Setting Captives Free: Personal Reflections on Ignatian Discernment of Spirits* (New York: Crossroad, 2018).
2. http://www.crossroadpublishing.com/crossroad/title/teaching-discernment

26 What about the Second Set of Rules?

1. Timothy Gallagher, OMV, *Spiritual Consolation: An Ignatian Guide for a Greater Discernment of Spirits* (New York: Crossroad, 2007), 11–29.
2. Gallagher, *Spiritual Consolation*, 26–27.
3. I have used the word *joy* rather than *spiritual consolation*, the more precise term, in order to avoid the confusion that Ignatius highlights in *SpirEx* 9. For a full discussion of this issue, see Gallagher, *Spiritual Consolation*, 11–29.

27 Resources for Learning the Rules

1. See the bibliography in Timothy Gallagher, OMV, *The Discernment of Spirits: An Ignatian Guide to Everyday Living* (New York: Crossroad, 2005), 207–8, and the many sources cited in that book, and Timothy Gallagher, OMV, *Setting Captives Free: Personal Reflections on Ignatian Discernment of Spirits* (New York: Crossroad, 2018).

Index

A
Accept/reject, 118–19
Accompaniment, 231–32
Action, 55, 56, 118–19, 165–66, 182–84
Agitations, 107
Angela of Foligno, Saint, 150–51
Apologia pro Vita Sua (Newman), 242
Augustine, Saint, 24, 28, 29–30, 57, 60–63
Availability to God, 92
Awareness, 53–54, 56, 57–59, 195, 199–200

B
Baptism, 66
Benedict, Saint, 51, 215–16
Benedict XVI, Pope, 231–32
Biting, 19–21, 63, 67–68, 75–76
Bonaventure, Saint, 183
Boudreaux, Claude, 3

C
Catechesis, 58
Changes, 121–26, 131–32, 144, 189, 217
Charity, 95
Chesterton, G. K., 245
Commentaries, 5, 23

Confession, 233
Confessions (Augustine), 24, 29, 57
Confessors, 220–21
Conscience, 68–70
Consolation, 81. *See also* Nonspiritual consolation; Spiritual consolation
Continence, 62, 80, 82–83
Conversation, 32, 217. *See also* Sharing, of spiritual burdens; Spiritual directors
Created things, 90–92

D
"Darkness of soul," 105
Demystifying, 37–38
Depression, 102–3
de Sales, Saint Francis, 53
Desolation, 101. *See also* Nonspiritual desolation; Spiritual desolation
Digital resources, 270
"Diligently using the means," 165–66
Discernment of spirits: basic paradigm, 55–56; demystifying, 37–38, 50–51
The Discernment of Spirits: An Ignatian Guide to Everyday Living (Gallagher), x, 10, 23, 49
Discussion groups, 263

"Disquiet from various agitations and temptations," 107

"Disquieting with False Reasons," 79–80

"Disturbance in the soul," 106

DVDs, 270

E

Easing and taking away obstacles, 82–83

Elizabeth Seton, Saint, 182–83, 184–85

Emmaus, 93

Encouragement and strengthening, 80–81

The enemy: defined, 66; tactics of. *See* Tactics of the enemy; terminology choice, 48–49, 64

Evangelization, 58

"Every Increase of Hope, Faith, and Charity," 94–95

The evil one, 48

Examen prayer, 31–32

Examination, 140–46

Examples. *See also individual rules*: choosing, 24–30; in Church tradition, 27–28; from classic figures, 24–25; finding, 24–26; Ignatius's conversion, 28; as pedagogy focus, 18–21; from personal experience, 25–26; relatability of, 27; role of, 70–71; that serve the teaching, 27–30

Exemplar presentation, 17–18

F

Faith, 95

Faults, 172

Fiorito, Miguel Ángel, 5

First Week, 55, 264–65, 266

Francis of Assisi, Saint, 8, 24, 51, 177–78, 183, 214

Frankl, Viktor, 153

Freedom, 12, 40

Fundamental spiritual orientation, 60

G

Gift of learning, 174–78

Gil, Daniel, 5, 6

Gives, 110–12

Good spirit: defined, 66; examples of, 67; tactics of. *See* Tactics of the good spirit

Grace, 39–41, 66, 156

Green, Thomas, 168

Groups for discussion, 263

H

Handouts, 254–55

Harmful changes, 126, 144

Heavenly things, 96

Helpful changes, 131–32

The Hidden Treasure (St. Leonard), 12
Hope, 94, 107, 235–243, 245–46
"The Hound of Heaven," (Thompson), 70
Humility, 178–180, 193–95
Hypostatic Union, 27

I

Identity, spiritual, 116–17
"As if separated from one's Creator and Lord," 109–10
Ignatian retreats, 32–33
Ignatius, Saint: conversion of, 28–29, 51–53; experience of desolation, 173–74; forty days' search, 128–130; Manresa experience, 75–76; pedagogical choices, 16, 45–46
Imagination, 63, 65–66
"Inflamed with love of Its Creator and Lord," 89–90
Inspirations and quiet, 82
"Instruments of Good Works," 215
Interior Castle (Teresa de Avila), 53
Interior joy, 95–96
Introduction to the Devout Life (Francis de Sales), 53
"Is ordinarily accustomed," 64–65
"It is better for you that I go," 170–71
"And It Is Proper to the Good Spirit to Give Courage and Strength," 80–81

J

John of the Cross, Saint, 51
Joseph, 185
Journaling, 32
Joy, 95–96
"Joy that calls and attracts to heavenly things," 95–97
Julian of Norwich, 8, 24, 166–67

K

Knox, Ronald, 96–97

L

Lacasse, Engelbert, 4
"Lack of confidence, without hope, without love," 107
Lanteri, Bruno, 3, 5
Leonard of Port Maurice, Saint, 12
Leseur, Elisabeth, 158–160
Lessons, given or permitted, 110–14
"Let him think that he will soon be consoled," 162–65
Litany of Spiritual Desolation, 156

"The Lord has left him in trial," 152–53
The Lord of the Rings (Tolkien), 127–28
Love, 107, 180
"Love of created things in their Creator," 90–92
Low and earthly things, 106–7

M
Man's Search for Meaning (Frankl), 153
Maritain, Jacques, 8
Maritain, Raïssa, 8, 84, 85, 86
Martini, Carlo Maria, 22
Meaning, 153
Meditation, 137–39, 187–88
Merton, Thomas, 227–29
Metaphors: attack of a stronghold, 236–38; dissolute man, 217–18; parent-child, 206, 208; woman fighting man, 206
Mortal sin, xiii, 63–64
Movements, 55
"Movement to low and earthly things," 106–7
Mullan, Eldar, 23

N
"Never," 125–26
"Never make a change," 121–26, 189
Newman, John Henry, 242

Nonspiritual consolation, 86–87
Nonspiritual desolation, 47, 101–5, 122, 156, 220
Normality, 168

O
Orientation, 60

P
Paradigms, 255–58, 259
Parent–child metaphor, 206, 208
The parish, 233
Pascal, Blaise, 58
Patience, 161–62, 163
Pedagogical choices, 16, 45–46
Penance, 146–48
Pensées (Pascal), 58
Permits, 110–12
"Persons who are going from mortal sin to mortal sin," 63–64
Peter's denial, 193–94
Philotheus, 227, 228
Pieper, Josef, 251
Placing obstacles, 76–79
Podcasts, 270
Ponticianus, 29, 61, 67
Poverty, 178–180
PowerPoint, 258–263
Prayer, 136–37, 187, 197–98, 211–12, 242, 250

Preparation for teaching: consolation and desolation in the teacher, 252–53; prayer, 250; proximate, 249–253; remote, 249; review of material, 250–52

Priests, 220–21

"To propose apparent pleasures," 65–66

Q

Questions, 44–45, 244–45

R

Reed, William, 154

Reinforcement, 47–48

Rejadell, Teresa, 19, 75, 76–77, 110–11

Resistance: of desolation, 113, 134–35, 153–57, 171, 181–82; of temptation, 209

Resources, 268–270

Retreats, 233

Revelations of Divine Love (Julian of Norwich), 24

Reverence, 41–42

Rhythm of presenting rules, 38–39

Ruiz, Jurado Manuel, 4, 5

Rule 1: example of Augustine, 60–63; exploring text of, 63–70; text of, 60

Rule 2: examples, use of, 20–21, 73–74, 80–81, 82–83; exemplar presentation, 17–18; linking to experience, 19–20; persons addressed, 72–74; tactics of the enemy, 75–80; text of, 16, 72

Rule 3: consolation, experiences of, 89–97; consolation, intensity and duration of, 97; consolation, spiritual and nonspiritual, 85–88; examples, use of, 84, 87–97 passim; text of, 84–85

Rule 4: desolation, spiritual and nonspiritual, 101–5; examples, use of, 99–101, 103, 105–10, 114–15; gives vs. permits, 110–14; spiritual desolation as spiritual identity, 116–17; text of, 101; thoughts from desolation, 114–16

Rule 5: examples, use of, 121, 122–25; experiences of, 126–131; harmful changes, 126, 144; helpful changes, 131–32; introduction to, 118–120; text of, 120; "In time of desolation never make a change," 120–26

Rule 6: examples, use of, 136, 141–44, 145; four spiritual means, 135–149; spiritual desolation, response to, 134–35; text of, 133

Rule 7: desolation, fruitfulness of, 153–55; desolation, resistance to, 155–57; desolation as trial, 152–53; examples, use of, 153, 154–55, 157; text and commentary, 151–52

Rule 8: examples, use of, 26, 158–160, 162, 163–65; patience, 161–62, 163; text and commentary, 161; will, effort of, 162

Rule 9: examples, use of, 170, 172–74, 175–77; first cause of desolation, 171–74; love, expressions of, 180; second cause of desolation, 174–78; text and commentary, 171, 175, 179; third cause of desolation, 178–180

Rule 10: examples, use of, 185–87; recipients of, 181; text of, 181

Rule 11: examples of, 193–94, 196–203; in practice, 196–203; recipients of, 192; text of, 192

Rule 12: examples of, 209–16; key point, 208–9; metaphors of, 206, 208–9; in practice, 209–16; text and commentary, 206–8

Rule 13: elements of, 218–221; enemy tactics, identifying, 229–231; keeping silent/ hidden, 219; metaphors of, 218; in practice, 221–27, 227–29; sharing, 219–221; the spiritual and nonspiritual, 219–220; text and commentary, 217–18

Rule 14: in practice, 241–43; text and commentary, 236–37; weak point, identifying, 239–240; weak point, metaphor of, 236–38

Rules for the discernment of spirits: applying to own life, 31–33; commentaries on, 5, 23; defined, 53; First Week, 55, 264–65, 266; introduction to, ix–xi; power of, 6–7, 13–14; reviewing, 189–190; Second Week, 264–67; text of, xiii–xvii; value of, 11

S

Sadness, 63, 76, 108–9

Second Week, 264–67

Self-knowledge, 240

Sessions, 38–39

Setting Captives Free: Personal Reflections on Ignatian Discernment of Spirits (Gallagher), x, 23, 49

The Seven Storey Mountain (Merton), 227

Shame, 42–44, 235–36

Sharing, of spiritual burdens, 213, 217, 219–221. *See also* Spiritual directors; Merton, Thomas, 227–29; Thérèse of Lisieux, Saint, 223–27

Showings (Julian of Norwich), 166–67

"Since he can resist," 155–57

Sloth, 108–9

Snowball metaphor, 208–9, 212

"To some extent," 54–55

"So that he may resist," 153–55

Spiritual consolation: accepting, 119, 182–84; alternations of, 166–68, 257; changes, making, 131; duration of, 97, 112; examples of, 89–97; future desolation and, 184–87; given, 110, 111; humility in, 193–95; Ignatius's experience of, 129; intensity of, 97; vs. nonspiritual, 85–88; in the teacher, 253

Spiritual Consolation: An Ignatian Guide to a Greater Discernment of Spirits (Gallagher), 266

Spiritual desolation: alternations of, 166–68, 257; Angela of Foligno, Saint, 150–51; causes of, 169–180; changes, making, 121–26, 128, 131, 134–35; examples of, 105–10; growth and, 188–89; Ignatius's experience of, 129–130; intensity of, 112–13; litany of, 156; vs. nonspiritual, 101–5; pedagogy and, 47; permitted, 110–12; planning for, 190–91; qualities of, 200; rejecting, 119–120; resistance to, 113, 134–35, 153–57, 171, 181–82; response to, 160; shame and, 42–44; as spiritual identity, 116–17; in the teacher, 252–53; temptation and, 107, 204–5; thoughts that come from, 114–16; as a trial, 152–53; 174–78; trusting in, 195–96; value of, 153–55, 171, 188–89

Spiritual Diary (Ignatius), 173

Spiritual directors: characteristics of, 221; spiritual desolation and, 100, 154, 176, 198–202 passim; temptation and, 213, 229; value of, 16, 32, 232

Spiritual energy, loss of, 11–12

Spiritual friends, 233

Spiritual identity, 116–17

Spirituality of redemption, 40, 66

Spiritual means, 135–149

Spiritual proposals, 122

Spiritual ups and downs, 11–12, 37, 168

Spouses, 233

"Stinging and biting," 63, 67–68

Supernatural organism, 66

T

Tactics of the enemy: biting, 75–76; disquieting, 79–80; identifying, 229–231; Ignatius's focus on, 40; imagination, 63, 65–66; listed, 17; placing obstacles, 76–79; saddening, 63, 76; secrecy, 219, 229–231; spiritual desolation. *See* Spiritual desolation; temptation. *See* Temptation

Tactics of the good spirit: consolation, 81; easing and taking away obstacles, 82–83; encouragement and strengthening, 80–81; inspirations and quiet, 82; listed, 18; stinging and biting, 63; tears, 81–82

"Taking New Strength," 187–191

Talbot, Matt, 241–43

Tears, 81–82

"Tears for the love of the Lord," 92–94

Temptation: examples of, 213–16; resisting, 209; responses to, 213–14; spiritual desolation and, 107, 204–5

Tepidness, 108–9

Teresa of Avila, Saint, 27, 51, 53

"Their Consciences through their rational power," 68–70

Thérèse of Lisieux, Saint, 24, 87–88, 221–27

"In these persons the good spirit," 66–67

Thompson, Francis, 70

"The thoughts that come from desolation," 114–16

Time limitations, 38–39

"In time of desolation," 120–21

Title statement: basic categories underlying, 52–53; demystifying discernment, 50–51; exploring text of, 53–55 Introduction to the Devout Life; text of, 50

Tolkien, J. R. R., 127

Toner, Jules, 5, 9, 193

Tools for teaching: discussion groups, 263; handouts, 254–55; paradigms, 255–58, 259; PowerPoint, 258–263

"Totally slothful, tepid, sad," 108–9

Translations, 23

Trials, 152–53, 174–78

U

Understanding, 54, 56, 201

"Uses a Contrary Method," xiii, 67

W

Waugh, Evelyn, 96

Weakest point, 235–240

Weakness of the enemy, 40

Within and without, 57–58

Woman healed by Jesus, 89–90

"Work to be in patience," 161–62